Some Heroes o

W. H. Davenport Adams

Alpha Editions

This edition published in 2023

ISBN : 9789357961912

Design and Setting By
Alpha Editions
www.alphaedis.com
Email - info@alphaedis.com

Contents

PREFACE.

THE present age is sometimes described as an Age of Commonplace; but it has its romance if we care to look for it. Assuredly, the adventures of its travellers and explorers do not lose in importance or interest, even when compared with those of their predecessors in days when a great part of the world was still "virgin ground." In the following pages, this thesis is illustrated by a summary of the narratives of certain "Heroes of Travel" belonging to our own time; and I believe it will be found that for "stirring scenes" and "hair-breadth escapes" they vie with any which the industrious Hakluyt, the quaint Purchas, or, coming down to a later date, the multifarious Pinkerton has collected. However, on this point the reader has an opportunity of satisfying himself, as, by way of contrast, I have prefixed to these Episodes of Recent Travel a succinct account of the enterprise of Messer Marco Polo, the Pioneer of Mediæval Travellers.

There is no pleasanter mode of learning geography than by studying the works of distinguished travellers; and therefore this little book may claim to possess some slight educational value, while primarily intended to supply the young with attractive but not unwholesome reading. The narratives which it contains have been selected with a view to variety or interest. They range over Mexico, Western Australia, Central Africa, and Central Asia. They include the experiences of the hunter, the war correspondent, and the geographical explorer; and, in recognition of the graceful influence of women, of a lady traveller, who showed herself as resolute and courageous as any of the so-called hardier sex. And, finally, they have the merit, it is believed, of not having appeared in previous compilations.

As a companion for the fireside corner, this little book will, I hope, be welcome to all English-speaking lads and lasses, who will learn from its pages how much may be accomplished by patience, perseverance, and energy.

SIR MARCO POLO, THE VENETIAN,
AND HIS TRAVELS IN ASIA.

WE should be inclined to consider Sir Marco Polo as one of the greatest travellers the world has ever seen. It is true he was not a man of genius; that he was not, like Columbus, inspired by a lofty enthusiasm; that he displayed no commanding superiority of character. But when we remember the vast compass of his journeys, and the circumstances under which they were carried out; when we remember, too, how close an observer he was, and how rigidly accurate, and his plenitude of energy and perseverance—we feel that he is, beyond all cavil or question, entitled to be recognized as the king of mediæval travellers. Let us take Colonel Yule's summary of his extraordinary achievements:—

"He was the first Traveller to trace a route across the whole longitude of Asia, naming and describing kingdom after kingdom which he had seen with his own eyes; the Deserts of Persia, the flowering plateaux and wild gorges of Badakshan, the jade-bearing rivers of Khotan; the Mongolian steppes, cradle of the power that had so lately threatened to swallow up Christendom; the new and brilliant Court that had been established at Cambaluc: the first Traveller to reveal China in all its wealth and vastness, its mighty rivers, its huge cities, its rich manufactures, its swarming population, the inconceivably vast fleets that quickened its seas and its inland waters; to tell us of the nations on its borders, with all their eccentricities of manners and worship; of Tibet, with its sordid devotees; of Burma, with its golden pagodas and their tinkling crowns; of Laos, of Siam, of Cochin China; of Japan, the Eastern Thule, with its rosy pearls and golden-roofed palaces: the first to speak of that Museum of Beauty and Wonder, still so imperfectly ransacked, the Indian Archipelago, source of those aromatics then so highly prized and whose origin was so dark; of Java, the Pearl of Islands; of Sumatra, with its many kings, its strange costly products, and its cannibal races; of the dusky savages of Nicobar and Andaman; of Ceylon, the Isle of Gems, with its sacred Mountain and its tomb of Adam; of India the Great, not as a dreamland of Alexandrian fables, but as a country seen and partially explored, with its virtuous Brahmans, its obscene ascetics, its diamonds and the strange tales of their acquisition, its sea-beds of pearl, and its powerful sun: the first in mediæval times to give any distinct account of the secluded Christian Empire of Abyssinia and the semi-Christian island of Socotra; to speak, though indeed dimly, of Zanzibar, with its negroes and its ivory, and of the vast and distant Madagascar, bordering on the Dark Ocean of the South, with its

Roc [3] and other monstrosities; and, in a remotely opposite region, of Siberia and the Arctic Ocean, of dog-sledges, white bears, and reindeer-riding Tunguses."

Who can dispute the fame of a man whose name and memory are associated with so marvellous a catalogue of discoveries, who anticipated the travellers of a later generation in many of their most remarkable enterprises? At one time, the authenticity of his statements was frequently and openly impugned; he was accused of exaggeration and inexactitude; but the labours of Marsden, Pauthier, and especially of Colonel Yule, have shown that his statements, so far as they are founded on personal observation, may be implicitly accepted.

In the early part of the fourteenth century there lived at Venice a patrician of good family, named Andrea Polo, to whom were born three sons, Marco, Nicolo, and Maffeo. Nicolo, the second of these sons, was the father of our traveller, Marco Polo, who was born in 1254. Engaged in extensive commercial operations, Nicolo, soon after his son's birth, journeyed to Constantinople, and thence proceeded on a trading venture to the Crimea, which led to his ascending the Volga for a considerable distance, and crossing the steppes to visit Bokhara and the Court of the great Kublai Khan, on or within the borders of Cathay. Kublai, the hero of so many legends, had never before seen a European. He tendered to Nicolo and his brother Maffeo (who travelled with him) a right royal welcome; was deeply interested in all they told him of the kingdoms and states of Europe; and finally resolved on sending them back, with one of his own nobles, as ambassadors to the Pope. In this capacity they arrived at Acre in 1269; but as Pope Clement IV. had died in the previous year, and no successor had as yet been elected, the two brothers thought they might reasonably indulge themselves in a visit to their Venetian homes, from which they had been absent for fifteen years.

Nicolo remained at Venice until 1271, when, no Pope having been elected, he deemed it well that he should return to the Great Khan to explain the delay which had taken place in the fulfilment of his mission. Accompanied by his brother Maffeo, and his son Marco, a lad of seventeen, he sailed to Acre, and thence to the port of Ayas on the gulf of Scanderoon, where he was overtaken by the news that a Pope had at last been elected in the person of an old friend of his, Tedoldo Visconti, or Pope Gregory X., at that time legate in Syria. The new Pope immediately sent for the two brothers to Acre, and charged them with a cordial message for the Khan. He also sent him two Dominican monks to teach the truths of science and Christianity; but they took fright at an early stage of the journey, and hurried back to Acre; while the two brothers, with young Polo, started overland for the Court of the Great Khan.

Reaching Hormuz, at the mouth of the Persian Gulf, they seem to have taken a northern route; traversing successively the regions of Kerman and Khorasan, Balkh and Badakshan, and ascending the Upper Oxus to the great plateau of Pamir—a route followed by no European traveller, except Benedict Goro, until it was undertaken by Captain John Wood, of the Indian navy, in his special expedition to the sources of the Oxus in 1838. Leaving the bleak wastes of the Pamir, the Polos descended into Kashgar, visited Yarkand and Khotand, passed near Lake Lob, and eventually traversed the great Desert of the Gobi, since explored by several European travellers, to Tangut, the name then applied by Mongols and Persians to territory at the extreme north-west of China, both within and without the famous Wall. Skirting the Chinese frontier, they came upon the Great Khan at his summer palace of Kaiping-fu, near the foot of the Khin-gan Mountains, and about fifty miles north of the Great Wall. This must have been in May, 1275, or thereabouts, when Marco Polo was close upon one and twenty.

"The king of kings" received the three bold Venetians with much favour. "He showed great pleasure at their coming, and asked many questions as to their welfare, and how they had sped. They replied that they had in verity sped well, seeing that they found the Khan well and safe. Then they presented the credentials and letters which they had received from the Pope, and those pleased him right well; and after that they produced some sacred oil from the Holy Sepulchre, whereat he was very glad, valuing it greatly. And next, spying Marco, who was then a young gallant (*jeune bacheler*), he asked who was that in their company. 'Sire,' said his father, Messer Nicolo, 'he is my son and your liegeman.' 'Welcome is he too,' quoth the Emperor. But why should I make a long story? There was great rejoicing at the Court because of their arrival; and they met with attention and honour from everybody. So there they abode at the Court with the other barons."

Among young Marco Polo's gifts appears to have been a facility for acquiring languages. He speedily mastered that of the Tartars, so as both to write and speak it; and in a brief space he came to know several other languages and four written characters. He studied also the customs of the Tartars and their mode of carrying on war. His ability and prudence greatly recommended him to Kublai, and he began to employ him in the public service. His first embassy was to a country lying a six months journey distant; apparently the province of Yun-nan, which he reached by way of Shansi, Shensi and Szechuen. He had been shrewd enough to observe that the Khan was disgusted with the rigid officialism of his ambassadors, who, on returning from their various missions, would speak only of the business they had transacted, whereas he would fain have heard of the strange things, peoples, and countries they had seen. And so he took full notes of all he saw, and returned to the Khan's Court brimful of surprising information, to which the prince listened with evident pleasure. "If this young man live," he said, "he will assuredly come to be a person of great work and capacity."

For seventeen years Marco Polo remained in the Khan's service, being sent on several important embassies, and engaged also in the domestic administration. For three years he held the government of the important city of Yangchau. On another occasion, with his uncle Maffeo, he spent a twelvemonth at Kangchau in Tangut. He also visited Karakorum, the old Mongolian capital of the Khans, and penetrated into Champa, or Southern Cochin China. Finally, he seems to have been sent on a mission to the Indian Seas, and to have explored several of the southern states of India. And thus it came about that Messer Marco Polo had knowledge of, or actually visited, a greater number of the different countries of the world than any other man; the more that he was always eager to gain information, and to examine and inquire into everything.

Meantime, the Venetians were growing wealthy, and Marco's father and uncle were growing old; and increasing wealth and increasing years raised in them an apprehension of what might befall them in case of the aged Khan's death, and a desire to return to their native land. Several times they applied to Kublai for permission to depart; but he was loth to say farewell to the men whom he had known and trusted so long, and, but for an opportune event, they might never have succeeded in carrying themselves and their jewels and gold back to Europe. In 1286 Arghún Khan, of Persia, Kublai's great-nephew, lost his favourite wife, the Khatun Bulaghán. On her death-bed she charged him to supply her place with a daughter of her own tribe, the Mongols of Bayaut; and, desirous of fulfilling her dying wish, the bereaved prince despatched three ambassadors to Kublai's Court to seek for him a fitting bride. The Great Khan received them with all honour and hospitality, and then sent for the lady Kukachiu, a maiden of seventeen, and a very beautiful and gracious person. On her arrival at Court she was presented to the three ambassadors, who declared that the lady pleased them well.

The overland route from Peking to Tabriz was long and dangerous, and the envoys decided, therefore, on returning, with their fair charge, by sea. While sojourning at the Khan's Court they had made the acquaintance of the three Venetians, and being greatly impressed by their marvellous good sense and experience, and by Marco Polo's extensive knowledge of the Indian seas and territories, they entreated the Khan to allow them the advantage and protection of their company. It was with profound reluctance that Kublai gave his consent; but when once he had done so, he behaved with his wonted splendour of generosity. Summoning the three Venetians to his presence, he placed in their hands two golden "tablets of authority," which secured them a free passage through all his dominions, and unlimited supplies of all necessaries for themselves and for their company. He entrusted them also with messages to the King of France, the King of England, the King of Spain, and other sovereigns of Christendom. Then he caused thirteen ships to be equipped, each with four masts and nine to twelve sails; and when all was ready, the ambassadors and the lady, with the three Venetians, took leave of the Great Khan, and went on board their ships, with a large retinue, and with two years' supplies provided by the Emperor (A.D. 1292).

The port from which they set out seems to have been that of Zaytou, in Fo-kien. The voyage was long and wearisome, and chequered by much ill fortune; and in the course of it two of the ambassadors died, and as many as six hundred of the mariners and attendants. They were detained for months on the coast of Sumatra, and in the south of India; nor did they arrive at Hormuz until the end of 1293. There they learned that Arghún Khan had been dead a couple of years, and that he had been succeeded by his brother Kaikhatu. The lady, according to the custom of the country, became the wife of Arghún's son, Prince Ghazan, who is spoken of as endowed with some of the highest qualities of a king, a soldier, and a legislator; but she wept much in bidding farewell to her noble Venetian friends.

As for Marco Polo, his father, and uncle, having discharged the trust placed in their hands by Kublai Khan, they proceeded to Tabriz, on a visit to Kaikhatu; and having sojourned there for some months, journeyed homeward by way of Trebizond, Constantinople, and Negropont, arriving in Venice in 1295, after an absence of four and twenty years.

The traditional story of their arrival is related by Ramusio:—

"Years of anxiety and travel, and the hardships of many journeys, had so changed the appearance of the three Venetians, who, indeed, had almost forgotten their native tongue, that no one in Venice recognized them. Their clothes, too, were coarse and shabby, and after the Tartar fashion. Proceeding to their house in Venice, a lofty and handsome palazzo, and known by the name of the Corte del Millioni, they found it occupied by some of their relatives, whom they had no small difficulty in convincing of their identity. To secure the desired recognition, and the honourable notice of the whole city, they adopted a quaint device.

"Inviting a number of their friends and kindred to an entertainment, they were careful that it should be prepared with great state and splendour; and when the hour came for sitting down to table, they came forth from their chamber, all clothed in crimson satin, fashioned in long robes reaching to the ground, such as in those days people wore within doors. And when water for ablutions had been served, and the guests were sat, they doffed these robes, and put on others of crimson damask, while the first suits were, by their orders, cut up and divided among the servants. After partaking of some of the dishes, they again retired, to come back resplendent in robes of crimson velvet, and when they had again taken their seats, the cast-off robes were divided as before. When dinner was over, they did the like with the robes of velvet, after they had attired themselves in dresses of the same fashion as those worn by the rest of the company. Much wonder and astonishment did the guests exhibit at these proceedings.

"Now, when the cloth had been removed, and all the servants had quitted the dining-hall, Messer Marco, as the youngest of the three, rose from table, and, going into another chamber, brought forth the three shabby dresses of coarse stuff which they had worn, on their arrival in the city. Straightway, with sharp knives they began to rip some of the seams and welts, and to draw forth vast quantities of jewels of the highest value—rubies and sapphires, carbuncles, diamonds, and emeralds—which had all been stitched up in those dresses so artfully that nobody could have suspected their presence. For when they took leave of the Great Khan, they had converted all the wealth he had bestowed upon them into this mass of precious stones, being well aware of the impossibility of carrying with them so great an amount in gold, over a journey of such extreme length and difficulty. The exhibition of this immense treasure of jewels and precious stones, all poured out upon the table, threw the guests into fresh amazement, so that they appeared bewildered and dumfounded. And straightway they recognized, what they had formerly doubted, that the three strangers were indeed those worthy and honoured gentlemen of the Polo family whom they had claimed to be; and paid them the greatest reverence. And the story being bruited abroad in Venice, the whole city, gentle and simple, hastened to the house to embrace them, and make much of them, with every demonstration of affection and respect. On Messer Maffeo, the eldest, they conferred an office that in those days was of high dignity; while the young men came daily to visit and converse with the ever polite and gracious Messer Marco, and to ask him questions about Cathay and the Great Khan, all of which he answered with such courtesy and kindliness, that every man felt himself in a manner in his debt. And as it chanced that in the narrative which he was constantly called on to repeat of the magnificence of the Great Khan, he would speak of his revenues as amounting to ten or fifteen 'millions' of gold, and, in like manner, when recounting other instances of great wealth in those remote lands, would always employ the term 'millions,' people nicknamed him Messer Marco *Millioni*—a circumstance which I have noted also in the public books of this

Republic where he is mentioned. The court of his house, too, at S. Giovanni Crisostomo has always from that time been popularly known as the Court of the Millioni." [12]

We pass on to 1298, a year which witnessed a fresh outburst of the bitter enmity between Genoa and Venice. The Genoese, intent upon crushing their formidable rival, despatched a great fleet into the Adriatic, under the command of Lamba Doria. Off the island of Curzola they were met by a more powerful armada, of which Andrea Dandolo was admiral, and one of the galleys of which was commanded by Marco Polo. The battle began early on the 7th of September, the Venetians entering into it with the glad confidence of victory. Their impetuous attack was rewarded by the capture of the Genoese galleys; but, dashing on too eagerly, many of their ships ran aground. One of these was captured, cleared of its crew, and filled with Genoese. Closing up into a column, the Genoese pushed the encounter hotly, and broke through the Venetian line, which the misadventure we have spoken of had thrown into disorder. Throughout the long September day the fight was bravely supported; but, towards sunset, a squadron of cruising ships arriving to reinforce Doria, the Venetians were taken in flank, and finally overpowered. The victory of the Genoese was complete; they captured nearly all the Venetian vessels, including the admiral's, and seven thousand men, among whom were Dandolo and Marco Polo. The former disappointed the triumph of his victors by dashing out his brains against the side of his galley; the latter was removed to Genoa.

During his captivity Polo made the acquaintance of a Pisan man of letters, named Rusticiano, or Rustichello, who was a prisoner like himself. When he learned the nature of Polo's remarkable experiences, this Pisan gentleman, not unnaturally, urged him to record them in writing; and it would seem that the great traveller complied with the request, and dictated to his new friend the narrative that has since excited so much curious interest. Through the intervention of Matteo Visconti, Captain-General of Milan, peace was concluded in May, 1299, between Genoa and Venice, and as one of the conditions was the release of prisoners on both sides, Messer Marco Polo soon afterwards obtained his freedom, and returned to his family mansion in the Corte del Sabbrin. He took with him the manuscript story of his world wanderings, and in 1306 presented a copy of it to a noble French knight, Thibault de Cipoy, who had been sent on a diplomatic mission to Venice by Charles of Valois.

The closing years of a life which, in its spring and summer, had been crowded with incident and adventures, were undisturbed by any notable event, and in his old age Marco Polo enjoyed the sweetness of domestic peace and the respect of his fellow-countrymen. On the 9th of January, 1324, "finding himself growing feebler every day through bodily ailment, but being by the grace of God of a meek mind, and of senses and judgment unimpaired, he made his will, in which he constituted as his trustees Donata, his beloved wife, and his dear daughters, Fantina, Bellola, and Monta," bequeathing to them the bulk of his property. How soon afterwards he died, there is no evidence to show; but it is at least certain that it was before June, 1325. We may conclude, therefore, that his varied life fulfilled the Psalmist's space of seventy years.

Marco Polo, says Martin Bucer, was the creator of the modern geography of Asia. He was the Humboldt of the thirteenth century; and the record of his travels must prove an imperishable monument of his force of character, wide intelligence and sympathy, and unshaken intrepidity. We have thus briefly summarized his remarkable career, and indicated the general extent of his travels. To follow him in detail throughout his extensive journeys would be impossible within the limits prescribed to us; and we shall content ourselves, therefore, with such extracts from his narrative as will best illustrate their more interesting and striking features, and indirectly assist us in forming some conception of the man himself.

And first, we take his description of the great river of Badakshan and the table-land of Pamir—which the wandering Kirghiz call "The Roof of the World"—substituting modern names of places for those in the original.

"In leaving Badakshan, you ride twelve days between east and north-east, ascending a river [the Upper Oxus] that runs through land belonging to a brother of the Prince of Badakshan, and containing a good many towns and villages and scattered habitations. The people are Mohammedans, and valiant in war. At the end of those twelve days you come to a province of no great size, extending indeed no more than three days' journey in any direction, and this is called Wakhan. The people worship Mohammed, and have a peculiar language. They are gallant soldiers, and have a chief whom they call *None* [No-no?], which is as much as to say Count, and they are liegemen to the Prince of Badakshan.

"There are numbers of wild beasts of all kinds in this region. And when you leave this little country, and ride three days north-east, always among mountains, you get to such a height that it is spoken of as the highest place in the world. And when you reach this height, you find a great lake between two mountains [Lake Sir-i-kol], and out of it a pure river [the Oxus] flows through a plain clothed with the most beautiful pasture in the world, so that a lean beast would fatten there to your heart's content in ten days. There are great numbers of all kinds of wild beasts; among others, wild sheep of large size, with horns six palms in length [the Rass, or *Ovis Poli*]. From these horns the shepherds make great bowls out of which to eat their food; and they use the horns also to enclose folds for their cattle at night. Messer Marco was told also that the wolves were numerous, and killed many of those wild sheep. Hence quantities of their horns and bones were found, and these were made into great heaps by the wayside, in order to direct travellers when snow lay on the earth.

"The plain is called Pamir, and you ride across it for twelve days together, finding nothing but a desert without habitation or any green thing, so that travellers are compelled to carry with them whatever they have need of. The region is so lofty and so cold, that not a bird is to be seen. And I must also observe that, owing to this extreme cold, fire does not burn so brightly, nor give out so much heat as usual, nor does it cook food so thoroughly.

"Now, if we continue our journey towards the east-north-east, we travel fully forty days, continually passing over mountains and hills, or through valleys, and crossing many rivers and wildernesses. And in all this extent you find neither habitation of man, nor any green thing, and must carry with you whatever you require. The country is called Bolor [the Tibetan kingdom of Balti]. The people dwell high up in the mountains, and are savage idolaters, living only by the chase, and clothing themselves in the skins of beasts. They are, in truth, an evil race."

[In February, 1838, Captain John Wood crossed the Pamir, and his description of it may be compared with the Venetian traveller's. "We stood, to use a native expression," he says, "upon the *Báni-i-Duniah*, or 'Roof of the World,' while before us lay stretched a noble, but frozen sheet of water, from whose western end issued the infant river of the Oxus. This fine lake (Sir-i-kol) lies in the form of a crescent, about fourteen miles long from east to west, by an average breadth of one mile. On three sides it is bordered by swelling hills about 500 feet high, while along its southern bank they rise into mountains 3500 feet above the lake, or 19,000 feet above the sea, and covered with perpetual snow, from which never-failing source the lake is supplied. Its elevation is 15,600 feet. . . . The appearance of the country presented the image of a winter of extreme severity. Wherever one's gaze rested, a dazzling bed of snow covered the soil like a carpet, while the sky above our heads was of a sombre and melancholy hue. A few clouds would have refreshed the eye, but none could be anywhere seen. Not a breath rippled the surface of the lake; not a living animal, not even a bird, presented itself to the view. The sound of a human voice had been harmonious music to the ear, but, at this inhospitable season of the year, no one ventured into these icy realms. Silence reigned everywhere around us; a silence so profound that it oppressed the heart."
[17]

Of the city of Lop (or Lob) and the great Desert of Gobi, Marco Polo writes:—

"Lop is a large town on the border of the desert which is called the Desert of Lop, and is situated between east and north-east. It belongs to the Great Khan, and the people worship Mohammed. Now, such persons as propose to cross the desert take a week's rest in this town to refresh themselves and their cattle; and then they make ready for the journey, taking with them a month's supply for man and beast. On quitting this city they enter the desert.

"The extent of this desert is so great, that it is said it would take a year and more to ride from one end of it to the other. And here, where its breadth is least, it takes a month to cross it. It is all composed of hills and valleys of sand, and contains not a thing to eat. But after riding for a day and a night you find fresh water, enough mayhap for some fifty or one hundred persons with their beasts, but not for more. And all across the desert you will find water in like manner, that is to say, in some twenty-eight places altogether you will find good water, but in no great quantity; and in four places also you find brackish water.

"Beasts there are none; for there is no food for them. But there is a marvellous thing related of this desert, which is that when travellers are on the march by night, and one of them chances to drop behind, or to fall asleep or the like, when he tries to regain his company, he will hear spirits talking, and suppose them to be his comrades. Sometimes the spirits will call him by name; and thus shall a traveller frequently be led astray so that he never finds his party. And in this way many have perished. Sometimes the travellers will hear as it were the tramp and murmur of a great cavalcade of people away from the real line of road, and taking this to be their own company, will follow the sound; and when day breaks they discover the deception, and perceive that they are in an evil plight. Even in the day time the spirits may be heard talking. And sometimes you shall hear the sound of various musical instruments, and still more commonly the rattle of drums. Hence, in performing this journey, it is customary for travellers to keep close together. All the animals, too, have bells at their necks, so that they cannot easily get astray. And at sleeping time a signal is hoisted to show the direction of the next march.

"And in this way it is that the desert is crossed."

As the sea has its mermaids, and the river its water-sprites, Undines, or Loreleys, which entice their victims to death, so the deserts and waste places of the earth have their goblins and malignant demons. The awe inspired by the vastness and dreary solitude of the wilderness suggests to the imagination only gloomy ideas, and it is conceived of as a place where no influences or beings favourable to man can exist. Its sounds are sounds of terror; its appearances all foster a sentiment of mystery. Pliny tells us of the phantoms that start up before the traveller in the African deserts; Mas'udi, of the Ghûls, which in night and solitude seek to lead him astray. An Arab writer relates a tradition of the Western Sahara:—"If the wayfarer be alone the demons make sport of him, and fascinate him, so that he wanders from his course and perishes." Colonel Yule remarks that the Afghan and Persian wildernesses also have their *Ghûl-i-Beában*, or Goblin of the Waste, a gigantic and fearful spectre which devours travellers; and even the Gaels of the West Highlands have the desert creature of Glen Eiti, which, one-handed, one-eyed, one-legged, seems exactly to answer to the Arabian Nesúas or *Empusa*. And it may be added that the wind-swept wastes of Dartmoor, limited as is their expanse, are, in the eyes of the peasantry, haunted by mysterious and malevolent spirits.

The effect of the Desert on a cultivated mind is well described by Madame Hommaire de Hell:—"The profound stillness," she says, "which reigns in the air produces an indescribable impression on our senses. We scarcely dare to interrupt it, it seems so solemn, so fully in harmony with the infinite grandeur of the desert. In vain will you seek a calm so absolute in even the remotest solitudes of civilized countries. Everywhere some spring murmurs, everywhere some trees rustle, everywhere in the silence of the nights some voices are heard which arrest the thought; but here nature is, so to speak, petrified, and we have before us the image of that eternal repose which the mind is hardly able to conceive."

Concerning the customs of the Tartars, Marco Polo writes:—

"The Tartar custom is to spend the winter in warm plains where they find good fodder for their cattle, while in summer they betake themselves to a cool climate among the mountains and valleys, where water is to be found, as well as woods and pastures.

"Their houses are circular, and are made of wands covered with felt. These are carried along with them whithersoever they go; for the wands are so strongly interwoven, and so well combined, that the framework can be made very light. Whenever these huts are erected, the door is always placed to the south. They also have waggons covered with black felt so efficaciously that no rain can enter. These are drawn by oxen and camels, and the women and children travel in them. The women do the buying and selling, and whatever is necessary to provide for the husband and household; for the men all lead the life of gentlemen, troubling themselves about nothing but hawking and hunting, and looking after their goshawks and falcons, unless it be the practice of warlike exercises.

"They live on the meat and milk which their birds supply, and on the produce of the chase; and they eat all kinds of flesh, including that of horses and dogs, and Pharaoh's rats, of which there are great numbers in burrows on these plains. Their drink is mare's milk. . . .

"This is the fashion of their religion: They say there is a most high God of Heaven, whom they worship daily with thurible and incense, but they pray to him only for health of mind and body. But they have also a certain other god of theirs called Natigay, and they say he is the God of the Earth, who watches over their children, cattle, and crops. They show him great worship and honour, and every man hath a figure of him in his house, made of felt and cloth; and they also make in the same manner images of his wife and children. The wife they put on the left hand, and the children in front. And when they eat, they take the fat of the meat and grease the god's mouth withal, as well as the mouths of his wife and children. Then they take of the broth and sprinkle it before the door of the house; and that done, they deem that their god and his family have had their share of the dinner.

"Their drink is mare's milk, prepared in such a way that you would take it for white wine, and a good right drink it is, called by them komiz.

"The clothes of the wealthy Tartars are for the most part of gold and silk stuffs, lined with costly furs, such as sable and ermine, vair and fox skin, in the richest fashion."

As in succeeding chapters of this volume we shall have something to say about the manners and customs of the Mongolian nomads, we may here be content with observing that Marco Polo's "Natigay" seems identical with the "Nongait" or "Ongotiu" of the Buriats, who, according to Pallas, is honoured by them as the tutelary god of sheep and other cattle. Properly the divinity consists of *two* figures, hanging side by side, one of whom represents the god's wife. These two figures are merely a pair of lanky flat bolsters with the upper part shaped into a round disc, and the body hung with a long woolly fleece; eyes, nose, breasts, and navel being indicated by leather knobs stitched upon the surface. The male figure commonly has at his girdle the foot-rope with which horses at pasture are fettered, whilst the female, which is sometimes accompanied by smaller figures representing her children, is adorned with all sorts of little nick-nacks and sewing implements.

The Tartar customs of war are thus described:—

"All their harness of war is excellent and costly. Their arms are bows and arrows, sword and mace; but, above all, the bow, for they are capital archers, indeed the best that are known. On their backs they wear armour of cuirbouly, [22] prepared from buffalo and other hides, which is very strong. They are excellent soldiers, and passing valiant in battle. They are also more capable of hardship than other nations; for many a time, if need be, they will go for a month without any supply of food, living only on the milk of their mares and on such game as their bows may win them. Their horses also will subsist entirely on the grass of the plains, so that there is no need to carry store of barley, or straw, or oats; and they are very docile to their riders. These, in case of need, will abide on horseback the livelong night, armed at all points, while the horse will be continually grazing.

"Of all troops in the world these are they which endure the greatest hardship and fatigue, and cost the least; and they are the best of all for making wide conquests of country. And there can be no manner of doubt that now they are the masters of the larger half of the world. Their armies are admirably ordered in the following manner:—

"You see, when a Tartar prince goes forth to war, he takes with him, say, a hundred thousand horse. Well, he appoints an officer to every ten men, one to every hundred, one to every thousand, and one to every ten thousand, so that his own orders have to be given to ten persons only, and each of these persons has to pass the orders only to other ten, and so on; none having to give orders to more than ten. And every one in turn is responsible only to the officer immediately over him; and the discipline and order that comes of this method is marvellous, for they are a people very obedient to their chiefs. . . . And when the army is on the march they have always two hundred horsemen, very well mounted, who are sent a distance of two marches in advance to reconnoitre, and these always keep ahead. They have a similar party detached in the rear and on either flank, so that there is a good look-out kept on all sides against surprise. When they are going on a distant expedition, they take no gear with them except two leather bottles for milk, and a little earthenware pot to cook their meat in, and a little tent to shelter them from rain. And in case of great urgency, they will ride ten days on end without lighting a fire or taking a meal. On such an occasion they will sustain themselves on the blood of their horses, opening a vein and letting the blood jet into their mouths, drinking till they have had enough, and then staunching it.

"They also have milk dried into a kind of paste to carry with them; and when they need food, they put this in water, and beat it up till it dissolves, and then drink it. It is prepared in this way: They boil the milk, and when the rich part floats on the top they skim it into another vessel, and of that they make butter; for the milk will not become solid till this is removed. Then they put the milk in the sun to dry. And when they go on an expedition, every man takes some ten pounds of this dried milk with him. And of a morning he will take a half-pound of it and put it in his leather bottle, with as much water as he pleases. So, as he rides along, the milk-paste and the water in the bottle get well churned together into a kind of pap, and that makes his dinner.

"When they come to an engagement with the enemy, they will gain the victory in this fashion: They never let themselves get into a regular medley, but keep perpetually riding round and shooting into the enemy. And as they do not count it any shame to run away in battle, they will sometimes pretend to do so, and in running away they turn in the saddle and shoot hard and strong at the foe, and in this way make great havoc. Their horses are trained so perfectly that they will double hither and thither, just like a dog, in a way that is quite astonishing. Thus they fight to as good purpose in running away as if they stood and faced the enemy, because of the vast volleys of arrows that they shoot in this way, turning round upon their pursuers, who are fancying that they have won the battle. But when the Tartars see that they have killed and wounded a good many horses and men, they wheel round bodily, and return to the charge in perfect order, and with loud cries; and in a very short time the enemy are routed. In truth, they are stout and valiant soldiers, and inured to war. And you perceive that it is just when the enemy sees them run, and imagines that he has gained the battle, that he has in reality lost it; for the Tartars wheel round in a moment when they judge the right time has come. And after this fashion they have won many a fight.

"All this that I have been telling you is true of the manners and customs of the genuine Tartars."

We come next to the magnificent city of Chandu—that is, Shangtu, or "Upper Towa," the Chinese title of Kublai Khan's summer palace at Kaiping-fu. The ruins, both of the city and palace, were extant as late as the end of the seventeenth century.

"When you have ridden three days from the city of Chagan Nor [Chagan Balghassan], between north-east and north, you come to a city called Chandu, which was built by the Khan now reigning. There is at this place a very fine marble palace, the rooms of which are all gilt and painted with figures of men and beasts and birds, and with a variety of trees and flowers, all wrought with such exquisite art that you regard them with delight and astonishment.

"Round this palace is built a wall, enclosing a compass of sixteen miles, and inside the park are fountains and rivers and brooks and beautiful meadows, with all kinds of wild animals (excluding such as are of ferocious nature), which the Emperor has produced and placed there to supply food for the gerfalcons and hawks which he keeps in mew. Of these the gerfalcons alone number more than two hundred, without reckoning the other hawks.

The Khan himself goes every week to see his birds sitting in mew, and sometimes he rides through the park with a leopard behind him on his horse's croup; and then, if he sees any animal that takes his fancy, he lets loose his leopard at it, and the game when taken is used to feed the hawks in mew. This he does for diversion.

"Further, at a point in the park where blooms a delightful wood, he has another palace built of bamboo, of which I must give you a description. It is gilt all over, and most elaborately finished inside. It is supported on gilt and lackered columns, on each of which stands a dragon all gilt, the tail being attached to the column, while the head uplifts the architrave, and the claws likewise being extended right and left as props to the architrave. The roof also is formed of bamboo, covered with a varnish so good and strong that no amount of rain will rot it. These canes are fully three palms in girth, and from ten to fifteen paces in length. They are cut across at each knot, and the pieces are then split so as to form from each two hollow tiles, and with them the house is roofed; only every such tile has to be nailed down to prevent the wind from lifting it. In short, the whole palace is built of these bamboos, which, I may mention, are employed for a great variety of other useful purposes. The construction of the palace is such that it can be taken down and put up again with great rapidity; and it can be removed to any place which he may desire. When erected, it is held up by more than two hundred (200) ropes of silk.

"The Emperor resides in this park of his, sometimes in the palace of marble, and sometimes in that of bamboo, for three mouths of the year, namely, June, July, and August; preferring this abode because it is by no means hot; in fact, it is very cool. When the 28th day of August arrives he takes his departure, and the bamboo palace is pulled to pieces. But I must tell you what happens when he takes his departure every year on the 28th of August.

"You must know that the Khan keeps an immense stud of white horses and mares; in truth, upwards of two hundred of them, and all pure white without a blemish. The milk of these mares is drunk by himself and family, and by no one else, except by the people of one great tribe who have also the privilege of drinking it—a privilege granted to them by Chingis Khan, on account of a certain victory which, long ago, they helped him to win. The name of the tribe is Horiad [the Uirad or Oirad].

"Now, when these mares are passing across the country, and any one falls in with them, be he the greatest lord in the land, he must not presume to pass until the mares have gone by; he must either tarry where he is, or go a half-day's round if so need be, so as not to come nigh them; for they are to be treated with the greatest respect. Well, when the Emperor sets out from the park on the 28th of August, as I have told you, the milk of all those mares is taken and sprinkled on the ground. And this is done at the bidding of the idolaters and idol-priests, who say that it is an excellent thing to sprinkle that milk on the ground every 28th of August, so that the earth and the air and the false gods shall have their share of it, and the spirits likewise that inhabit the air and the earth. And thus those beings will protect and bless the Khan, and his children, and his wives, and his folk, and his gear, his cattle and his horses, his corn, and all that is his. After this is done, the Emperor is off and away.

"But I must now tell you a strange thing that hitherto I have omitted to mention. During the three months of every year that the Khan resides at that place, if it should chance to be bad weather, there are certain crafty enchanters and astrologers in his train who are such adepts in necromancy and the diabolic arts, that they are able to prevent any cloud or storm from traversing the spot whereon the imperial palace stands. The sorcerers who do this are called Tcbit and Kesomin, which are the names of two nations of idolaters. Whatever they do in this way is by the help of the devil, but they make these people believe that it is compassed by their own sanctity and the help of God. They always go in a state of dirt and uncleanness, devoid of respect for themselves, or for those who see them, unwashed, unkempt, and sordidly attired.

"These people have another custom which I must describe to you. If a man is condemned to death, and executed by the lawful authority, they take his body, and cook and eat it. But if any one die a natural death, then they will not eat his body.

"There is another marvel performed by these Bacsi [*Bakhshi*, or *Bhikshu*], of whom I have spoken as skilled in so many enchantments. For when the Great Khan is at his capital and in his great palace, seated at his table, which stands on a platform some eight cubits above the ground, his cups are set before him on a great buffet in the middle of the hall pavement, at a distance of some ten paces from his table, and filled with wine, or other good spiced liquor such as they use. Now, when the lord desires to drink, these necromancers, by the power of their enchantments, cause the cups to move from their place without being touched by anybody, and to present themselves to the Emperor! This every one present may witness, and ofttimes there are more than two thousand persons present. 'Tis a truth, and no lie; and so will the sages of your own country who understand necromancy, tell you, for they also can perform this marvel.

"And when the idol festivals come round, these Bacsi go to the prince and say, 'Sire, the feast of such a god is come' (naming him). 'My lord, you know,' the enchanter will say, 'that this god, when he gets no offerings, always sends bad weather and spoils our seasons. So we pray you to give us such and such a number of black-faced sheep' (naming whatever number they please). 'And we also beg, good my lord, that we may have such a quantity of incense, and such a quantity of lign-aloes, and'—so much of this, so much of that, and so much of t'other, according to their fancy—'that we may perform a solemn service and a great sacrifice to our idols, and that so they may be induced to protect us and all that is ours.'

"The Bacsi say these things to the nobles entrusted with the stewardship, who stand round the Great Khan, and then repeat them to the Khan, and he then orders the nobles to give to the Bacsi anything they have demanded. And when they have received the articles, they go and make a great feast in honour of their god, and hold grand ceremonies of worship, with grand illuminations and quantities of incense of a variety of odours, which they make up from different aromatic spices. And then they cook the meat, and set it before the idols, and sprinkle their broth hither and thither, saying that in this way the idols obtain their bellyful. In this way it is that they keep their festivals. You must know that each idol has a name of his own, and a feast-day, just as our saints have their anniversaries.

"They have also immense minsters and monasteries, some as big as a small town, with upwards of two thousand monks, so to speak, in a single monastery. These monks dress more decently than the rest of the people, and shave the head and beard. Some among these Bacsi are allowed by their rule to take wives, and they have plenty of children.

"Another kind of devotees is the Sunni, who are more remarkable for their abstemiousness, and lead a life of such austerity as I will describe. All their life long they eat only bran, which they take mixed with hot water. That is their food; bran, and nothing but bran; with water for their drink. Their life is one long fast; so I may well speak of its asceticism as extraordinary. They have great idols, and very many; but they sometimes also worship fire. The other idolaters who are not also of this sect call these people heretics—*Palamis*, as we should say—because they do not worship the idols after their fashion. Those of whom I am now speaking would not take a wife on any consideration. They wear dresses of hempen stuff, black and blue, and sleep upon mats; in fact, their asceticism is something astonishing. Their idols are all feminine; that is, they bear women's names."

[It was after reading Marco Polo's account of the Great Khan's palace, as it is given in Purchas's "Pilgrims," that the poet Coleridge, falling asleep, dreamed his melodious dream of Kublai's Paradise. When he awoke he was able to recall a portion of it, beginning thus:—

"In Xanadu did Kubla Khan
    A stately pleasure-dome decree:

Where Alph, the sacred river, ran,
By caverns measureless to man,
    Down to a sunless sea.
So twice five inches of fertile ground
With walls and towers were girdled round;
And there were gardens bright with sinuous rills,
Where blossomed many an incense-bearing tree;
And here were forests, ancient as the hills,
    Enfolding sunny spots of greenery."]

The principal palace of the Great Khan was situated, however, at Cambaluc (the modern Peking), and is thus described by our Venetian:—

"It is enclosed all round by a great wall, forming a square, each side of which is a mile in length; that is to say, the whole compass thereof is four miles. This you may depend on; it is also very thick, and a good ten paces in height, whitewashed and loop-holed all round. At each angle of the wall is situated a very fine and rich palace, in which the war harness of the Emperor is kept, such as bows and quivers, saddles and bridles, and bowstrings, and everything needful for an army. Also, midway between every two of these corner palaces is another of the like; so that, taking the whole circuit of the enclosed, you will find eight vast palaces stored with the great lord's harness of war. And you must understand that each palace is reserved for only one kind of article; one being stored with bows, a second with saddles, a third with bridles, and so on, in succession, right round.

"The great wall has five gates on its southern face, the central being the great gate, which is opened only for the egress or admission of the Great Khan himself. Close on either side is a smaller one, through which all other people pass; and then, towards each angle, is another great gate, also open to people in general; so that on that side are five gates in all.

"Inside of this wall is a second, enclosing a space that is somewhat longer than it is broad. This enclosure has its eight palaces also, corresponding to those of the outer wall, and stored like them with the Emperor's harness of war. There are likewise five gates on the southern face, answering to those in the outer wall; and one gate on each of the other faces. In the centre of the second enclosure stands the Emperor's Great Palace, and I will tell you what it is like

"You must know that it is the greatest palace ever erected. Towards the north it is in contact with the outer wall, while towards the south lies a vacant space which the nobles and the soldiers are constantly traversing.

The palace itself hath no upper story, but is all on the ground floor; only the basement is raised some ten palms above the surrounding soil. And this elevation is retained by a wall of marble raised to the level of the pavement, two paces in width, and projecting beyond the base of the palace so as to form a kind of terrace-walk, by which people can pass round the building, and this is exposed to view; while along the outer edge of the wall runs a very fine pillared balustrade, up to which the people are allowed to come. The roof is very lofty, and the walls are covered with gold and silver. They are also adorned with representations of dragons, sculptured and gilt, beasts and birds, knights and idols, and divers other subjects. And on the ceiling, too, can nothing be seen but gold and silver and painting. On each of the four sides is a great marble staircase, leading to the top of the marble wall, and forming the approach to the palace.

"The hall of the palace is so large that it could easily dine six thousand people; and it is quite a marvel to see how many rooms there are besides. The building is altogether so vast, so rich, and so beautiful, that no man on earth could design anything superior to it. The outside of the roof also is all coloured with vermilion and yellow and green and blue and other hues, which are fixed with a varnish so fine and exquisite, that they shine like crystal, and lend a resplendent lustre to the palace, visible far around. This roof is so solidly and strongly constructed that it is fit to last for ever.

"On the inner side of the palace are large buildings with halls and chambers, where the Emperor's private property is placed, such as his treasures of gold, silver, gems, pearls, and gold plate, and in which the ladies and concubines reside. He occupies himself there at his own convenience, and no one else has access to it.

"Between the two walls of the enclosure which I have described are two fine parks, and beautiful trees bearing a variety of fruits. There are beasts also of sundry kinds, such as white stags and fallow deer, gazelles and roebucks, and fine squirrels of various kinds, with numbers also of the animal that gives the musk, and all manner of other beautiful creatures, insomuch that the whole place is full of them, and no spot remains void except where there is traffic of people going to and fro. The parks are covered with abundant grass; and the roads through them being all paved and raised two cubits above the surface, they never become muddy, nor does the rain lodge on them, but flows off into the meadows, quickening the soil and producing that fertility of herbage.

"From the north-western corner of the enclosure extends a fine lake, containing abundance of fish of different kinds, which the Emperor hath caused to be put in there, so that, whenever he desires any, he can have them at his pleasure. A river enters this lake and issues from it; but a grating of iron or brass is put up to prevent the escape of the fish.

"Moreover, about a bowshot from the north side of the palace is an artificial hill, made with the earth out of the lake; it is a good hundred paces in height, and a mile in compass, and is entirely covered with evergreen trees which never lose their leaves. And I assure you that wherever a beautiful tree exists, and the Emperor hears of it, he sends for it and has it transported bodily, with all its roots and the earth attached to them, and planted upon his hill. No matter how huge the tree may be, he has it carried by his elephants, and in this way he has formed the finest collection of trees in all the world. And he has also caused the whole hill to be covered with ore of azure, [35] which is very green. And thus not only are the trees all green, but the hill itself is all green likewise; and there is nothing to be seen on it that is not green; and hence it is called the Green Mount; and, in good sooth, it is well named.

"On the top of the hill, too, stands a fair large palace, which is all green outside and in, so that the hill, and the trees, and the palace form together a charming spectacle; and it is wonderful to see their uniformity of colour. Everybody who sees it is delighted. And the Great Khan has ordered this beautiful prospect for the comfort, solace, and delectation of his heart.

"You must know that besides the palace I have been describing, *i.e.* the Great Palace, the Emperor has caused another to be built, resembling his own in every respect; and this he has done for his son, when he shall reign and be Emperor after him. Hence it is made just in the same fashion, and of the same size, so that everything can be carried on in the same manner after his death. It stands on the other side of the lake from the Great Khan's palace, and a bridge is thrown across from one to the other. The prince I speak of holds now a seal of empire, but not with such complete authority as the Great Khan, who remains supreme as long as he lives."

Let us now accompany the Emperor on a hunting expedition:—

"After he has sojourned in his capital city for three months, December, January, and February, the Great Khan starts on the first day of March, and travels southward towards the Ocean Sea, a two days' journey. He takes with him fully ten thousand falconers and some five hundred falcons, besides peregrines, sakers, and other hawks in great number; and goshawks also, for flying at the water-fowl. But do not suppose that he keeps all these together by him; they are distributed hither and thither, one hundred together, or two hundred at the utmost, as he thinks proper. But they are always fowling as they advance, and the greater part of the quarry taken is carried to the Emperor. And let me tell you, when he goes thus a-fowling with his gerfalcons and other hawks, he is attended by fully ten thousand men, who are placed in couples; and these are called *Toscach*, which is as much as to say, 'Watchers.' The name describes their business. They are posted from spot to spot, always in couples, so that they cover a good deal of ground. Each of them is provided with whistle and hood, so as to be able to call in a hawk, and hold it in hand. And when the Emperor makes a cast, there in no need that he should follow it up, for the men I speak of keep so close a watch that they never lose sight of the birds, if the hawks require help, they are ready to render it.

"The Emperor's hawks, as well as those of the nobles, have a little label attached to the leg to mark them, whereon are written the names of the owner and the keeper of the bird. So that the hawk, when caught, is at once identified, and handed over to its owner. But if not, the bird is carried to a certain noble, styled the *Bulargachi*, that is, 'the Keeper of Lost Property.' And I tell you that anything found without a proper owner, whether horse, sword, or hawk, or what not, is taken immediately to that official, and he holds it in charge. Should the finder neglect to carry his trover to the Bulargachi, the latter punishes him. Likewise, the loser of any article goes to him, and should it be in his hands, he immediately gives it up to its owner. Moreover, the said noble always pitches on the highest point of the camp, with his banner displayed, in order that those who have lost or found should have no difficulty in making their way to him. Thus, nothing can be lost without being quickly found and restored. . . .

"The Emperor, on his journey, is borne upon four elephants in a fine pavilion made of timber, lined inside with plates of beaten gold, and outside with lion's skins. He always travels in this fashion on his hunting expeditions, because he is troubled with gout. He invariably keeps beside him a dozen of his choicest gerfalcons, and is attended by several of his nobles, who ride on horseback by his side. And sometimes, as they go along, and the Emperor from his chamber is discoursing with his nobles, one of the latter will exclaim, 'Sire, look out for cranes!' Then the Emperor has the top of his chamber instantly thrown open, and, having marked the cranes, he casts one of his gerfalcons, whichever he pleases; and often the quarry is struck in his sight, so that he has the most exquisite sport and diversion, as he sits in his chamber or lies on his bed; and all the nobles in attendance share the enjoyment with him! So it is not without reason I tell you that I do not believe there ever existed in the world, or will exist, a man with such sport and enjoyment as he has, or with such rare opportunities.

"And when he has travelled until he reaches a place called Cachar Modem, there he finds his tents pitched, with the tents of his sons, and his nobles, and those of his ladies, and their attendants, so that there shall be fully ten thousand in all, and all costly and handsome. And I will tell you how his own quarters are disposed. The tent in which he held his courts is large enough to accommodate a thousand persons. It is pitched with its door to the south, and the nobles and knights remain in attendance in it, while the Emperor abides in another close to it on the west side. When he wishes to speak with any person, he causes him to be summoned to the great tent. Immediately behind the latter is a spacious chamber, where he sleeps. . . . The two audience-tents and the sleeping-chamber are thus constructed:— Each of the audience-tents has three poles, which are of spice-wood, and most artfully covered with lion's skins, striped with black and white and red, so that they do not suffer from any weather. All three apartments are also covered outside with similar skins of striped lions, a substance that lasts for ever. Inside they are lined with sable and ermine, which are the finest and costliest furs in existence. . . . All the tent-ropes are of silk. In short, I may say that these tents, namely, the two halls of audience and the sleeping-chamber, are so costly, that it is not every king could afford to pay for them.

"Round about these tents are others, also fine ones and beautifully pitched, in which abide the imperial ladies, and the ladies of the different princes and officers. Tents are there also for the hawks and their keepers, so that altogether the number of tents on the plain is something wonderful. To see the many people who are thronging to and fro on every side and every day there, you would take the camp for a good large city. For you must include the physicians and astrologers and falconers, and all the other attendants on so numerous a company; and add that everybody has his own household with him, for such is their custom.

"There until the spring the Emperor remains encamped, and all that time he does nothing but go hawking among the cane brakes that fringe the abundant lakes and rivers in that region, and across broad plains plentifully frequented by cranes and swans, and all other kinds of fowl. Nor are the rest of the nobles of the camp ever weary of hunting and hawking, and daily they bring home great store of venison and feathered game of every kind. Indeed, unless you witnessed it, you would never believe what quantities of game are taken, and what marvellous sport and diversion they have while residing there in camp.

"Another thing I must mention, namely, that for twenty days' journey round the spot nobody is allowed, whoever he may be, to keep hawks or hounds, though anywhere else whoever chooses may keep them. And furthermore, throughout all the Emperor's territories, nobody, however audacious, dares to hunt any of these four animals, namely, hare, stag, buck, and roe, from the month of March to the month of October. Whoever should do so would rue it bitterly. But these people are so obedient to their Emperor's commands, that even if a man were to find one of those animals asleep by the roadside, he would not touch it for the world. And thus the game multiplies at such a rate, that the whole country swarms with it, and obtains as much as he could desire. Beyond the time I have mentioned, however, to wit, that from March to October, everybody may take these animals as he chooses.

"After the Emperor has tarried there, enjoying his sport, as I have related, from March to the middle of May, he moves with all his people, and returns straight to his capital city of Cambaluc (which is also the capital city of Cathay, as you have been told), but all the while continuing to take his diversion in hunting and hawking as he travels."

We pass on to Marco Polo's description of Tibet, which at one time was considered a part of the empire of the Mongol Khans. Its civil administration is ascribed to Kublai Khan:—

"In this region you find quantities of bamboos, full three palms in girth, and fifteen paces in length, with an interval of about three palms between the joints. And let me tell you that merchants and other travellers through that country are wont at nightfall to gather these canes and make fires of them; for as they burn they make such loud reports, that the lions and bears and other wild beasts are greatly frightened, and make off as fast as possible; in fact, nothing will induce them to come near a fire of that kind. [41] So, you see, the travellers make these fires to protect themselves and their cattle from the wild beasts, which have so greatly multiplied since the devastation of the country. And it is this multiplication of the wild beasts that prevents the country from being reoccupied. In fact, but for the help of these bamboos, which make such a noise in burning that the beasts are terrified and kept at a distance, no one would be able even to travel through the land.

"I will tell you how it is that the canes make such a noise. The people cut the green canes, of which there are vast numbers, and set fire to a heap of them at once. After they have been burning awhile they burst asunder, and this makes such a loud report, that you might hear it ten miles off. In fact, a person unused to this noise, hearing it unexpectedly, might easily go into a swoon or die of fright. But those accustomed to it care nothing about it. Hence those who are not used stuff their ears well with cotton, and wrap up their heads and faces with all the clothes they can muster; and so they get along until they have become used to the sound. It is just the same with horses. Those unused to these noises are so terrified that they break away from their halters and heel-ropes, and many a man has lost his beasts in this way. So all who do not wish to lose their horses are careful to tie all four legs, and peg the ropes down strongly, and wrap the heads and eyes and ears of the animals closely, and so they save them. But horses also, when they have heard the noise several times, cease to mind it. I tell you the truth, however, when I say that the first time you hear it nothing can be more alarming. And yet, in spite of all, the lions, bears, and other wild beasts will sometimes come and do great mischief; for in those parts they are very numerous.

"You ride for twenty days without finding any inhabited spot, so that travellers are obliged to carry all their provisions with them, and are constantly falling in with those wild beasts which are so numerous and so dangerous. After that you come at length to a tract where there are very many towns and villages. . . .

"The people are idolaters and an evil generation, holding it no sin to rob and maltreat; in fact, they are the greatest brigands on earth. They live by the chase, as well as on their cattle and the fruits of the earth.

"I should tell you also that in this country are many of the animals that produce musk, which are called in the Tartar language *Gudderi*. These robbers have great numbers of large and fierce dogs, which are of much service in catching the musk-beasts, and so they procure an abundance of musk. They have none of the Great Khan's paper money, but use salt instead of money. They are very poorly clad, for their clothes are only of the skins of beasts, and canvas, and buckram. They have a language of their own, and are called *Tebit*."

Speaking of the people who dwell in the provinces to the north-west of China, Marco Polo relates the following curious custom:—

"When any one is ill, they send for the devil-conjurors, who are the keepers of their idols. When these are come, the sick man tells what ails him, and then the conjurors incontinently begin playing on their instruments, and singing, and dancing; and the conjurors dance to such a pitch, that at last one of them will fall to the ground lifeless, like a dead man. And then the devil entereth into his body. And when his comrades see him in this plight, they begin to put questions to him about the sick man's ailment. And he will reply, 'Such or such a spirit hath been meddling with the man, for that he hath angered it and done it some despite.' Then they say, 'We pray thee to pardon him, and to take of his blood or of his goods what thou wilt in consideration of thus restoring him to health.' And when they have so prayed, the malignant spirit that is in the body of the prostrate man will, perhaps, answer, 'The sick man hath also done great despite unto such another spirit, and that one is so ill-disposed that it will not pardon him on any account.' This, at least, is the answer they get if the patient be like to die. But if he is to get better, the answer will be that they are to bring two sheep, or maybe three; and to brew ten or twelve jars of drink, very costly and abundantly spiced. Moreover, it will be announced that the sheep must be all black-faced, or of some other particular colour, as it may happen; and then all these things are to be offered in sacrifice to such and such a spirit whose name is given. And they are to bring so many conjurors, and so many ladies, and the business is to be done with a great singing of lauds, and with many lights and store of good perfumes. That is the sort of answer they get if the patient is to get well. And then the kinsfolk of the sick man go and procure all that has been commanded, and do as has been bidden, and the conjuror springs to his feet again.

"So they fetch the sheep of the prescribed colour, and slaughter them, and sprinkle the blood over such places as have been enjoined, in honour and propitiation. And the conjurors come, and the ladies, in the number that was ordered, and when all are assembled and everything is ready, they begin to dance and play and sing in honour of the spirit. And they take flesh-broth, and drink, and lign-aloes, and a great number of lights, and go about hither and thither, scattering the broth and the drink, and the meat also. And when they have done this for a while, one of the conjurors will again fall flat, and wallow there foaming at the mouth, and then the others will ask if he have yet pardoned the sick man. And sometimes he will answer 'Yes,' and sometimes he will answer 'No.' And if the answer be 'No,' they are told that something or other has to be done all over again, and then he will be pardoned; so this they do. And when all that the spirit has commanded has been done with great ceremony, then it will be announced that the man is pardoned, and will be speedily cured. So when they at length receive this reply, they announce that it is all made up with the spirit, and that he is propitiated, and they fall to eating and drinking with great joy and mirth, and he who had been lying lifeless on the ground gets up and takes his share. So when they have all eaten and drunken, every man departs home. And presently the sick man gets sound and well."

[Sir A. Phayre testifies that this account of the exorcism of evil spirits in cases of obstinate illness tallies exactly with what he himself has seen in similar cases among the Burmese; and, in truth, the practice extends widely among the non-Aryan races. Bishop Caldwell furnishes the following description of "devil-dancing" as it still exists among the Shanars of Tinnevelly:—

"When the preparations are completed and the devil-dance is about to commence, the music is at first comparatively slow; the dancer seems impassive and sullen, and he either stands still or moves about in gloomy silence. Gradually, as the music becomes quicker and louder, his excitement begins to rise. Sometimes, to help him to work himself up into a frenzy, he uses medicated draughts, cuts and lacerates himself till the blood flows, lashes himself with a huge whip, presses a burning torch to his breast, drinks the blood which flows from his own wounds, or drains the blood of the sacrifice, putting the throat of the decapitated goat to his mouth. Then, as if he had acquired new life, he begins to brandish his staff of bells, and to dance with a quick, but wild, unsteady step. Suddenly the afflatus descends; there is no mistaking that glare, or those frantic leaps. He snorts, he stares, he gyrates. The demon has now taken bodily possession of him; and though he retains the power of utterance and motion, both are under the demon's control, and his separate consciousness is in abeyance. The bystanders signalize the event by raising a long shout, attended with a peculiar vibratory noise, caused by the motion of the hand and tongue, or the tongue alone. The devil-dancer is now worshipped as a present deity, and every bystander consults him respecting his diseases, his wants, the welfare of his absent relatives, the offerings to be made for the accomplishment of his wishes, and, in short, everything for which superhuman knowledge is supposed to be available."]

"And now," says Marco Polo, in concluding his wonderful narrative,— "and now ye have heard all that we can tell you about the Tartars and the Saracens and their customs, and likewise about the other countries of the world, so far as our researches and information extend. Only we have said nothing whatever about the Greater Sea [the Mediterranean], and the provinces that lie round it, although we know it thoroughly. But it seems to me a needless and endless task to speak about places which are visited by people every day. For there are so many who sail all about that sea constantly, Venetians, and Genoese, and Pisans, and many others, that everybody knows all about it, and that is the reason that I pass it over and say nothing of it.

"Of the manner in which we took our departure from the Court of the Great Khan you have already heard, and we have related the fortunate chance that led to it. And you may be sure that, but for that fortunate chance, we should never have got away, in spite of all our trouble, and never have returned to our country again. But I believe it was God's pleasure we should return, in order that people might learn about the things the world contains. For according to what has been said in the introduction at the beginning of the book, there never was man, be he Christian or Saracen or Tartar or heathen, who ever travelled over so much of the world as did that noble and illustrious citizen of the city of Venice, Messer Marco, the son of Messer Nicolo Polo.

"Thanks be to God! Amen! Amen!"

We incline to believe, out of consideration for the modesty of "Messer Marco, the son of Messer Nicolo Polo," that he finished his narrative at the word "contains," and that the last sentence was added by his amanuensis. Yet the assertion it contains does not go beyond the truth. Of all the mediæval travellers it may be repeated that Marco Polo is the first and foremost; and the world is indebted to him for a vast amount of valuable information, which, but for his industry, his perseverance, and his intelligence, would have been wholly or partly lost. We owe to him a graphic and, as it is now known to be, an accurate picture of the condition of Asia in the thirteenth century; a picture full of lights and shadows, but interesting and instructive in every detail.

MR. GEORGE F. RUXTON,
AND HIS ADVENTURES IN MEXICO AND THE
ROCKY MOUNTAINS.

A.D. 1847.

MR. RUXTON'S sweeping condemnation of the Mexicans is, unfortunately, confirmed by most reputable authorities, or we might hesitate to reproduce it here. "From south to north," he says, "I traversed the whole of the Republic of Mexico, a distance of nearly ten thousand miles, and was thrown amongst the people of every rank, class, and station; and I regret to have to say that I cannot remember to have observed one single commendable trait in the character of the Mexican; always excepting from this sweeping clause the women of the country, who, for kindness of heart and many sterling qualities, are an ornament to their sex, and to any nation." Whatever may be affirmed to the discredit of the people, it cannot be doubted that they inhabit a country which was at one time the seat of a remarkable civilization, which presents to the traveller a succession of remarkable and frequently romantic scenery, and a wonderful variety and luxuriance of vegetation.

From the southern frontier of the United States it stretches down to the isthmus which connects the northern and southern mainlands of the great American continent. On the west its shores are washed by the waters of the Pacific; on the east, by those of the Mexican Gulf and Caribbean Sea. Roughly speaking, its area is about 850,000 square miles; its population may number ten souls to a square mile. Its form of government is pseudo-republican; and for administrative purposes it is divided into twenty-five provinces. Its capital, Mexico, has 200,000 inhabitants: its only other important towns are Puebla, 75,000 inhabitants; Guadalajara, 65,000; Guanajuata, 50,000; and San Luis and Merida, about 45,000 each.

A glance at the map will show you that Mexico consists in the main of an elevated table-land, which in the south rises up into the Cordilleras of Central America, and on the east and west descends, by more or less gradual terraces, to the sea-coast. Owing to its geographical position, this table-land enjoys the profuseness and beauty of a tropical vegetation; on the other hand, its climate is so tempered by its various elevations, which lie between 5000 and 9000 feet, that it has been found possible to naturalize the European fauna and flora. A remarkable geological feature is the volcanic belt or chain that runs from ocean to ocean between the parallels of 18° 15' and 19° 30' north latitude, and is marked by several active as well as extinct volcanoes. Among them may be named Orizaba, Cittalapetl

("The Mountain of the Star"), Popocatapetl ("The Smoking Mountain"), 17,884 feet, Istaccihuatl ("The White Woman"), and Toluca. Most of the mountain chains that break up the table-land are of comparatively low altitude; the principal is the Sierra Madre, or Tepe Serene. The two chief streams are the Rio Santiago and the Rio Grande del Norte.

In company with a young Spaniard who was travelling as far as Durango, Mr. Ruxton quitted Mexico one fine day in September, 1847, bent on crossing the country to the United States. He passed at first through a mountainous district, covered with dwarf oak and ilex; afterwards he entered upon a tract of open undulating downs, dotted with thickets. Villages were few and far between, and when found, not very attractive, consisting only of a dozen huts built of adobes, or sun-dried bricks. Crossing a rocky sierra, he came to the town of San Juan del Rio; its one-storied houses of stone, whitewashed, with barred windows, looking out upon a fair expanse of vineyard and garden. Forty miles beyond lay Queretaro; a large and well-built town of 40,000 inhabitants, surrounded by gardens and orchards. Its chief trade is the manufacture of cigars. These, as made at Queretaro, are of a peculiar shape, about three inches long, square at both ends, and exceedingly pungent in flavour. Excellent pulque is another of its products. Pulque, the national liquor of Mexico, is made from the saccharine juice of the American aloe, which attains maturity at the age of eight or fourteen years, and then flowers. Only while it is flowering may the juice be collected. The central stem which encloses the coming flower is cut off near the bottom, and a basin or hollow exposed, over which the surrounding leaves are closely gathered and fastened. The juice distils into the reservoir thus provided, and is removed three or four times during the twenty-four hours, by means of a syphon made of a species of gourd called acojote. One end is placed in the liquor, the other in the mouth of the operator, who by suction draws up the sweet fluid into the pipe, and forces it out into a bowl. Afterwards it receives the addition of a little old pulque, and is allowed to ferment for two or three days in earthen jars. When fresh, pulque, according to Mr. Ruxton, is brisk and sparkling, and the most cooling, refreshing, and delectable drink ever invented for mortals when athirst. The Mexicans call it "vino divino;" but, admirable as may be its qualities, it needs to be very temperately used.

Between Queretaro and Celaya the traveller gradually descends from the table-lands, and the air comes upon him with a warm tropical breath. Nopalos, or prickly-pears, line the road; the Indians collect the fruit— which is savoury and invigorating—with a forked stick. At Silao striking evidence of the geniality of the climate is supplied by the variety of fruit exposed for sale: oranges, lemons, grapes, chirimoyas, batatas, platanos, plantains, cumotes, grenadillas, mamayos, tunas, pears, and apples—a list which would have delighted Keats's Porphyro when he was preparing a refection for his lady-love Madeline. But if fruit be abundant, so are beggars and thieves; and Silao is not a comfortable place to live in! Mexico, according to its climatic conditions, is divided into three great divisions— the *Tierras Frias*, or Cold lands; the *Tierras Templadas*, or Temperate lands; and the *Tierras Calientes*, or Hot lands. From Celaya our travellers stooped down rapidly into the *Tierra Caliente*, and the increased temperature was every day more perceptibly felt. Jalisco, the most important town on their route, is situated on the western declivity of Anahuac, a Cordillera which unites the Andes of South and Central America with the great North American chain of the Rocky Mountains. Mr. Ruxton describes the table-land on the western ridge of the Cordillera as blessed with a fertile soil and a temperate climate. It is studded with the populous towns of Silao, Leon, Lagos, and Aguas Calientes. The central portion, of a lower elevation and consequently higher temperature, produces cotton, cochineal, vanilla, as well as every variety of cereal produce. While the littoral, or coast region, teems with fertility, and lies in the shadow of immense forests, unfortunately it is cursed by the ever-prevalent vomito, or yellow fever, and its climate is scarcely less fatal to its inhabitants than to strangers.

At La Villa de Leon, a town celebrated for robbers and murderers, Mr. Ruxton met with an adventure. About nine o'clock in the evening he was returning from the plaza, which with its great lighted fires, the stalls of the market-people, the strange garb of the peasantry, and the snow-white sarapos, or cloaks, of the idlers of the town, presented a stirring aspect, when, striking into a dark and narrow street, a group of vagabonds, at the door of a pulque shop, detected that he was a stranger, and, mistaking his nationality, yelled at him: "Let's kill him, the Texan!" Having no weapon but a bowie-knife, and not desiring an encounter with such overwhelming numbers, he turned off into another street; but the rascals followed him, renewing their wild cries. Happily, a dark doorway invited him to seek its shelter, and while crouching in its obscurity, he could see them rush by, knives in hand. When he thought they had all passed, he stepped forth, to find himself confronted by three wretches who brought up the rear, and who, brandishing their knives and rushing headlong at him, cried, "Here he is, here he is; kill him!" As the foremost rushed at him with uplifted blade, he swiftly stepped aside, and at the same moment thrust at him with his bowie. The robber fell on his knees with a cry of "Me ha matado!" ("He has killed me!"), and fell on his face. One of his companions hastened to his assistance; the other dashed upon Mr. Ruxton, but, confused by his calm attitude of preparation, fell back a few paces, and finally slunk away. Mr. Ruxton returned at once to his quarters, ordered out the horses, and in a few minutes was on his road.

By way of Aguas Calientes, a very pretty town, and Zacatecas, a populous mining town, he proceeded towards the Hacienda (or farm) of San Nicolas, with the view of traversing that singular volcanic region, the *Mal Pais*. Down to a comparatively recent period, it would seem to have been the theatre of plutonic phenomena of an extraordinary character. The convexity of the district enables the traveller to judge very readily of the extent of the convulsion, which has spread to a distance of twelve or fourteen miles from the central crater. The said crater measures about fifteen hundred feet in circumference, and its sides are covered with dwarf oaks, mezquito, and cocoa trees, which find a rich nourishment in the chinks and crevices of the lava. At the bottom stagnate the green and slimy waters of a small lake, which is fringed with rank shrubs and cacti, growing among huge blocks of lava and scoriæ. Not a breath of air disturbs its inky surface, save when a huge water-snake undulates across it, or a duck and her progeny swim out from their covert among the bushes.

"I led my horse," says Mr. Ruxton, "down to the edge of the water, but he refused to drink the slimy liquid, in which frogs, efts, and reptiles of every kind were darting and diving. Many new and curious water-plants floated near the margin, and one, lotus-leaved, with small delicate tendrils, formed a kind of network on the water, with a superb crimson flower, which exhibited a beautiful contrast with the inky blackness of the pool. His Mexicans, as they passed this spot, crossed themselves reverently, and muttered an *Ave Maria*; for in the lonely regions of the Mal Pais, the superstitious Indian believes that demons and gnomes and spirits of evil persons have their dwelling-places, whence they not unfrequently pounce upon the solitary traveller, to carry him into the cavernous bowels of the earth. The arched roof of the supposed prison-house resounding to the tread of their horses as they pass the dreaded spot, they feel a sudden dread, and, with rapidly muttered prayers, they handle their amulets and charms to drive away the treacherous bogies who invisibly beset the path."

From the Mal Pais Mr. Ruxton travelled onward to the rancho of La Punta, a famous cattle-breeding station.

In the preceding autumn it had been harried by a party of Comanche Indians, who, one day, without warning, rode across the sierra and swooped down upon it, killing, as they passed, the peones, or labourers, whom they found at work in the road. On their appearance the men made no attempt to defend the rancho, but fled at full speed, abandoning the women and children to their terrible fate. Some were carried away captives; some pierced with arrows and lances, and left for dead; others made the victims of unspeakable outrages. The ranchero's wife, with her two adult daughters and several younger children, fled from the rancho at the first alarm, to conceal themselves under a wooden bridge, which crossed a neighbouring stream. For several hours they escaped detection; but at last some Indians drew near their hiding-place, and a young chief took his station on the bridge to issue his commands. With keen eyes he examined the spot, and discovered the terror-stricken fugitives; but he pretended not to have seen them, playing with them as a cat might with a mouse. He hoped, he was heard to say, that he should find out where the women were concealed, for he wanted a Mexican wife and a handful of scalps. Then he leaped from the bridge, and thrust his lance under it with a yell of exultation; the point pierced the woman's arm, and she shrieked aloud. She and her children were forthwith drawn from their retreat.

"Alas, alas, what a moment was that!" said the poor woman, as she told her painful story. The savages brandished their tomahawks around her children, and she thought that the last farewell had been taken. They behaved, however, with unusual clemency; the captives were released, and allowed to return to their home—to find it a wreck, and the ground strewn with the dead bodies of their kinsmen and friends.

"Ay de mi!" ("Woe is me!")

While at La Punta, our traveller was witness of the Mexican sport of the "Coléa de toros" (or "bull-tailing"), for the enjoyment of which two or three hundred rancheros had assembled from the neighbouring plantations.

A hundred bulls were shut up in a large corral, or enclosure, at one end of which had been erected a building for the convenience of the lady spectators. The horsemen, brave in their picturesque Mexican costume, were grouped around the corral, examining the animals as they were driven to and fro in order to increase their excitement, while the ranchero himself, and his sons, brandishing long lances, were busily engaged in forcing the wilder and more active bulls into a second enclosure. When this had been effected, the entrance was thrown open, and out dashed, with glaring eyes, tossing head, and lashing tail, a fine bull, to gallop at his topmost speed over the grassy plain before him, followed by the whole crowd of shouting, yelling horsemen, each of whom endeavoured to outstrip the other, and overtake the flying animal. At first they all kept close together, riding very equally, and preserving excellent order, but very soon superior skill or strength or daring began to tell, and in front of the main body shot forth a few of the cavaliers. Heading them all, in swift pursuit of the rolling cloud of dust which indicated the bull's track, rode the son of the ranchero, a boy about twelve years old; and as he swayed this way and that when the bull doubled, the women made the air ring with their shrill vivas. "Viva, Pepito! viva!" cried his mother; and, dashing his spurs into his horse's streaming flanks, the brave lad ran the race. But before long the others came up with stealthy strides; soon they were abreast of him. The pace quickened; the horses themselves seemed to share the excitement; the men shouted, the women screamed; each urged on her favourite—"Alza!—Bernardo!—Por mi amor, Juan Maria!—Viva, Pepitito!" A stalwart Mexican, mounted on a fine roan, eventually took the lead, and every moment increased the distance between himself and his competitors. But Pepito's quick eyes detected a sudden movement of the bull, and saw that, concealed by the dust, he had wheeled off at a sharp angle from his former course. In an instant Pepe did the same, and dashed in front of him, amid a fresh outburst of cheers and vivas. Getting on the bull's left quarter, he stooped down to seize his tail, and secure it under his right leg, so as to bring him to the ground. But for a manœuvre which requires great muscular power, Pepe's strength was not equal to his spirit, and, in attempting it, he was dragged from his saddle, and thrown to the ground, senseless. Several horsemen had by this time come up, and the bold rider of the roan galloping ahead, threw his right leg over the bull's tail, and turning his horse sharply outwards, upset the brute in the midst of his fiery charge, rolling him over and over in the dust.

Another bull was then let loose, and the wild ride recommenced; nor, until the corral was empty, and every horse and horseman completely spent, did the game cease. It is a rude game, though full of excitement; a rude game, and, perhaps, a cruel one; but we must not be harsh in our judgment, remembering that our English sports and pastimes have not always been exempt from a taint of ferocity.

A less manly and much more cruel equestrian game is called "el Gallo" ("the Cock"). Poor chanticleer is tied by the leg to a post driven into the ground, or to a tree, his head and neck being well greased. At a given signal the horsemen start all together, and he who first reaches the bird, and seizing it by its neck, releases it from the fastenings, carries off the prize. The well-greased neck generally eludes the eager fingers of him who first clutches it; but whoever gets hold of the prize is immediately pursued by the rest, intent upon depriving him of it. In the *mêlée* the unfortunate rooster is literally torn to pieces, which the successful horsemen present as *gages d'amour* to their lady-loves.

At Durango, the capital of Northern Mexico, popularly known as "the City of Scorpions," the traveller was shown a large mass of malleable iron, which lies isolated in the centre of the plain. It is supposed to be an aerolite, because identical in physical character and composition with certain aerolites which fell in some part of Hungary in 1751. Durango is 650 miles from Mexico, and, according to Humboldt, 6845 feet above the sea. At the time of Mr. Ruxton's visit, it was expecting an attack from the Comanche Indians, of whose sanguinary ferocity he tells the following "owre true" story:—

Half-way between Durango and Chihuahua, in the Rio Florido valley, lived a family of hardy vaqueros, or cattle-herders, the head of whom, a stalwart man of sixty, rejoiced in the sobriquet of El Coxo ("The Cripple"). He had eight sons, bold, resolute, vigorous fellows, famous for their prowess in horsemanship, their daring and skill at the "colea" or "el Gallo." Of this goodly company, reminding us of the Nortons in Wordsworth's "White Doe of Rylstone"—

> "None for beauty or for worth
> Like those eight sons—who, in a ring
> (Ripe men, or blooming in life's spring),
> Each with a lance, erect and tall,
> A falchion and a buckler small,
> Stood by their sire,"—

the handsomest and most skilful was, perhaps, the third, by name Escamilla, "a proper lad of twenty, five feet ten out of his zapatos, straight as an organo, and lithesome as a reed." Having been educated at Queretaro, he was more refined than his brothers, and had acquired a taste for dress, which enabled him to set off his comeliness to the best advantage, and made him the cynosure of "the bright eyes" of all the neighbouring rancheras. Next to him came Juan Maria, who was scarcely less skilful, and certainly not less daring than his brother, and by good judges was reputed to be even handsomer, that is, manlier and more robust, though inferior in polish of manner and picturesqueness of appearance. Until Escamilla's return from Queretaro, he had always been victor at "el Gallo" and the "colea," and had laid his spoils at the feet of the beauty of the valley, Isabel Mora, a charming black-eyed damsel of sixteen, called from the hacienda where she resided, Isabel de la Cadena. It was understood that she accepted them with pleasure, and rewarded the suitor with her smiles.

But the course of true love never does run smooth, and in this instance it was fated to be interrupted by fraternal treachery. Escamilla contrived to win the fickle beauty's affections from his brother, who, however, instead of resenting the deceit, magnanimously forgave it, and withdrew all pretensions to her hand. Escamilla and Isabel were duly affianced, and a day was fixed for their marriage, which was to take place at the bride's hacienda; and in honour of the occasion a grand "funcion de toros" was proclaimed, to which all the neighbours (the nearest of whom, by the way, was forty miles distant) were duly invited.

Two days before the appointed wedding-day, El Coxo and his eight sons made their appearance, extorting an admiring murmur from all beholders as, mounted on superb steeds, they rode gaily into the hacienda.

On the following day, leaving Escamilla at home El Coxo and the rest of his sons accompanied the master of the hacienda into the plains, to assist him in the arduous work of driving in the bulls required for the morrow's sport; while the other rancheros were busy in constructing the large corral intended to secure them.

Evening was drawing near; the sun dropped rapidly behind the rugged crest of the sierra, investing each ridge and precipice with a luminous glory of gold and purple; while the cold grey shadow of the coming night was swiftly creeping over the plain beneath. The cry of the cranes was heard in the silence, as, wedge-shaped, like the Macedonian phalanx of old, they pursued their aerial flight; the shrill pipe of the mother quail summoned together her foraging progeny; the brown hare stole from its covert and prowled about in search of food; and the lowing cattle assembled on the bank of the stream to quench their thirst before they were driven to their stalls. The peones, or labourers of the farm, with slow gait were returning from the scene of their day's work; while at the doors of the cottages the women, with naked arms, were pounding the tortillas on stone slabs in preparation for the evening meal. Everything indicated that the hours of labour had passed, and those of rest and refreshment come.

Escamilla and Isabel were wandering among the hushed pastures, where the last rays of the sun still lingered with a soft subdued radiance, building those airy castles in the construction of which happy youth is always so eager and so dexterous. In the distance they saw a little cloud of dust rising from the plain; in another direction they heard the shouts of the returning cowherds, and the heavy hoofs of the bulls they were driving towards the corral. In advance rode a single horseman, swiftly making for the hacienda.

Meanwhile, the cloud of dust rolled onwards rapidly, and out of it emerged several cavaliers, who suddenly dashed towards the two happy lovers. "Here come the bull-fighters," exclaimed Isabel; and with natural modesty she added, "Let us return."

"Perhaps they are my father and brothers," answered Escamilla. "Yes, look; there are eight of them. Do you not see?"

Ay, she *did* see, as her gaze rested on the group of horsemen, who, thundering across the mead, were now within a few yards of them. She *did* see, and the blood ran cold in her veins, and her face turned white with fear; for they were Comanche Indians, naked to the waist, horrible in their war-paint, and fierce with brandished spears. Escamilla saw them, too, and shrieking, "Los barbaros! los barbaros!" he fled with rapid foot, and, like a coward, abandoned his affianced to her fate.

A horseman met him: it was Juan Maria, who, having lassoed a little antelope on the plains, was riding in advance of his company to present it to the fickle Isabel. Glancing around, he saw her imminent danger; flung down the animal he was carrying in his arms, dashed his spurs desperately into his horse's sides, and hastened to her rescue. "Salva me, Juan Maria!" she cried, "salva me!" ("save me"). But the bloodthirsty savages were before him. With a ferocious whoop, the foremost plunged his spear into her heart, and in a moment her scalp was hanging from his saddle-bow. He did not long enjoy his triumph. A clatter of hoofs caused him to turn; and, behold, Juan Maria, with lasso swinging round his head, and his heart beating with the desire of vengeance, rode fiercely towards the murderer, heedless of the storm of arrows that rained upon him. The savage shrank from the encounter; but the open coil of the lasso, whirling through the air, fell over his head, and dragged him to the ground with a fatal crash.

The odds, however, were against Juan Maria, who, surrounded by Indians, had no other weapon than a small machete, or rusty sword. Bating not one jot of heart or hope, he rushed on the nearest Indian, and dealt a blow at his head, which cleft it open; the savage fell dead. Daunted by the Mexican's surpassing courage, the others kept at a distance, discharging their swift arrows, and piercing him with many wounds. Spurring his horse towards them, he fought on bravely, cheered by the shouts of his father and brothers, who were galloping full speed to his support. Before they could reach him, an arrow, discharged at but a few paces' distance, penetrated his heart. He slipped heavily from his horse, and one of the Comanches rode away in triumph, with the heroic Mexican's scalp as a trophy.

At that moment the Indians were reinforced by some thirty or forty of their tribe, and a desperate struggle ensued between them and El Coxo and his sons. The latter, burning with rage at the death of their brother, fought with such eager courage, that, outnumbered as they were, they slew half a dozen of the Comanches. It is probable, however, they would have been overpowered but for the arrival of the rancheros, who, coming up from the hacienda, put the Indians to flight. As night had darkened in the sky, they did not pursue; but returned to the hacienda with the dead bodies of Juan Maria and Isabel, who were buried the next day, side by side, at the very hour that had been fixed for the unfortunate Isabel's marriage. As for Escamilla, ashamed of his cowardice, he was seen no more in the valley of the Rio Florido, but settled at Queretaro, where he afterwards married.

This tragedy occurred on the 11th of October, 1845.

From Durango Mr. Ruxton proceeded westward for Chihuahua and New Mexico. On the second day of his journey an unpleasant incident very sternly convinced him of the treachery and bloodthirstiness of the lower Mexicans. He was riding slowly ahead of his native attendant, whom he had hired at Durango, when the sudden report of fire-arms, and the whiz of a bullet close to his head, caused him to turn sharply round, and he beheld his amiable mozo [young man], pistol in hand, some fifteen yards behind him, looking guilty as well as foolish. Drawing a pistol from his holsters, Mr. Ruxton rode up to him immediately, and was about to blow out his brains, when his terror-stricken and absurdly guilty-looking face turned his employer's wrath into "an immoderate fit of laughter."

"Amigo," said Mr. Ruxton, "do you call this being skilled, as you boasted, in the use of arms, to miss my head at fifteen yards?"

"Ah, caballero, in the name of all the saints, I did not fire at you, but at a duck which was flying over the road. Your worship cannot believe I would do such a thing." Now, the pistols which Mr. Ruxton had given him to carry were secured in a pair of holsters tightly buckled and strapped round his waist. To unbuckle them at any time was difficult; to unbuckle them in time to get one out to fire at a flying duck, was impossible. Mr. Ruxton knew that the duck was an invention, and a clumsy one, and to prevent another treacherous attack, took from the fellow everything in the shape of offensive weapon, including even his knife. Then, after lecturing him severely, he administered a sound thrashing with the buckle-end of his surcingle, and promised him that, if he were suspected of even dreaming of another attempt at murder, he would be pistolled without a moment's hesitation.

After narrowly escaping a collision with a party of Indians, Mr. Ruxton reached a place called El Gallo, where he resided for a couple of days in the house of a farmer. He tells us that in a rancho the time is occupied as follows:—The females of the family rise at daybreak, and prepare the chocolate, or alde, which is eaten the first thing in the morning. About nine o'clock, breakfast is served, consisting of chile colorado, frijoles (beans), and tortillas (omelettes). Dinner, which takes place at noon, and supper at sunset, are both substantial meals. Meanwhile, the men employ themselves in the fields or attending to the animals; the women about the house, making clothes, cleaning, cooking, washing. In the evening the family shell corn, and chat; or a guitar is brought, and singing and dancing are continued until it is time to retire.

Riding onward from El Gallo, Mr. Ruxton turned aside from the regular route to kill an antelope and broil a collop for breakfast. He was descending the sierra to quench his thirst at a stream which flowed through a cañon, or deep ravine, when a herd of antelopes passed him, and stopped to feed on a grassy plateau near at hand. He started in pursuit. As soon as he got within rifle-shot, he crept between two rocks at the edge of the hollow, and raised his head to reconnoitre, when he saw a sight which startled him, as the footprint on the sand startled Robinson Crusoe. About two hundred yards from the cañon, and scarcely twice that distance from his place of concealment, eleven Comanches, duly equipped for war, each with lance and bow and arrow, and the chief with a rifle also, were riding along in Indian file. They were naked to the waist, their buffalo robes being thrown off their shoulders, and lying on their hips and across the saddle, which was a mere pad of buffalo-skin. Slowly they drew towards the cañon, as if to cross it by a deer-path near the spot where Mr. Ruxton lay concealed. The odds were great; but he was advantageously posted, and he held in readiness his rifle, a double-barrelled carbine, and a couple of pistols. If he were attacked, he thought he could make a good defence; but, if unobserved, he had nothing to gain by attacking them. On they came, laughing and talking, and Mr. Ruxton, raising his rifle and supporting it in the fork of a bush which served as a screen, covered the chief with deadly aim. On they came, but suddenly diverged from the deer-path and struck across the plain, thereby saving the chief's life, and probably Mr. Ruxton's. As soon as they had disappeared, he recrossed the sierra, and returned for the night to El Gallo.

The next stage from El Gallo was Mapimi, situated at the foot of a range of mountains which teems with the precious metals. There he got rid of his mozo, or native attendant, and engaged in his place a little Irishman, who had been eighteen years in Mexico, and had almost forgotten his own language. He readily agreed to accompany him to Chihuahua, having no fear of the Indians, though they infested the country through which the travellers would have to pass. They reached Chihuahua, however, without misadventure. Its territory is described as a paradise for sportsmen. The common black or American bear, and the formidable grizzly bear, inhabit the sierras and mountains; and in the latter is found the carnero cimarron, or big-horn sheep. Elk, black-tailed deer, cola-arieta (a large species of the fallow deer), the common American red deer, and antelope, are everywhere abundant. Of smaller game the most numerous are peccaries, hares, and rabbits; and in the streams the beavers still construct their dams. There are two varieties of wolf—the white, or mountain wolf, and the cayeute, or coyote, commonly called the prairie-dog. Of birds the most common are the faisan (a species of pheasant), snipe, plover, crane, and the quail, or rather a bird between a partridge and a quail.

The entomologist would find much to interest him in the plains of Chihuahua, and especially an insect which seems almost peculiar to that part of Mexico. From four to six inches in length, it has four long slender legs. Its body, to the naked eye, seems nothing more than a blade of grass, and has no apparent muscular action or vitality except in the two antennæ, which are about half an inch long. It moves very slowly upon its long legs, and altogether looks not unlike a blade of grass carried by ants. The Mexicans assert that if horse or mule swallow these zacateros (so called from *zacato*, grass), it invariably dies; but the assertion may well be doubted. The variety of spiders, bugs, and beetles is endless, including the tarantula and the cocuyo, or lantern-bug. Of reptiles the most common are the rattlesnake and the copper-head: both are poisonous; and the sting of the scorpion is fatal under some conditions. The grotesque but harmless cameleon abounds in the plains. On the American prairies it is known as the "horned frog."

Vegetation is very scanty in Chihuahua. The shrub that covers its plains, the mezquit, is a species of acacia, growing to a height of ten or twelve feet. The seeds, contained in a small pod, resemble those of the laburnum, and are used by the Apache Indians to make a kind of bread, or cake, which is not unpleasant to the taste. This constantly recurring and ugly shrub, according to Mr. Ruxton, becomes quite an eyesore to the traveller who crosses the mezquit-covered plains. It is the only thing in the shape of a tree seen for hundreds of miles, except here and there a solitary alamo or willow, overhanging a spring, and invariably bestowing its name on the rancho or hacienda which may generally be found in the vicinity of water. Thus day after day the traveller passed the ranchos of El Sauz, Los Sauzes, Los Sauzilles—the willow, the willows, the little willows,—or El Alamo, Los Alamitos—the poplar, the little poplars. The last is the only timber found on the streams in northern Mexico, and on the Del Norte and the Arkansas it grows to a great size.

Leaving Chihuahua, Mr. Ruxton set out for the capital of New Mexico, escorted by three dragoons of the regiment of Vera Cruz, and carrying despatches from the governor to the commander of the American troops then posted on the frontier. At El Paso del Norte he entered a valley of great fertility; but this delightful change of scenery lasted only as far as San Diego, where begins the dreaded and dreadful wilderness significantly known as the *Jornada del Muerto*, or "Dead Man's Journey." Not only is it cursed by an absolute want of water and pasture, but it is the favourite foraging-ground of the Apache Indians, who are always on the alert to surprise the unwary traveller, to plunder and kill him. There is no vegetation but artemisia (sago) and screw-wood (torscilla). About half-way lies a hollow or depression called the *Laguna del Muerto*, or "Dead Man's Lake," but this is hard and dry except in the rainy season. Mr. Ruxton's horses suffered considerably, but the "Dead Man's Journey" of ninety-five or one hundred miles was performed, nevertheless, without accident in twenty-four hours.

At Fray Cristoval Mr. Ruxton came upon the river Del Norte, and thence pushed along its banks to the ruins of Valverde, where, encamped in the shade of noble trees, he found a trading caravan and a United States surveying party, under the command of a Lieutenant Abert. The traders' waggons were drawn up so as to form a corral, or square—a laager, as the Boers of South Africa call it—constituting a truly formidable encampment, which, lined with the fire of some hundred rifles, could defy the attacks of Indians or Mexicans. "Scattered about," says Mr. Ruxton, "were tents and shanties of logs and branches of every conceivable form, round which lounged wild-looking Missourians; some looking at the camp-fires, some cleaning their rifles or firing at targets—'blazes' cut in the trees—with a bull's-eye made with wet powder on the white bark. From morning till night the camp resounded with the popping of rifles, firing at marks for prizes of tobacco, or at any living creature which presented itself. The oxen, horses, and mules were sent out at daylight to pasture on the grass of the prairie, and at sunset made their appearance, driven in by the Mexican herders, and were secured for the night in the corrals. My own animals roamed at will, but every evening came to the river to drink, and made their way to my camp, where they would frequently stay round the fire all night. They never required herding, for they made their appearance as regularly as the day closed, and would come to my whistle whenever I required my hunting mule."

Mr. Ruxton remained several days at Valverde in order to recruit his animals. He amused himself by hunting. Deer and antelope were plentiful; so were turkeys, hares, rabbits, and quail on the plain, geese and ducks in the river; and he had even a shot—an unsuccessful one—at a painter, or panther. In some men the love of sport amounts to a passion, and in Mr. Ruxton it seems to have been equalled or surpassed only by his love of adventure. But about the middle of December the camp broke up, the traders departing for Fray Cristoval; while Mr. Ruxton resumed his northward journey, in company with Lieutenant Abert's party. Crossing the Del Norte, he arrived at Socorro, the first settlement of New Mexico upon this river. Here the houses are *not* painted, but the women *are*; they stain their faces, from forehead to chin, with the fire-red juice of the alegria, to protect the skin from the effects of the sun. At Galisteo he met with a typical Yankee, of the kind Sam Slick has made us familiar with—a kind that is rapidly dying out,—sharp, active, self-reliant; a cunning mixture of inquisitiveness, shrewdness, and good nature. On reaching Mr. Ruxton's encampment he unyoked his twelve oxen, approached the camp-fire, and seated himself almost in the blaze, stretching his long lean legs at the same time into the ashes. Then he began: "Sich a poor old country, I say! Wall, strangers, an ugly camp this, I swar; and what my cattle ull do I don't know, for they have not eat since we put out of Santa Fé, and are very near give out, that's a fact; and thar's nothin' here for 'em to eat, surely. Wall, they must jist hold on till to-morrow, for I have only got a pint of corn apiece for 'em tonight anyhow, so there's no two ways about that. Strangers, I guess now you'll have a skillet among ye; if yev a mind to trade, I'll jist have it right off; anyhow, I'll jist borrow it to-night to bake my bread, and, if you wish to trade, name your price. . . . Sich a poor old country, say I! Jist look at them oxen, wull ye!—they've nigh upon two hundred miles to go; for I'm bound to catch up the sogers afore they reach the Pass, and there's not a go in 'em."

"Well," remarked Mr. Ruxton, "would it not be as well for you to feed them at once and let them rest?"

"Wall, I guess if you'll some of you lend me a hand, I'll fix 'em right off; tho', I tell you! they've give me a pretty lot of trouble, they have, I tell you! but the critturs will have to eat, I b'lieve!"

The aid asked for was given, and some corn added to the scanty rations which he put before his wearied and hungry oxen. When they had been fixed, the Yankee returned to the fire and baked his cake, fried his bacon, and made his coffee, while his tongue kept up an incessant clatter. He was all alone, with a journey of two hundred miles before him, and his waggon and twelve oxen to look after; his sole thought and object, however, were dollars, dollars, dollars! He caught up every article he saw lying about, wondered what it cost and what it was worth, offered to trade for it, or for anything else which anybody might be disposed to offer, never waiting for an answer, but rattling on, eating and drinking and talking without pause; until at last, gathering himself up, he said, "Wall, I guess I'll turn into my waggon now, and some of you will, maybe, give a look round at the cattle every now and then, and I'll thank you." No sooner said than done. With a hop, step, and a jump, he sprang into his waggon, and was snoring in a couple of minutes.

Next morning, at daybreak, while he was still asleep, Mr. Ruxton resumed his journey, and before evening entered Santa Fé, after a ride in all of nearly two thousand miles.

There was nothing in Santa Fé to repay him for all he had undergone in getting there. The houses were built of sun-dried mud, and every other one was a grocery, that is, a gin or whisky shop, where Mexicans and Americans were drinking eagerly or playing monté. The streets were filled with brawlers, among whom Pueblo Indians and priests endeavoured to make their way. Donkey-loads of hoja, or corn-shucks, were hawked about for sale. It was noise everywhere; noise and filth, dirt and drink. The town contains about 3500 inhabitants, and lies at the foot of a summit of the eastern chain of the Rocky Mountains, about fourteen miles from the river Del Norte. As for the province, it covers an area of 6000 square miles, with a population of 70,000, divided among the Mexico-Spanish (descendants of the original settlers), the Mestizos (or half-castes), and the Indian Manzos or Pueblos (the aboriginal inhabitants).

Mr. Ruxton was so disgusted with Santa Fé, that in a very few days he had packed his mules, taken his leave of its profanity, drunkenness, and squalidness, and, through the valley of Taos, continued his northward route. The landscape was now ennobled by the majesty of the Rocky Mountains, with cool green valleys and misty plains lying among them, through which the river had hewn its way in deep rocky cañons. The scenery had assumed a new character of grandeur, and Mr. Ruxton surveyed it with admiration. At the Rio Colorado he crossed the United States frontier, and plunged into the wild expanse of snow, with towering peaks rising on every side, that lay before him; his object being to cross the Rocky Mountains by the trail or track of the Ute Indians, and strike the river Arkansas near its head-waters. The cold was intense, and when a cutting wind swept over the bleak plains or roared through the wooded valleys, the hardy traveller found scarcely endurable.

Stricken almost to the heart, he suffered the antelope that bounded past— hunter as he was!—to go unscathed. His hands, rigid as those of "the Commandant" in the statue-scene of Mozart's "Don Giovanni," dropped the reins of his horse, and allowed him to travel as he pleased. The half-breed who attended him, wrapped himself round in his blanket, and heaved a sigh at the thought of the fine venison that was being lost. At length, a troop of some three thousand swept almost over them, and Mr. Ruxton's instincts as a sportsman prevailed over the inertness and deadness induced by the icy air; he sprang from his horse, knelt down, and sent a bullet right into the midst. At the report two antelopes leaped into the air, to fall prostrate in the dust; one of them shot in the neck, through which the ball had passed into the body of the other. While he was cutting up the prize, half a dozen wolves howled around, drawn to the spot by the scent of blood. A couple of these creatures, tamed by hunger, gradually drew nearer, occasionally crouching on their haunches, and licking their eager lips as if already partaking of the banquet. Mr. Ruxton flung at them a large piece of meat; whereupon the whole pack threw themselves upon it, growling and fighting, and actually tearing each other in the wild, fierce fray. "I am sure," says our traveller, "I might have approached near enough to have seized one by the tail, so entirely regardless of my vicinity did they appear. They were doubtless rendered more ravenous than usual by the uncommon severity of the weather, and from the fact of the antelope congregating in large bands, were unable to prey upon these animals, which are their favourite food. Although rarely attacking a man, yet in such seasons as the present I have no doubt that they would not hesitate to charge upon a solitary traveller in the night, particularly as in winter they congregate in troops of from ten to fifty. They are so abundant in the mountains, that the hunter takes no notice of them, and seldom throws away upon the skulking beasts a charge of powder and lead."

Mr. Ruxton pitched his camp at Rib Creek one night; at La Culebra, or Snake Creek, the next; at La Trinchera, or Bowl Creek, on the third. The cold continued excessive. The blast seemed to carry death upon its wings; snow and sleet fell in heavy showers; the streams were covered with a solid crust of ice. But the worst part of the journey was through the Vallerito, or Little Valley—the "Wind-trap," as the mountaineers expressively call it—a small circular basin in the midst of rugged mountains, which receives the winds through their deep gorges and down their precipitous sides, and pens them up in its confined area to battle with one another, and with the unfortunates who are forced to traverse it. How they beat and rage and howl and roar! How they buffet the traveller in the face, and clasp him round the body as if they would strangle him! How they dash against the stumbling mules, and whirl the thick snow about them, and plunge them into dense deep drifts, where they lie half buried! This "Wind-trap" is only four miles long; and yet Mr. Ruxton was more than half a day in getting through it.

Once clear of it, he began the ascent of the mountain which forms the watershed of the Del Norte and Arkansas rivers. The view from the summit was as wild and drear as one of the circles in Dante's "Inferno." Looking back, the traveller saw everywhere a dense white pall or shroud of snow, which seemed to conceal but partially the rigid limbs of the dead and frozen earth. In front of him stretched the main chain of the Rocky Mountains, dominated by the lofty crest of James's or Pike's Peak; to the south-east, large against the sky, loomed the grim bulk of the two Cumbres Españolas. At his feet, a narrow valley, green with dwarf oak and pine, was brightened by the glancing lights of a little stream. Everywhere against the horizon rose rugged summits and ridges, snow-clad and pine-clad, and partly separated by rocky gorges. To the eastward the mountain mass fell off into detached spires and buttresses, and descended in broken terraces to the vast prairies, which extended far beyond the limit of vision, "a sea of seeming barrenness, vast and dismal." As the traveller gazed upon them, billows of dust swept over the monotonous surface, impelled by a driving hurricane. Soon the mad wind reached the mountain-top, and splintered the tall pines, and roared and raved in its insatiable fury, and filled the air with great whirls of snow, and heaped it up in dazzling drifts against the trees. Its stern voice made the silence and the solitude all the more palpable. For not a sound of bird or beast was to be heard; nor was there sign or token of human life. In such a scene man is made to feel his own littleness. In the presence of the giant forces of Nature he seems so mean and powerless that his heart sinks within him, and his brain grows dizzy, until he remembers that behind those forces is a Power, eternal and supreme—a Power that seeks not to destroy, but to bless and comfort and save.

With no little difficulty, Mr. Ruxton and his guide conveyed their mules and horses down the steep eastern side of the mountain into the valley beneath. Across Greenhorn Creek they pushed forward to the banks of the San Carlos; and fourteen miles beyond, they struck the Arkansas, a few hundred yards above the mouth of Boiling Spring River. There he was hospitably entertained in the "lodge" of a certain mountaineer and ex-trapper, John Hawkins.

The home and haunt of the trapper is the vast region of forest and prairie known as the Far West. He extends his operations from the Mississippi to the mouth of the western Colorado, from the frozen wastes of the north to the Gila in Mexico; making war against every animal whose skin or fur is of any value, and exhibiting in its pursuit the highest powers of endurance and tenacity, a reckless courage, and an inexhaustible fertility of resource. On starting for a hunt, whether as the "hired hand" of a fur company, or working on his own account, he provides himself with two or three horses or mules—one for saddle, the others for packs—and six traps, which are carried in a leather bag called a "trap-sack." In a wallet of dressed buffalo-skin, called a "possible-sack," he carries his ammunition, a few pounds of tobacco, and dressed deerskins for mocassins and other articles. When hunting, he loads his saddle mule with the "possible" and "trap-sack;" the furs are packed on the baggage mules. His costume is a hunting shirt of dressed buckskin, ornamented with long fringes; and pantaloons of the same material, but decorated with porcupine quills and long fringes down the outside of the leg. His head bears a flexible felt hat; his feet are protected by mocassins. Round his neck is slung his pipe-holder, generally a love token, in the shape of a heart, garnished with beads and porcupine quills. Over his left shoulder and under his right arm hang his powder-horn and bullet-pouch, in which are stored his balls, flint and steel, and all kinds of "odds and ends." A large butcher-knife, in a sheath of buffalo-hide, is carried in a belt, and fastened to it by a chain or guard of steel. A tomahawk is also often added, and a long heavy rifle is necessarily included in the equipment.

Thus provided (we quote now from Mr. Ruxton), and having determined the locality of his trapping-ground, he starts for the mountains, sometimes with three or four companions, as soon as the worst of the winter has passed. When he reaches his hunting-grounds, he follows up the creeks and streams, vigilantly looking out for "sign." If he observes a cotton-wood tree lying prone, he examines it to discover if its fall be the work of the beaver; and, if so, whether "thrown" for the purpose of food, or to dam the stream, and raise the water to a level with its burrow. The track of the beaver on the mud or sand under the bank is also examined; and if the "sign" be fresh, he sets his trap in the run of the animal, hiding it under water, and attaching it by a stout chain to a picket driven in the bank, or to a bush or tree. A "float-stick" is fastened to the trap by a cord a few feet long, which, if the animal carry away the trap, floats on the water and indicates its position. The trap is baited with the "medicine," an oily substance obtained from a gland in the scrotum of the beaver. Into this is dipped a stick, which is planted over the trap; and the beaver, attracted by the smell, and wishing a close inspection, very foolishly puts his leg into the trap, and falls a victim to his curiosity.

When "a lodge" is discovered, the trap is set at the edge of the dam, at the point where the amphibious animals pass from deep to shoal water, but always beneath the surface. In early morning the hunter mounts his mule, and examines his traps. The captured animals are skinned, and the tails, a great dainty, carefully packed into camp. The skin is then stretched over a hoop or framework of osier twigs, and is allowed to dry, the flesh and fatty substance being industriously scraped or "grained." When dry, it is folded into a square sheet, with the fur turned inwards, and the bundle of ten to twenty skins, well pressed and carefully corded, is ready for exportation.

During the hunt, regardless of Indian vicinity, the fearless trapper wanders far and near in search of "sign." His nerves must always be in a state of tension; his energies must always rally at his call. His eagle eye sweeps round the country, and in an instant detects any unusual appearance. A turned leaf, a blade of grass pressed down, the uneasiness of the wild animals, the flight of birds, are all paragraphs to him, written in Nature's legible hand and plainest language. The subtle savage summons his utmost craft and cunning to gain an advantage over the wily white woodman; but, along with the natural instinct of primitive man, the white hunter has the advantages of the civilized mind, and, thus provided, seldom fails to baffle, under equal advantages, his Indian adversary.

While hunting in the Arkansas valley, Mr. Ruxton met with many exciting experiences; the most serious being that of a night in the snow. Suspecting that some Indians had carried off his mules, he seized his rifle, and went in search of them, and coming upon what he supposed to be their track, followed it up with heroic patience for ten miles. He then discovered that he had made a mistake; retraced his steps to the camp, and, with his friend, struck in another direction. This time he hit on the right trail, and was well pleased to find that the animals were not in Indian hands, as their ropes evidently still dragged along the ground. Carrying a lariat and saddle-blanket, so as to ride back on the mules if they were caught, away went the two dauntless hunters, nor did they stop to rest until midnight. Then, in the shelter of a thicket and on the bank of a stream, they kindled a fire, and thankfully lay down within reach of its genial influence. Alas! a gale of wind at that moment arose, and scattering the blazing brands to right and left, soon ignited the dry grass and bushes; so that, to prevent a general conflagration, they were compelled to extinguish their fire. To prevent themselves from being frozen to death, they started again in pursuit of the missing animals, following the trail by moonlight across the bare cold prairies. Next day their labours were rewarded by the recovery of the mules, and Mr. Ruxton and his Irish companion began to think of returning. The latter, by agreement, made at once for the trapper's cabin; Ruxton, with the animals, turned off in search of some provisions and packs that had been left in their hunting encampment. Since morning the sky had gradually clouded over, and towards sunset had blackened into a dense, heavy, rolling darkness. The wind had gone down, and a dead, unnatural calm, the sure precursor of a storm, reigned over the face of nature. The coyote, mindful of the coming disturbance, was trotting back to his burrow, and the raven, with swift wings, laboured towards the shelter of the woods.

Lower and lower sank the clouds, until the very bases of the mountains were hidden, and the firmament and the earth seemed mingled together. Though neither branch nor spray was stirred, the valley rang with a hoarse murmur. Through the gloom the leafless branches of the huge cotton-wood trees protruded like the gaunt arms of fleshless phantoms. The whole scene was eery and weird, impressing the mind with an indefinable sense of awe, with an apprehension of approaching disaster. The traveller turned his animals towards the covert of the wood; and they, quivering with terror, were not less eager than himself to gain it. Two-thirds of the distance still lay before them, when the windows of heaven opened, and the storm broke, and a tremendous roar filled the valley, and thick showers of sleet descended, freezing as it fell. The lonely traveller's hunting-shirt was soaked through in a moment, and in another moment frozen hard. The enormous hailstones, beating on his exposed head and face—for the wind had carried away his cap—almost stunned and blinded him. The mule he bestrode was suddenly caparisoned with a sheet of ice. To ride was impossible. He sprang to the ground, and wrapped himself in the saddle-cloth. As the storm beat in front of them, the animals wheeled away from the wood, turned their backs upon it, and made for the open prairies; still, through the intense darkness, whirled and buffeted in clouds of driving snow, Mr. Ruxton steadfastly followed them. His sufferings were indescribable; but he persevered. The wind chilled his blood; the sleet wounded his eyes; with difficulty his weary feet toiled through the gathering snow, which was soon two feet in depth; but he persevered. This quality of tenaciousness, without which no man can become a successful traveller, any more than he can become a successful musician, painter, sculptor, engineer, Mr. Ruxton possessed in an eminent degree. He pursued the frightened animals across the darkening prairie, until, suddenly, on the leeward side of a tuft of bushes, they stood still. Some vain attempts he made to turn them towards the wood; they would not move; so that at length, completely exhausted, and seeing before him nothing but inevitable death, he sank down behind them in the deep snow, covering his head with his blanket—far away from human habitation,—far away from all help, but that of God!

Ah, what a night was that! How the wind roared over the frozen plain! How the snow rolled before it in dense huge billows, that took in the darkness a sombre greyish colour! What horrible sounds surged upon the ear and brain of the benumbed watcher, as, with his head on his knees, pressed down by the snow as by a leaden weight, with the chilled blood scarcely flowing in his veins, and an icy torpor threatening to arrest the very motion of his heart, he struggled against the temptation of a slumber from which he knew that he should wake no more on earth! Once yield to that fatal sleep, and farewell to life! Yet how he longed to close his aching eyes, to rest his weary brain, to cease from the tumult of thought and feeling that confused and exhausted him! Every now and then the mules would groan heavily, and fall upon the snow, and again struggle to their legs. Every now and then the yell of famished wolves arose in the pauses of the storm. So passed the night, or, rather, to the hunter it seemed as if it were prolonging itself into day; each second was lengthened into a minute, each minute into an hour. At last, by keeping his hands buried in the bosom of his hunting-shirt, he so far restored their natural warmth, that he was able to strike a match and set light to his pipe, a large one made of cotton-wood bark, that chanced, by great good fortune, to be filled with tobacco to the brim. This he smoked with intense delight, and no doubt the stimulus it afforded saved his life.

He was sinking, however, into a dreamy drowsiness, when he was roused by a movement among the mules, which cheered him by proving that they were still alive. With some difficulty he lifted his head to get a look at the weather, but all was pitch dark. Was it still night? Suddenly he remembered that he was buried deep in snow, and thrusting his arm above him, he worked out a hole, through which he could see the sheen of stars and the glimmer of blue sky. After one or two efforts, he contrived to stand on his feet, and then he discovered that morning was dawning slowly in the east, whore the horizon was clear of clouds. By dint of constant exertion he regained the use of his limbs, and, springing on his horse, drove the mules before him at full speed across the prairie, and through the valley, until he reached the Arkansas, where he was welcomed as one who had risen from the grave. It took him two days, however, to recover from the effects of that fearful night among the snow.

One of Mr. Ruxton's most agreeable excursions was to the Boiling Spring River and the Boiling Fountains, which he found to be situated in the midst of picturesque combinations of wood and rock. These celebrated springs issue from round holes in a large, flat white rock, at some distance from each other; the gas escapes with a hissing sound, like that of water in a state of ebullition; and the taste is peculiarly refreshing, like that of, but seeming more pungent than, the very best soda-water. The Indians call them the "medicine" springs, and regard them with superstitious reverence as the haunts of a spirit, who, by breathing through the transparent fluid, causes the perturbation of its surface. As to this water-spirit the Arapahoes attribute the power of preventing the success or bringing about the failure of their war expeditions, they never pass the springs without leaving there some propitiatory offerings, such as beads, wampum, knives, pieces of red cloth, strips of deerskin, and mocassins. The country round about was formerly in the hands of the Shoshone, or Snake Indians, of whom the Comanches are a branch: the latter now dwell to the east of the Rocky Mountains; the former to the west, or in the recesses of the mountains themselves.

The Snake Indians connect a curious legend with these two springs of sweet and bitter water.

They say that, hundreds of years ago, when the cotton-wood trees on the Rio Colorado were no higher than arrows, and the red man hunted the buffalo on the plains, all people spoke the same language, and two parties of hunters never met without smoking together the pipe of peace. In this happy age, it chanced on one occasion that a couple of hunters, belonging to different tribes, met on the bank of a small rivulet, in which they designed to quench their thirst. A bright clear thread of water, trickling from a spring in a rock a few feet from the bank, it wound its silvery way into the river. Now, while one of the hunters threw himself at once on the ground, and plunged his face into the running stream, the other first flung from his back a fine deer, and then, turning towards the spring, poured some of the water out as a libation to the Great Spirit, who had rewarded his prowess with bow and arrow, and caused the fountain to flow, at which he was about to refresh himself.

And it came to pass that the other hunter, who had killed no fat buck, and had forgotten to make the usual peace-offering, felt his heart swell with rage and jealousy; and the Evil Spirit taking possession of him, he sought for an excuse to quarrel with the stranger Indian. Rising to his feet with a moody frown upon his brow, he exclaimed—

"Why does a stranger drink at the spring-head, when one to whom the spring belongs is content to drink of the water that runs from it?"

"The Great Spirit," replied the other, "places the cool water at the spring, that his children may drink it pure and undefiled. The running water is for the beasts that inhabit the plains. Au-sa-qua is a chief of the Shoshone, and he drinks at the head of the waters."

"The Shoshone," answered the first speaker, "is but a tribe of the Comanche. Wa-co-mish is the chief of the great nation. Why does a Shoshone dare to drink above him?"

"He has said it. The Shoshone drinks at the spring-head; let other nations be satisfied with the water of the stream that runs into the fields. Au-sa-qua is chief of his nation. The Comanche are brothers; let them both drink of the same water."

"The Shoshone pays tribute to the Comanche. Wa-co-mish leads that nation to war. Wa-co-mish is chief of the Shoshone, as he is of his own people."

"Wa-co-mish lies," said Au-sa-qua coldly; "his tongue is forked like the rattlesnake's; his heart is as black as the Misho-tunga (evil spirit). When the Manitou made his children, whether Shoshone or Comanche, Arapaho, Shi-an, or Pá-ui, he gave them buffalo to eat, and the pure water of the crystal fountain to quench their thirst. He said not to one, 'Drink here,' or to the other, 'Drink there,' but gave to all the bright clear fountain, that all might drink."

A tempest of fury swept over the soul of Wa-comish as he listened to these words; but he was a coward at heart, and durst not openly encounter the cooler and more courageous Shoshone. But when the latter, hot with speaking, again stooped to drink of the refreshing waters, Wa-co-mish suddenly threw himself upon him, pressed his head beneath the surface, and held it there, until his victim, suffocated, ceased to struggle, and fell forward into the spring, dead.

The murderer had satisfied his passion; but was he happy? No; as he gazed at the corpse of his victim, he was seized with a passionate sense of remorse and regret. Loathing himself for the crime he had committed, he proceeded to drag the body a few paces from the water, which, thereupon, was suddenly disturbed. The wave trembled to and fro, and bubbles, rising to the surface, escaped in hissing gas. And, as a vaporous cloud gradually rose and sank, the figure of an aged Indian was revealed to the murderer's straining eyes, whom, by his noble countenance, his long sinewy hand, and his silvery beard, he knew to be the great Wau-kan-aga, the father of the Shoshone and Comanche nation, still remembered and revered for the good deeds and the heroic acts he had done in life.

Stretching out a war-club towards the shrinking, trembling Wa-co-mish, he said:

"Accursed of my tribe! this day hast thou snapt the link that bound together the mightiest nations of the world, while the blood of the brave Shoshone cries to the Manitou for vengeance. May the water of thy tribe be rank and bitter in their throats!" And, swinging round his ponderous war-club, he dashed out the brains of the treacherous Comanche, so that he fell headlong into the spring, which, from that day, has ever been nauseous to the taste, and an offence to thirsty lips. But at the same time, to preserve the memory of the noble Au-sa-qua, he struck a hard flint rock, higher up the rivulet, with his club, and called forth a fountain of crystal water, which, even in our own times, is the joy and the delight of men.

"Never," says Mr. Ruxton, "never was there such a paradise for hunters as this lone and solitary spot. The shelving prairie, at the bottom of which the springs are situated, is entirely surrounded by rugged mountains, and, containing perhaps about two or three acres of excellent grass, affords a safe pasture to their animals, which would hardly care to wander from such feeding. Immediately overhead, Pike's Peak, at an elevation of 12,000 feet above the level of the sea, towers high into the clouds; whilst from the fountain, like a granitic amphitheatre, ridge after ridge, clothed with pine and cedar, rises and meets the stupendous mass of mountains, well called 'Rocky,' which stretches far away north and southward, their gigantic peaks being visible above the strata of clouds which hide their rugged bases."

But here our companionship with Mr. Ruxton ceases. His travels in the United States do not present any uncommon or remarkable feature; do not differ from those of the thousand and one sightseers who yearly cross the Atlantic, and survey the broad territories of the great Western Republic. With a small party he crossed the wide-rolling prairies to Fort Leavenworth; thence, passing the Kansas or Caro river, and entering upon a picturesque country of hill and dale, well wooded and watered, he penetrated into the valley of the Missouri. Down that noble stream he made his way to St. Louis, and afterwards traversed the prairies of Illinois to Chicago; not then, as it is now, the capital of the West, and the great corn depôt of the Mississippi States. From Chicago he crossed Lake Michigan to Kalamazoo, where he took the rail to Detroit. A Canadian steamer conveyed him to Buffalo. Thence, by rail, he travelled to Albany, and descended the majestic Hudson to New York. His home voyage was swift and prosperous, and he arrived at Liverpool in the middle of August, 1847. [89]

DOCTOR BARTH,
AND CENTRAL AFRICA.

A.D. 1850.

I.

DR. HEINRICH BARTH, a native of Hamburg, and lecturer at the University of Berlin upon geography, had already had some experience of African travel, when, in 1849, he learned that Mr. James Richardson had planned an expedition from London to Central Africa, with the view of opening up the Soudan to European commerce, and substituting for the cruel slave-trade the legitimate enterprise of working the natural riches of the country. Dr. Barth obtained permission to accompany it, and with another volunteer, also a German, named Overweg, he repaired to head-quarters. The expedition was authorized and supported by the British Government. It met, therefore, with no preliminary difficulties; and we may begin our summary of its adventures at Tripoli, whence it started for the south on the 24th of March, 1850. Entering the Fezzan, it crossed the rocky and elevated plateau known as the Hammada, and through fertile wadys, or valley-basins, separated by precipitous ridges and broad wastes of sand, made its way to Mourzouk, the capital, situated in a sandy plain, where agricultural labour is possible only under the shelter of the date-palms. The town has no rich merchants, and is not so much a commercial depôt as a place of transit. For Dr. Barth and his companions it was, however, the first stage of their journey, and, indeed, their true point of departure. They made all haste, therefore, to leave it, and on the 13th of June entered upon their great undertaking. On the 25th, after an unavoidable delay, they quitted Tasua, crossed a considerable mass of sand-hills, and descended into a more agreeable district, where the heights were crowned by tamarisk trees, each height standing alone and isolated, like sentinels along the front of an army. This pleasant variety of scenery did not last long, however; they came again upon a soil as rocky as that of the Hammada, and met with an alternation of green valleys and sterile promontories, similar to that which they had explored before they reached Mourzouk.

They had reached the Wady Elaveu, a huge depression running north and south, when, at a distance of two hundred yards from their camp, they discovered a pond, forming a centre of life in that solitary region. Everybody hastened to enjoy a bath; a crowd of pintados and gangas hovered, with bright-coloured wings, above the laughing, frolicking company, waiting until they could take their places. While in this vicinity the travellers were disturbed by the conduct of some Towaregs, who had been engaged to conduct them to Selompih. Eventually, some slight change was made in the plans of the expedition, which, it was determined, should go on to Ghat, and remain there for six days; while the Towaregs, on their part, undertook to set out immediately afterwards for the Asben. Striking into the valley of Tanesof, they saw before them, revelling in the glow and gleam of the sunset, the Demons' Mountain, or Mount Iniden; its perpendicular summit, adorned with towers and battlements, showed its white outlines vividly against a dark-blue sky. Westward, the horizon was bounded by a range of sand-hills, which the wind swept like a mighty besom, filling the air with sharp, gritty sand, and covering the entire surface of the valley.

On the following morning, their course carried them towards an enchanted mountain, which the wild legends of the natives have invested with picturesque interest. In spite of the warnings of the Towaregs, or perhaps because they had cautioned Dr. Barth not to risk his life in scaling that palace of the evil spirits, he resolved on attempting the sacrilegious enterprise. Unable to obtain guides, neither threats nor bribes prevailing over their superstitious terrors, he set out alone, in the belief that it had been formerly a place of religious worship, and that he should find there either sculptures or curious inscriptions. Unfortunately, he took with him no provisions but some biscuits and dates, and worse food cannot be imagined where there is a want of water. Crossing the sand-hills, he entered upon a bare and sterile plain, strewn with black pebbles, and studded with little mounds or hillocks of the same colour. Then he followed the bed of a torrent, its banks dotted with herbage, which offered an asylum to a couple of antelopes. Anxious for the safety of their young, the timid animals did not move at his approach. Affection inspired them with courage; they raised their heads boldly, and waved their tails. The enchanted palace seemed to recede as he advanced; finding himself in front of a dark deep ravine, he changed his course, only to find the passage barred by a precipice. Under the glare and glow of a burning sun he undauntedly pursued his way, and at last, spent with fatigue and exertion, reached the summit, which was only a few feet wide, and could boast neither of sculptures nor inscriptions.

From so lofty a watch-tower the prospect was necessarily extensive; but on surveying the plain below with anxious glance, Dr. Barth failed to detect any sign of the caravan. He was hungry and athirst; but his dates and biscuit were not eatable, and his supply of water was so limited that he durst not indulge himself with more than a mouthful. Feeble and spent as he was, to descend was imperative; he had no water left when he once more stood upon the plain. He dragged his weary limbs onward for some time, but at length was forced to own to himself that he did not know the direction he ought to take. He fired his pistol; but it elicited no reply. Wandering further and further from the route, he came upon a small grassy oasis, where some huts had been constructed of the branches of the tamarisk. With hopeful heart he hurried towards them; they were empty. Then in the distance he saw a long train of loaded camels ploughing their slow way through the sand; no, it was an illusion!—the illusion of fever. When night fell, he descried a fire gleaming redly against the darkened sky; it must be that of the caravan! Again he fired his pistol, and again there was no answer. Still the flame rose steadily towards heaven, and seemed to beckon him to a place where he should find rest and safety; but he was unable to profit by the signal. He fired again; no answering sound came forth from the silence of the mysterious night, and Dr. Barth, on his knees, entrusted his life to the Divine Mercy, and waited and watched for the dawn of day. The dawn came, as it comes to all God's creatures, whether rich or poor, happy or wretched—comes with a blessing and a promise that are too often accepted without thought or emotion of gratitude; the dawn came, and still the calm of the desert remained unbroken. He loaded his pistol with a double charge, and the report, travelling from echo to echo, seemed loud enough to awaken the dead; it was heard by no human ear but his own. The sun, for whose beams he had prayed in the night-watches, rose in all its glory; the heat became intense; slowly the belated wayfarer crawled along the hot sand to seek the scanty shelter afforded by the leafless branches of the tamarisk. At noon there was scarcely shade enough to protect even his head, and in an agony of thirst, he opened a vein, drank a little of his own blood, and lost all consciousness. When he recovered his senses, the sun had set behind the mountain. He dragged himself a few paces from the tamarisk, and was examining the dreary level with sorrowful eyes, when he suddenly heard the voice of a camel. Never had he listened to music so delightful! For twenty-four hours had his sufferings been prolonged, and he was completely exhausted when rescued by one of the Towaregs of the caravan who had been sent in search of him.

The caravan spent six days in the double oasis of Ghat and Barakat, where crops of green millet, taking the place of barley and rye, indicated the neighbourhood of Nigritiá. The gardens were neatly fenced and carefully cultivated; turtle-doves and pigeons cooed among the branches; the clean, well-built houses were each provided with a terraced roof. Dr. Barth observed that the male inhabitants worked with industry and intelligence; as for the women, almost every one had a babe on her shoulders, and children swarmed by the wayside. As a whole, the population was far superior, physically and morally, to the mixed, hybrid race of the Fezzan.

They left the gracious and grateful oasis to plunge into the desert, a chaos of sandstone and granite rocks. On the 30th of July, they reached the junction-point of two ravines which formed a sort of "four-ways" among these confused masses. The wady which crossed their route was about sixty feet broad, but, at a short distance, narrowed suddenly into a defile between gigantic precipices upwards of a thousand feet in height—a defile which in the rainy season must be converted into a veritable cataract, to judge from an excavated basin at the mouth, which, when Dr. Barth and his companions passed, was full of fresh and limpid water. This "four-ways," and these defiles, form the valley of Aguéri, long known to European geographers by the name of Amaïs.

The unpleasant intelligence now arrived that a powerful chief, named Sidi-Jalef-Sakertaf, projected an expedition against their peaceful caravan. Fortunately, it was only a question of the tribute which, by right of might, the Towaregs levy from every caravan that crosses the desert. Sidi-Jalef-Sakertaf was pacified; and the enthusiasts went on their way through sterile valleys and frowning defiles that would have daunted the courage of any but a votary of science and adventure.

They next arrived at Mount Tiska, which is six hundred feet in height, and surrounded by numerous lesser cones. It forms a kind of geological landmark; for the soil, hitherto so broken and irregular, thenceforward becomes smooth and uniform, while rising gradually, and the vast plain stretches far beyond the limit of vision without anything to interrupt its arid monotony. A two days' journey brought our travellers to the well of Afelesselez. It is utterly wanting in shade; only a few clumps of stunted tamarisks grow on the sandy hillocks; but, desolate as it is and uninviting, the caravans resort to it eagerly, on account of its supply of fresh water.

Sand; stones; little ridges of quartzose limestone; granite mixed with red sandstone or white; a few mimosas, at intervals of one or two days' march; abrupt pinnacles breaking the dull level of the sandstones; dry and bushless valleys—such were the features of the country through which Dr. Barth and his companions wearily plodded. Herds of buffaloes, however, are numerous; as is also, in the higher ground, the *Ovis tragelaphis*.

On the 16th of August the travellers, while descending a rocky crest covered with gravel, came in sight of Mount Asben. The Asben or A'ir is an immense oasis, which has some claim to be considered the Switzerland of the Desert. The route pursued by Dr. Barth on his way to Agadez traversed its most picturesque portion, where, almost every moment, the great mountain revealed itself, with its winding gorges, its fertile basins, and its lofty peaks.

Agadez is built on a plain, where it seems to lament that the day of its prosperity has passed. At one time it was the centre of a considerable commerce; but, since the close of the last century, its population has sunk from sixty thousand to seven or eight thousand souls. Most of its houses lie in ruins; the score of habitations which compose the palace are themselves in a deplorably dilapidated condition; of the seventy mosques which it previously boasted only two remain. The richer merchants shun the market of Agadez, which is now in the possession of the Touats, and supported by small traders, who do a little business in the purchase of millet when the price is low.

The day after his arrival, Barth repaired to the palace, and found that the buildings reserved for the sovereign were in tolerably good repair. He was introduced into a hall, from twelve to fifteen yards square, with a low daïs or platform, constructed of mats placed upon branches, which supported four massive columns of clay. Between one of these columns and the angle of the wall was seated Abd-el-Kadir, the Sultan, a vigorous and robust man of about fifty years old, whose grey robe and white scarf indicated that he did not belong to the race of the Towaregs. Though he had never heard of England, he received Dr. Barth very kindly, expressed his indignation at the treatment the caravans had undergone on the frontier of A'ir, and, by-and-by, sent him letters of recommendation to the governors of Kanó, Katséna, and Daoura. Dr. Barth remained for two months at Agadez, and collected a number of interesting details respecting its inhabitants and their mode of life. Thus, he describes a visit which he paid to one of its more opulent female inhabitants. She lived in a spacious and commodious house. When he called upon her, she was attired in a robe of silk and cotton, and adorned with a great number of silver jewels. Twenty persons composed her household; including six children, entirely naked, their bracelets and collars of silver excepted, and six or seven slaves. Her husband lived at Katséna, and from time to time came to see her; but it appears that she scarcely awaited his visits with the loving expectancy of a Penelope. No rigid seclusion of women is insisted upon at Agadez. During the Sultan's absence, five or six young females presented themselves at Dr. Barth's house. Two of them were rather handsome, with black hair falling down their shoulders in thick plaits, quick lively eyes, dark complexion, and a toilette not wanting in elegance; but they were so importunate for presents, that Dr. Barth, to escape their incessant petitions, shut himself up.

Barth rejoined his companions in the valley of Tin-Teggana. On the 12th of December they resumed their march, crossing a mountainous region, intersected by fertile valleys, in which the Egyptian balanite and indigo flourished, and finally emerging on the plain which forms the transition between the rocky soil of the desert and the fertile region of the Soudan—a sandy plain, the home of the giraffe and the antelope leucoryx. By degrees it became pleasantly green with brushwood; then the travellers caught sight of bands of ostriches, of numerous burrows, especially in the neighbourhood of the ant-hills, and those of the Ethiopian orycteropus, which have a circumference of three yards to three yards and a half, and are constructed with considerable regularity.

The wood grew thicker, the ground more broken, the ant-hills more numerous. As the travellers descended an abrupt decline of about one hundred feet, they found the character of the vegetation entirely changed. Melons were abundant; the dilon, a kind of laurel, dominated in the woods; then appeared an euphorbia, a somewhat rare tree in this part of Africa, in the poisonous juice of which the natives steep their arrows; parasites were frequent, but as yet lacked strength and pith; in a pool some cows were cooling themselves in the shades of the mimosas that fringed its banks; the thick herbage flourishing along the track impeded the progress of the camels, and against the horizon were visible the fertile undulating meads of Damerghue. Continuing their journey, they came upon a scattered village, where, for the first time, they saw that kind of architecture which, with some unimportant modifications, prevails throughout Central Africa. Entirely constructed of the stems of the sorghum and the *Asclepias gigas*, the huts of Nigritiá have nothing of the solidity of the houses of the A'ir, where the framework is formed of the branches and trunks of trees; but they are incontestably superior in prettiness and cleanliness. The traveller, in examining them, is impressed by their resemblance to the cabins of the aborigines of Latium, of which Vitruvius, amongst others, has furnished a description. More remarkable still are the millstones scattered round the huts; they consist of enormous panniers of reeds, placed on a scaffolding two feet from the ground, to protect them from the mice and termites.

On their arrival at Tagilet, the travellers separated. Mr. James Richardson undertook the road to Zindu, Overweg that to Marádi, and Barth to Kanó. Kúkáwa was named as the place, and about the 1st of April as the date, of their reassembling. Our business here is with Dr. Barth.

At Tasáwa he gained his first experience of a large town or village in Negroland proper; and it made a cheerful impression upon him, as manifesting everywhere the unmistakable marks of the comfortable, pleasant sort of life led by the natives. The courtyard, fenced with a hedge of tall reeds, excluded to a certain degree the gaze of the passer-by, without securing to the interior absolute secrecy. Then, near the entrance, were the cool and shady "runfá," for the reception of travellers and the conduct of ordinary business; and the "gída," partly consisting entirely of reed of the best wicker-work, partly built of clay in the lower parts, while the roof is constructed only of reeds,—but whatever the material employed, always warm and well adapted for domestic privacy; while the entire dwelling is shaded with spreading trees, and enlivened with groups of children, goats, fowls, pigeons, and, where a little wealth has been accumulated, a horse or a pack-ox.

Dr. Barth afterwards arrived at Katséna, a town of considerable size, with a population of eight thousand souls. It was formerly the residence of one of the richest and most celebrated princes in Nigritiá, though he paid a tribute of a hundred slaves to the King of Bornu as a sign of allegiance.

For two centuries, from 1600 to 1800, Katséna appears to have been the principal town in this part of the Soudan. Its social condition, developed by contact with the Arabs, then reached its highest degree of civilization; the language, rich in form and pure in pronunciation, and the polished and refined manners of the inhabitants, distinguished it from the other towns of the Háusa. But a complete and pitiful change took place when, in 1807, the Fulbi, raised to the highest pitch of fanaticism by the preaching of the reformer, Othmán dan Fódiye, succeeded in gaining possession of the town. The principal foreign merchants then emigrated to Kanó; the Asbenáwa also transferred their salt-market thither; and Katséna, notwithstanding its excellent position and greater salubrity, is now but of secondary importance as the seat of a governor. Mohammed Bello, who held that post at the time of Barth's visit, either through capriciousness or suspicion, was very desirous of sending him on to Sokoto, the residence of the Emir. At first he employed persuasion, and when that failed, resorted to force, detaining Barth a prisoner for five days. However, the energy and perseverance of the traveller overcame every difficulty; and, having obtained his freedom, he directed his steps towards the celebrated commercial entrepôt of the Central Soudan.

Kanó, as he says, was an important station for him, not only from a scientific, but a financial point of view. After the extortions of the Towaregs, and his long delay in A'ir, he was entirely dependent upon the merchandise which had been forwarded thither in advance. On his arrival, he had to liquidate a debt which had risen to the large amount of 113,200 kurdi; and he was much disheartened by the low value set upon the wares which were his sole resource. Lodged in dark and uncomfortable quarters, destitute of money, beset by his numerous creditors, and treated with insolence by his servant, his position in the far-famed African city, which had so long occupied his thoughts and excited his imagination, was the reverse of agreeable. Anxiety acted upon his physical health, and a severe attack of fever reduced him to a state of great weakness. Yet the gloomy colours in which he naturally paints his own condition do not extend to his description of Kanó. *That* is bright, vivid, and graphic.

The whole scenery of the town—with its great variety of clay houses, huts, and sheds; its patches of green pasture for oxen, horses, camels, donkeys, and goats; its deep hollows containing ponds overgrown with water-plants; its noble trees, the symmetric gónda or papaya, the slender date-palm, the spreading alléluba, and the majestic bombyx, or silk-cotton tree; the inhabitants, gay in diversified costumes, from the half-naked slave to the most elaborately dressed Arab—forms an animated picture of a world complete in itself; a strange contrast to European towns in external form, and yet, after all, in social inequalities, in the difference of happiness and comfort, activity and laziness, luxury and poverty, exactly similar.

Here a row of shops is filled with articles of native and foreign produce, with noisy buyers and sellers in every variety of figure, complexion, and dress, yet all intent upon gain, and endeavouring to get the advantage of each other; there, a large shed, like a hurdle, full of half-naked, half-starved slaves, torn from their quiet homes, from their wives, husbands, parents, arranged in rows like cattle, and staring with hopeless eyes upon the purchasers, wondering, perhaps, into whose hands it would be their lot to fall. How dark to them the mystery of life! In another part may be seen all that can minister to human ease and comfort, and the wealthy buying dainties and delicacies for his table, while the poor man eyes wistfully a handful of grain. Here a rich governor, dressed in silk and gaudy clothes, mounted upon a spirited and richly caparisoned horse, is followed by a troop of idle, insolent menials; there, a blind pauper gropes his way through the restless, excited multitude, and fears at every step to be trodden underfoot. Observe yonder a yard neatly fenced with mats of reed, and provided with all the comforts which the country affords; a clean, neat-looking cottage, with nicely polished clay walls, a shutter of reeds placed against the low, well-rounded door, to forbid abrupt intrusion on the privacy of domestic life; a cool shed for the daily household work; a fine spreading alléluba tree, affording a pleasant shade in the noontide hours, or a stately gónda or papaya lifting its crown of feather-like leaves on a slender, smooth, and undivided stem, or the tall and useful date-tree, adding its charm to the fair scene of domestic peace and comfort,—the matron, in a clean black cotton gown wound round her waist, and with her hair trimly dressed, busily preparing the meal for her absent husband, or spinning cotton, and at the same time urging the female slaves to pound the corn; the children, naked and merry, playing about in the sand, or chasing a straggling, stubborn goat; earthenware pots and wooden bowls, cleanly washed, all standing in order. Our survey also includes a "mácina"—an open terrace of clay, with a number of dyeing-pans, and people actively employed in various processes of their handicraft: one man stirring the juice, and mixing some colouring wood with the indigo in order to secure the desired tint; another drawing a shirt from the dye-pot, or suspending it to a rope fastened to the trees; and a couple of men busily beating a well-dyed shirt, and singing the while in good time and tune. Further on, a blacksmith with rude tools that an European would disdain, is fashioning a dagger, the sharpness of which will surprise you, or a formidable barbed spear, or some implement of husbandry; beyond, men and women turn an unfrequented thoroughfare to account by hanging up, along the fences, their cotton thread for weaving; and, lastly, close at hand, a group of loiterers idle away the sunny hours.

Ever and anon comes upon the scene a caravan from Gónja, with the much-prized kola-nut, chewed by all who can spare as much or as little as "ten kurdi;" or a caravan passes, laden with natron, bound for Núpa; or a troop of Asbenáwa, going off with their salt for the neighbouring towns; or some Arabs lead their camels, heavily charged with the luxuries of the north and east, to the quarters of the opulent; or a troop of gaudy, warlike-looking horsemen dash towards the palace of the governor with news from some distant province. Everywhere you see human life in its varied forms, the brightest and the most gloomy closely mixed together, as in life itself happiness and sorrow are never divided; every variety of national form and complexion—the olive-coloured Arab; the dark Kanuri, with his wide nostrils; the small-featured, light, and slender Ba-Fillanchi; the broad-faced Ba-Wángara; the stout, large-boned, and masculine-looking Núpa female; the well-proportioned and comely Ba-Haúshe woman.

The regular population of Kanó numbers about 30,000 souls, but is raised to 60,000, from January to April, by the influx of strangers. Its trade principally consists of cotton stuffs sold under the form of tebi, a kind of blouse; tenkédi, the long scarf or dark blue drapery worn by the women; the zunie, a kind of plaid, very bright in colour; and the black turban, worn by the Towaregs. At Kanó are concentrated also the products of northern, eastern, and western Africa, flowing thither through the channels of Mourzouk, Ghat, Tripoli, Timbúktu, and the whole of Bornú.

Early in March the intrepid traveller resumed his journey, across an open and pleasant country. At Zurrikulo he entered Bornú proper. The beautiful fan-palm was here the prevailing tree; but as Barth advanced, he met with the kuka, or *Adansonia digitata*, and the landscape brightened with leafiness, and soon he entered upon a pleasant tract of dense green underwood. "The sky was clear," he says, "and I was leaning carelessly upon my little nag, musing on the original homes of all the plants which now adorn different countries, when I saw advancing towards us a strange-looking person, of very fair complexion, richly dressed and armed, and accompanied by three men on horseback, likewise armed with musket and pistols. Seeing that he was a person of consequence, I rode quickly up to him and saluted him, when he, measuring me with his eyes, halted and asked me whether I was the Christian who was expected to arrive from Kanó; and on my answering him in the affirmative, he told me distinctly that my fellow-traveller, Yakúb (Mr. Richardson), had died before reaching Kúkáwa, and that all his property had been seized. This sad intelligence deeply affected me; and, in the first moment of excitement, I resolved to leave my two young men behind with the camels, and to hurry on alone on horseback. But as I could not reach Kúkáwa in less than four days, and as part of the road was greatly infested by the Tawárek (or Towaregs), such an attempt might have exposed me to a great deal of inconvenience. Therefore, we determined to go on as fast as the camels would allow us."

Four days later, and Dr. Barth saw before him the wall of white clay which surrounds the capital of Bornú. He entered the gate, and of some people assembled there inquired the way to the sheikh's residence. Passing the little market-place, and following the dendal, or promenade, he rode straight up to the palace which flanks the palace on the east. The sheikh received him cordially, and provided him with quarters closely adjoining the vizier's house; these consisted of two immense courtyards, the more secluded of which enclosed, besides a half-finished clay dwelling, a spacious and neatly built hut, which, he ascertained, had been specially prepared for the reception and accommodation of the English mission. It taxed all Dr. Barth's energy and perseverance to obtain the restoration of Mr. Richardson's property; but he finally succeeded. He also obtained a loan of money on the credit of the British Government, which enabled him to satisfy his creditors, pay Mr. Richardson's servants, and provide for the prosecution of the labours which had been so unhappily interrupted.

The capital of Bornú consists of two towns, each surrounded by a wall: one, inhabited by the rich, is well built, and contains some very large residences; the other is a labyrinth of narrow streets of small and squalid houses. Between the two towns spreads an area of about eight hundred yards each way, which, throughout its length, is traversed by a great highway, serving as a channel of intercommunication. This area is largely peopled; and a picturesque aspect it presents, with its spacious mansions and thatched huts, its solid walls of mud and its fences of reeds, varying in colour, according to their age, from the brightest yellow to the deepest black.

In the surrounding district are numerous little villages, hamlets, and isolated farms, all walled. Every Monday a fair is held between two of these villages, lying beyond the western gate; to which the inhabitant of the province brings, on the back of his camel or his ox, his store of butter and corn, with his wife perched upon the top of the burden; and the Yédiná, that pirate of Lake Tchad, who attracts our admiration by the delicacy of his features and the suppleness of his figure, his dried fish, flesh of hippopotamus, and whips made of the animal's leathery hide. Provisions are abundant; but to lay in at one time a week's supply is a wearisome and troublesome task, and a task all the more wearisome and burdensome, because there is no standard money for buying and selling. The ancient standard of the country, the pound of copper, has fallen into disuse; and the currency partly consists of "gábagá," or cotton-strips, and "kungóna," or cowries. A small farmer, who brings his corn to the market, will refuse cowries, however, and will rarely accept of a dollar. The would-be purchaser, therefore, must first exchange a dollar for cowries; then, with the cowries, must buy a "kúlgu," or shirt; and in this way will be able at last to obtain the required quantity of corn.

Provisions are not only abundant, but cheap, and the variety is considerable. For corn,—wheat, rice, and millet; for fruits,—ground-nuts, the bito, or fruit of the *Balanites Ægyptiaca*, a kind of *physalis*, the African plum, the *Rhamnus lotus*, and the dúm-palm; for vegetables—beans and onions, and the young leaves of the monkey-bread tree.

Dr. Barth had spent three weeks at Kúkáwa, when, on the evening of the 14th of April, the Sheikh Omar and his vizier departed on a short visit to Ngornu, and at their invitation he followed next morning. The road thither was marked with the monotony which distinguishes the neighbourhood of the capital. At first, nothing is seen but the *Asclepias gigas*; then some low bushes of cucifera; and gradually trees begin to enliven the landscape. The path is broad and well trodden, but generally consists of a deep sandy soil. There are no villages along the road, but several at a little distance. Two miles and a half from Ngornu the trees cease, giving way to an immense fertile plain where cereals are cultivated as well as beans.

At Ngornu, the town of "the blessing," our traveller arrived about an hour after noon. The heat being very great, the streets were almost deserted; but the houses, or rather yards, were crowded, tents having been pitched for the accommodation of the visitors. Except the sheikh's residence, scarcely a clay house was to be seen; yet the town gave a general impression of comfort and prosperity, and every yard was fenced with new "séggadé" mats, and well shaded by leafy koma-trees, while the huts were large and spacious.

Early next morning the indefatigable traveller started forth on horseback to refresh himself with a view of Lake Tchad, which he supposed to be at no great distance, and of which he indulged the brightest visions. But no shining expanse of fair waters greeted his eye; wherever he directed his gaze, he saw only an endless grassy, treeless plain, stretching to the farthest horizon. At length, riding through grass of constantly increasing freshness and luxuriance, he reached a shallow swamp, the irregular and deeply indented margin of which greatly impeded his progress. After struggling for some time to get clear of it, and vainly straining his eyes to discover a shimmer of water in the distance, he retraced his steps. Mentioning on his return the ill success he had met with, the vizier undertook to send some horsemen to conduct him along the shore as far as Káwa, whence he could cross the country to Kúkáwa.

When the time came, however, the vizier's promise was represented by two horsemen only. With them Dr. Barth started on his excursion, taking a north-east direction. The broad grassy plain seemed to roll away to an immeasurable distance, unrelieved by tree or shrub; not a living creature was visible, and the hot rays of the sun fell all around like burning arrows. After about half an hour's ride, he reached swampy ground, through which he and his companions forced their horses, often up to the saddle. Thus they arrived on the margin of a fine open sheet of water, fringed thickly with papyrus and tall reed, from ten to fourteen feet high, among which wound and interwound the garlands of a yellow-flowered climbing plant, called "boibuje." Turning to the north, and still pushing onward through deep water and grass, he made a small creek called Dímbebú, and caught sight of a couple of small flat boats, each about twelve feet long, and manned by a couple of men, who, on descrying the stranger, pulled off from the shore. They were Búdduma, or Yédiná, the pirates of the Tchad, in search of human prey; and Dr. Barth hastened to warn of their presence some villagers who had come to cut reeds for the roofs of their huts, and evidently had not caught sight of their enemies. He then continued his march. The sun's heat was intense, but a fresh cooling breeze blowing from the lagoon rendered it endurable. Large herds of kelára, a peculiar kind of antelope, started up as he advanced, bounding swiftly over the rushes, and sometimes swimming on the silent waters. They are like the roe in shape and size, with their under parts white as snow. At another creek, which the lake pirates sometimes use as a harbour, river-horses abounded, and the air echoed with their snorting. This was the easternmost period of Dr. Barth's ride; turning then a little west from north, he and his escort marched over drier pasture-grounds, and, in about three miles, struck a deeply indented and well-sheltered creek, called Ngómaíen. Here the curiosity of the traveller was rewarded by the sight of eleven boats of the Yédiná. Each was about twenty feet long, tolerably broad, with a low waist, and a high pointed prow. They are made of the narrow planks of the fógo-tree, fastened together with ropes from the dúm-palm, the holes being stopped with bast.

Another ride, and Dr. Barth turned westward—a course which brought him to Maduwári, a pleasant village, lying in the shade of trees, where he resolved on halting for the night. From its inhabitants, who belong to the tribe of the Sagárti, he obtained much information respecting the numerous islands that stud the surface of the lake. They also told him that the open water begun one day's voyage from Káya, the small harbour of Maduwári, and is from one to two fathoms deep. It stretches from the mouth of the Sháry towards the western shore; all the rest of the lake consisting of swampy meadow-lands, occasionally inundated. Next morning, on resuming his journey, he was charmed by the bright and gracious picture before him. Clear and unbroken were the lines of the horizon, the swampy plain extending on the right towards the lake, and blending with it, so as to allow the mind that delights in wandering over distant regions a boundless expanse to rove in—an enjoyment not to be found in mountainous regions, be the mountains ever so distant. Thus they travelled slowly northwards, while the sun rose over the patches of water which brightened the grassy plain; and on their left the village displayed its snug yards and huts, neatly fenced and shaded by spreading trees. At Dógoji he came upon a hamlet or station of cattle-breeders, where a thousand head were collected; the herdsmen being stationed on guard around them, armed with long spears and light shields. Equidistant poles were fixed in the ground, on which the butter was hung up in skins or in vessels made of grass.

Turning to the eastward, Dr. Barth reached the creek "Kógorani," surrounded by a belt of dense reeds, and was there joined by a Kánemma chief, named Zaitchua, with five horsemen. The party rode on towards Bolè, passing through very deep water, and obtained a view of the widest part of the lake they had yet seen. A fine open sheet of water, agitated by a light easterly wind, rippled in sparkling waves upon the shore. A reedy forest spread all around, while the surface was bright with aquatic plants, chiefly the beautiful water-lily, or *Nymphoea lotus*. Flocks of waterfowl of every description played about. At length they reached Káwa, a large straggling village, lying among magnificent trees, where Dr. Barth's' excursion terminated; thence he returned to Kúkáwa.

On the 7th of May he was joined there by Mr. Overweg, and the two travellers immediately made their preparations for resuming the work of exploration with which they had been charged by the British Government. These were completed by the 29th of May (1851), and the two travellers then set out for the southward, accompanied by an officer of the sheikh, and attended by a small company of servants and warriors. A singular variety of country greeted them as they moved forward: at first it was low and swampy; then came a bare and arid soil, planted with scattered tamarisks; next, a dense forest, partly inundated in the rainy season, and, afterwards, a broad and fertile plain, sprinkled with villages, and white with thriving crops of cotton. This was the district of Uji, which comprises several places of a considerable size. Thence they entered upon a fine open country, a continuous corn-field, interrupted only by pleasant villages, and shaded here and there by single monkey-bread trees, or Adansonias, and various kinds of fig-trees, with their succulent dark-green foliage, or large fleshy leaves of emerald green. A fiumara, or water-course, which rises near Aláwó, traverses the plain with numerous curves and bends, and passing Dekùa, falls into the Tchad. The travellers crossed it twice before they reached Mabani, a large and prosperous town, with a population of nine or ten thousand souls, which covers the sides and summit of a hill of sand. From this point their road lay through fertile fields, where they were greeted by the sight of the first corn-crop of the season, its fresh and vivid green sparkling daintily in the sunshine. Having crossed and recrossed the fiumara, they ascended its steep left bank, which in some places exhibited regular strata of sandstone. Here they passed a little dyeing-yard of two or three pots, while several patches of indigo flourished at the foot of the bank, and a bustling group of men and cattle were gathered round the well. Villages were seen lying about in every direction; and single cottages, scattered about here and there, gave evidence of a sense of security. The corn-fields were most agreeably broken by tracts covered with bushes of the wild gónda, which has a most delicious fruit, of a fine creamy flavour, and of the size of a peach, but with a much larger stone.

Mount Délabida marked the border line of a mountainous region. After entering upon the district of Shamo, Barth observed that millet became rare, and that the sorghum was generally cultivated. Here he and his party were joined by some native traders; for robbers haunted the neighbourhood, and safety was to be found in numbers. At every step they came upon evidences of the misfortunes which had swept and scathed the country: traces of ancient cultivation and ruined huts; and thick interwoven jungles, where the grass grew so high as to hide both horse and rider. After three hours' march through this land of desolation, they arrived at what had once been a considerable village, but was then inhabited only by a few natives, recently converted to the religion of the Crescent. As but a single hut could be found for the accommodation of the whole company, Dr. Barth preferred to encamp in the open air. But he had scarcely laid down to rest, when a terrible storm arose, sweeping his tent to the ground, and flooding his baggage with torrents of rain. To such adventures is the daring traveller exposed!

Though they had embraced Islam, the natives wore no other clothing than a strip of leather passed between the legs, and even this seemed by some of them to be considered a superfluity. The observer could not fail to remark their harmonious proportions, their regular features, undisfigured by tattooing, and, in not a few cases, presenting no resemblance to the negro type. The difference of complexion noticeable in individuals presumably of the same race, was remarkable. With some it was a brilliant black; with others a rhubarb colour, and there was no example of an intermediate tint; the black, however, predominated. A young woman and her son, aged eight years, formed a group "quite antique," and worthy of the chisel of a great artist. The child, especially, in no respect yielded to the ancient Discophorus; his hair was short and curled, but not woolly; his complexion, like that of his mother and the whole family, was of a pale or yellowish red.

Re-entering the forest, Dr. Barth observed that the clearings bore the imprints of the feet of elephants of all ages. A wealth of flowers loaded the atmosphere with fragrant incense. But the soil soon deteriorated; the trees were nearly all mimosas, and nearly all of indifferent growth, with here and there a large leafless Adansonia flinging abroad, as if in despair, its gaunt gigantic arms; while the herbage consisted only of single tufts of coarse grass, four or five feet high. When things are at their worst they begin to mend; and for the traveller there is no motto more applicable than the old proverb, that it is a long lane which has no turning. With intense delight Dr. Barth and his companions saw the monotonously gloomy forest giving way to scattered clusters of large and graceful trees, such as generally indicate the neighbourhood of human labour. And they soon emerged upon bright green meadow-lands extending to the base of the Wandala mountain-range, which rose like a barrier of cloud upon the horizon, from north to south. The highest elevation of this range is about 3000 feet; its average elevation does not exceed 2500 feet. Behind it, to a point of 5000 feet above the sea, rises the conical mass of Mount Mendefi, first seen by gallant Major Denham. The country now gradually assumed a wilder aspect; rocks of sandstone and granite projected on all sides, while, in front, a little rocky ridge, densely crowded with bush and tree, seemed to form a *ne plus ultra*. Suddenly, however, a deep recess opened in it, and a village was seen, lying most picturesquely in the heart of the rocks and woods. This was Laháula, where the travellers rested for the night. Next day they reached Uba, on the border of A'damáwa; A'damáwa, described by Dr. Barth as "a Mohammedan kingdom engrafted upon a mixed stock of pagan tribes—the conquest of the valorous and fanatic Pállo chieftain, A'dáma, over the great pagan kingdom of Fúmbiná."

Here the camels greatly excited the curiosity of the population; for they are rarely seen in A'damáwa, the climate of which these animals are unable to endure for any length of time. Still more vivid was the curiosity of the governor and his courtiers, when they saw Dr. Barth's compass, chronometer, telescope, and the small print of his Prayer-Book. The Fulbi, he says, are intelligent and civilized, but prone to malice; they lack the good nature of the real blacks, from whom they differ more in their character than their colour.

At Bagma our travellers were struck by the size and shape of the huts, some of them being from forty to sixty feet long, about fifteen broad, and from ten to twelve feet high. They narrowed above to a ridge, and were thatched all over, no distinction being made between roof and wall. They are so spaciously constructed, in order to provide a shelter for the cattle against the inclemency of the weather. The river separates the village, which is inhabited entirely by Mohammedans, into two quarters. "The news of a marvellous novelty soon stirred up the whole place, and young and old, male and female, all gathered round our motley troop, and thronged about us in innocent mirth, and as we proceeded the people came running from the distant fields to see the wonder; but the wonder was not myself, but the camel, an animal which many of them had never seen, fifteen years having elapsed since one had passed along this road. The chorus of shrill voices, 'Gelóba, gelóba!' was led by two young wanton Púllo girls, slender as antelopes, and wearing nothing but a light apron of striped cotton round their loins, who, jumping about and laughing at the stupidity of these enormous animals, accompanied us for about two miles along the fertile plain. We passed a herd of about three hundred cattle. Gradually the country became covered with forest, with the exception of patches of cultivated ground." Through scenery of this interesting character, the travellers pushed on to Mbtudi.

Next day their route laid through well-wooded and well-watered pastures, and immense fields of millet and ground-nuts, which here form as large a proportion of the food of the people as potatoes do in Europe. Dr. Barth liked them very much, especially if roasted, for nibbling after supper, or even as a substitute for breakfast on the road. From Segero the travellers proceeded to Sara'wu, and thence to Béhur. Forest and cultivated land alternated with one another to the margin of a little lake, lying in a belt of tall thick grass, where the unwieldy river-horse snorted loud. The sky was dark with clouds, and a storm was gathering, when the caravan entered the narrow streets of Salléri. That night it obtained but scanty accommodation, and everybody was glad to find the next morning bright and cheerful, so that the march could be resumed. Their course was directed towards the river Bénuwé. The neighbourhood of the water was first indicated by numerous high ant-hills, which, arranged in almost parallel lines, presented a sufficiently curious spectacle. To the north-west towered the insulated colossal mass of Mount Atlantika, forming a conspicuous and majestic object in the landscape. The savannas were now overgrown with tall rank grass, and broken by many considerable pools, lying in deep hollows; every year, in the rainy season, they are under water. Crossing these low levels with some difficulty, Dr. Barth arrived on the banks of the Bénuwé. A broad and noble stream, it flowed from east to west through an entirely open country. The banks were twenty to thirty feet high; while, immediately opposite to the traveller's station, behind a pointed headland of sand, the river Fáro, which has its source on the eastern side of Mount Atlantika, came in with a bold sweep from the south-east, and poured its tributary waters into the Bénuwé. The Bénuwé, below the point of junction, bends slightly to the north, runs along the northern foot of Mount Bágelé, thence traverses the mountainous region of the Báchama and Zina to Hamárruwa and the industrious country of Korórofa, until it joins the great western river of the Kwára, or Niger.

The passage of the Bénuwé, which is here about eight hundred yards wide, was safely accomplished in the native canoes, nor did any mishap occur in the transit of the Fáro, which measures about six hundred yards. The current of the Fáro has a velocity of about five miles an hour; that of the Bénuwé does not exceed three miles and a half. By way of Mount Bágelé, and through the rich low lands of Ribágo, the travellers repaired to Yola, the capital of A'damáwa.

II.

Yola, the capital of A'damáwa, lies four degrees to the south of Kuka, on the Fáro, in a marshy plain, which presents nothing attractive to the eye of an artist. Dr. Barth describes it as a large open place, consisting mainly of conical huts, surrounded by spacious court-yards, and even by corn-fields; only the houses of the governor and his brothers being built of clay. When he entered it, Lowel, the governor, was in his fields, and could not be seen; but on his return the travellers proceeded to his "palace" to pay their respects. They were not allowed an interview, however, until the following day, and then it was anything but satisfactory. The officer who had accompanied them from Kuka took the opportunity of delivering certain despatches; and as they proved displeasing to the governor, he immediately vented his wrath upon Dr. Barth, accusing him of treacherous intentions. The audience terminated in confusion, and next day but one, Dr. Barth was ordered to leave Yola, on the pretence that his sojourn there could not be allowed unless he obtained the authorization of the Sultan of Sokoto. He was suffering from fever, and the heat of the day was excessive, but at once made preparations for departure. Sitting firmly in his large Arab stirrups, and clinging to the pommel of his saddle, he turned his horse's head towards Bornú, and, though he fainted twice, was soon invigorated by a refreshing breeze, which opportunely rose with healing on its wings.

But he was really ill when he arrived at Kúkawa, and, unhappily, the rainy season had begun. During the night of the 3rd of August, the storm converted his sleeping apartment into a small lake, and his fever was seriously aggravated. The pools which formed in every nook and corner of the town were rendered pestiferous by the filth of all kinds which stagnated in them. He ought to have withdrawn to some healthier country, but, in order to pay the debts of the expedition and prepare for new explorations, was compelled to remain and sell the merchandise which had arrived in his absence. He made all haste, however, to discharge this duty; and when, early in September, the Government despatched a body of the Welád Shinán—Arab mercenaries whom they had enlisted—to reconquer the eastern districts of the province of Kánem, he attached himself to the expedition, accompanied by his fellow-traveller, Overweg.

In the course of this new journey they obtained another view of Lake Tchad, under peculiar circumstances. It was about seven o'clock in the morning. Far to their right, a whole herd of elephants, arranged in almost military array, like an army of rational beings, slowly proceeded to the water. In front appeared the males, as was evident from their size, in regular order; at a little distance followed the young ones; in a third line were the females; and the whole were brought up by five males of immense size. The latter, though the travellers were riding along quietly, and at a considerable distance, took notice of them, and some were seen throwing dust into the air; but no attempt was made to disturb them. There were altogether about ninety-six.

Barth and Overweg returned to Kúkáwa on the 14th of November, but ten days afterwards they again sallied forth, accompanying another warlike expedition, which had been ordered to march against Mánderá. It presented, however, few features of interest or importance. The indefatigable pioneers were back again in Kúkáwa on the 1st of February, 1852, and there they remained until the 1st of March. Though crippled by want of means, enfeebled by fever, and beset by a thousand difficulties, Dr. Barth resolved on continuing his work of exploration, and, on the 17th of March, entered into Bagirmi, a region never before visited by Europeans.

Bagirmi forms an extensive table-land, with an inclination towards the north, and an elevation of 900 to 1000 feet above the sea-level. It measures about 240 miles from north to south, and 150 from east to west. In the north lie some scattered mountain ranges, which separate the two basins of Lake Fittri and Lake Tchad. The chief products are sorghum, millet, sesamum, poa, wild rice, haricot beans, water-melons, citron, and indigo. Very little grain is cultivated. The population numbers about 1,500,000 souls.

On reaching the broad stream of the Koloko, Dr. Barth found that he was suspected of treacherous designs against the throne of Bagirmi, and the boatmen refused to ferry him across, unless he obtained the Sultan's permission. Resolved not to be baffled on the threshold of his enterprise, he retraced his steps for about two miles, then turned to the north-east, and at Mili succeeded in effecting the passage of the river. The country through which he advanced was fertile and well cultivated; village succeeded village in an almost unbroken series; here and there groups of natives issued from the thick foliage; numerous herds of cattle were feeding in the rich green water-meadows, and among them birds of the most beautiful plumage, and of all descriptions and sizes, sported upon nimble wing. The gigantic pelican dashed down occasionally from some neighbouring tree; the marabout stood silent, with head between its shoulders, like a decrepit old man; the large-sized azure-feathered "dédegami" strutted proudly along after its prey, the plotus, and extended its long snake-like neck; and the white ibis searched eagerly for food, with various species of ducks, and numerous other lesser birds, in larger or smaller flights.

But an unexpected obstacle arrested his progress; an official arrived with an intimation that he could not be allowed to continue his advance without the formal consent of the supreme authority. He therefore sent forward a messenger with letters to the capital, and retraced his steps to Mili, to await his return. He had not long to wait. The messenger made his appearance on the following day, bearing a document with a large black seal, which directed him to proceed to Búgomán, a place higher up the river, until an answer could be obtained from the Sultan, who was then absent on a campaign in Gógomi. But on his arrival at Búgomán, the governor refused to receive him, and the unfortunate traveller was glad to find a resting-place at Bákadá. There he had time and opportunity to meditate on the vast numbers of destructive worms and ants which afflicted the land of Bagirmi; especially a terrible large black worm, as long as, but much bigger than, the largest of European grubs, which, in its millions, consumes an immense proportion of the produce of the natives. There is also an injurious beetle, yellow as to colour, and half an inch as to length; but the people of Bagirmi take their revenge upon this destroyer by eating him as soon as he has grown fat at their expense. As for the ants, both black and white, they are always and everywhere a scourge and a calamity. Of the termites, or so-called white ants, which, by the way, are not really ants, Dr. Barth had unpleasant experience. As early as the second day of his sojourn at Bákadá, he observed that they were threatening his couch, which he had spread on a mat of the thickest reeds, with total destruction. To circumvent their devices, he elevated it upon three large poles; but in two days' time they had not only raised their entrenchments along the poles to the very top, but had eaten through mat and carpet, and accomplished much general depredation

No reply arriving from the Sultan, Barth not unnaturally lost patience, and decided on quitting the inhospitable Bagirmi, and returning to Kúkáwa. But he was closely watched; and on arriving at Mili, was arrested by order of the governor, who took possession of his arms, his baggage, his watch, his papers, his compass, and his horse, and placed him in charge of a couple of sentinels. Happily, while at Bákadá he had made a powerful friend, who, making his appearance at Mili, interfered on his behalf, obtained the restoration of his property, and conducted him in person to Má33sená, the capital. There he was lodged in a clay house standing in an open courtyard, which was likewise fenced by a low clay wall. The house contained an airy front room, which he found very comfortable, and four small chambers at the back, useful for stowing away luggage and provisions.

Másená occupies a considerable area, the circumference of which measures about seven miles; but only about half this space is inhabited, the principal quarter being formed in the midst of the town on the north and west of the Sultan's palace, while a few detached quarters and isolated yards lie straggling about as outposts. Its most distinctive feature is a deep trough-like bottom, running from east to west, which in the rainy season is filled with water, in the summer with verdure of the greatest luxuriance. To the south of this hollow, or bedá, lies the principal quarter, which, however, is by no means thickly inhabited. In the centre stands the palace; which is simply an irregular cluster of clay buildings and huts, surrounded by a wall of baked bricks. Generally speaking, the appearance of the town was one of decay and dilapidation; yet, as all the open grounds were enlivened with fresh green pasture, it was not deficient in a certain charm. There are no signs of industrial activity. The market-place is rather small, and without a single stall or shed. The chief feature of interest is the bedá, which is bordered on the south-west by picturesque groups of dúm-palms and other trees of fine foliage; while at the western end, as well as on the south-east, spreads a large tract of market-gardens.

In general, the houses are well built, and the thatched roofs are formed with care, and even with neatness; but the clay is not of a good kind for building, and the clay houses afford so little security from the rains, that most persons prefer to reside during that part of the year in huts of straw and reed.

While waiting the Sultan's arrival, Dr. Barth's time was chiefly occupied in defending himself against the attacks of the large black ant (*Termes mordax*). One day, in particular, he maintained a long and desperate encounter with a host of these voracious little insects. In a thick unbroken column, about an inch broad, they had marched over the wall of the courtyard, and entering the hall where he abode both day and night, advanced right upon the store-room. But his couch being in their way, they immediately assailed his own person, and compelled him to decamp. Assisted by his servants, he then fell upon the bandits, killing all the stragglers and foragers, and burning the main body of the army as it proceeded on its way. But fresh legions arrived on the scene of war, and it took a struggle of two hours' duration thoroughly to break up their lines, and put them to flight.

The insects seemed to have been attracted by the corn which Dr. Barth had stored up. But it must be owned that, if inconvenient in one respect, their attacks are beneficial in another; for they destroy all kinds of vermin, mice included. And while they thus act as the "scavengers of the houses," in many parts of Negroland they also render service through their very greediness in gathering what man would fain appropriate for himself. They lay in such considerable stores of corn, that the poor natives frequently dig out their holes in order to gain possession of their supplies.

It was on the 3rd of July that the Sultan appeared before the walls of his capital, escorted by about eight hundred cavalry. At the head of the *cortége* rode the lieutenant-governor, surrounded by a troop of cavaliers. Then came the Barma, followed by a man carrying a spear of ancient and peculiar shape, designed to represent the "fetish," or idol of Kénga-Matáya, the original patrimony of the kings of Bagirmi. Next rode the Fácha, or commander-in-chief, who is the second person in the kingdom; and after him the Sultan himself, attired in a yellow burnous, and mounted on a grey charger, the points of which could hardly be seen owing to the amplitude of the war-trappings that hung about him. Nor was the head of his rider much more plainly visible, not only on account of the horsemen gathered round him, but more particularly owing to two umbrellas—one of green, the other of red—borne on each side of him by a couple of slaves.

Six slaves, their right arms clad in iron, fanned the magnificent prince with ostrich feathers attached to long poles, while round about him were gathered a motley array of his captains and courtiers, gay in burnouses of various colours, or in shirts of black or blue. Behind them followed the war-camel, bestridden by the drummer, Kodgánga, who made the echoes resound with the clang of a couple of kettle-drums, fastened on each side of the animal; and the charivari was swelled by the exertions of three musicians, two of whom played upon horns, and the third upon a bugle. Mention must be made of the long train of the Sultan's female slaves, or favourites, forty-five in number, all mounted upon horseback, all dressed from head to foot in black cloth, and all guarded by a slave on either side. The procession was terminated by a train of eleven camels, carrying the baggage.

A day or two afterwards, an officer of the Sultan demanded Dr. Barth's attendance at the palace. He hastened thither; and being admitted into an inner courtyard, found the courtiers sitting on either side of a door, which was protected by screenwork made of very fine reeds. Being desired to sit down, along with his companions, and ignorant whom he should address, he asked in a loud voice if the Sultan 'Abdel-Kadir were present. A clear voice, from behind the screen, answered that he was. When fully satisfied that he was addressing the prince, he proceeded to offer his respects, and present the compliments of the great and powerful British Government, which desired to be on terms of unity with so illustrious a prince. His speech, which he delivered in Arabic, was translated by an interpreter, and received a favourable reply. His presents also were accepted with satisfaction, and the audience ended. Next day he had a second audience, at which he expressed his desire to return to Kúkáwa. After some slight delay, he obtained the Sultan's leave to depart, and was supplied with a camel and two horsemen to assist him on his journey. Well pleased with the result of his visit to Máºená, after the inauspicious circumstances which had attended its commencement, he set out on his return to the capital of Bornú, and arrived there in safety on the 21st of August. He was glad to find Mr. Overweg in excellent spirits, for liberal supplies had been forwarded by the British Government, though looking physically weak and exhausted. The sheikh received him with great cordiality, and he enjoyed a degree of comfort and repose to which he had long been a stranger.

His business, however, was to explore unknown countries, and to open up new paths to the enterprise of commerce. Considering it almost impossible to penetrate southward, on account of the obstacles thrown in his way by the native princes, he meditated a journey westward in the hope of reaching the celebrated city of Timbúktu, at one time the centre of so many extravagant legends. The fulfilment of his projects was delayed by an unhappy calamity. During a short excursion in the neighbourhood of Kúkáwa, Mr. Overweg got wet, caught a chill, and was afterwards seized with a violent fever, which carried him off in a few hours (September 27th). He died, a martyr to science, and one of the many victims of African exploration, in his thirtieth year.

A delay of some weeks was the necessary result of this melancholy event; but Barth, though left alone, was not to be turned aside from the great object of all his labours. His gaze was directed towards the Niger— towards the *terra incognita* which lay between the route pursued by the French traveller, Caillé, and the region in which Lander and Major Clapperton had achieved so many important discoveries. His preparations completed, he took final leave of Kúkáwa on the 25th of November; and on the 9th of December had crossed the frontier of Háusa. On the 12th he directed his course towards the north-east, and the mountain region of Múniyo. The road waved, serpent-like, through a succession of valleys, the green sides of which were covered with groves and villages. Múniyo takes the form of a wedge, or triangle, the apex projecting towards the desert. The home of a peaceful and industrious population, who flourish under a mild and orderly government, it presents an agreeable contrast to the neighbouring territories, inhabited by nomads. Its rulers, men of courage and energy, have not only been able to defend their country against the attacks of the Babus, but to encroach upon the district of Diggéra, which had submitted to the latter. The chief of this independent province can bring into the field, it is said, an army of 1500 horse and 9000 or 10,000 archers; and his revenue amounts to 30,000,000 kurdi (about £6000) a year, without counting the tax which he levies on the crops.

Barth diverged somewhat to the westward in order to visit U'shek, the largest corn-producing district in western Bornú; it is characterized by a curious alternation of luxuriance and sterility. At the foot of a mountain lies a barren, desolate tract, on the very threshold of which lies an undulating country, bright with date-palms and tamarisks, with crystal pools and rich grasses. Around the town of U'shek spreads a glittering girdle of corn-fields, onion-beds, cotton-fields, in various stages of development. Here the labourer is breaking up the clods and irrigating the soil; there, his neighbour is weeding out his blooming crops. The vegetation everywhere is abundant. The accumulation of refuse prevents you, however, from gaining a general view of the village, which lurks in the sheltering folds of the soil; but the main group of houses surrounds the foot of an eminence, crowned by the habitation of the chief. Observe that while the huts are made of reeds and the stems of millet, the towers in which the grain is pounded are constructed of clay, and ten feet in height.

Beyond U'shek stretches a sandy table-land, waving with a dense growth of reeds, and intersected by fertile valleys. Then comes a spur of the mountain-range which rises in the south-west; an irregular and broken plain, carpeted with grass and broom; a jungle of mimosas, dense thickets of capparis, and at intervals small patches of cultivated land. The climate is intensely hot; the very soil seems to burn; and our traveller, feeling himself ill, was forced to rest. During the night, a cold north-east wind covered him and his followers with the feathery awns of the pennixtum; and they rose in the morning in a condition of indescribable uneasiness. The next night was also cold; but there was no wind.

At Badámuni, the fertile fields are brightened with springs, which feed a couple of lakes, connected by a canal. Notwithstanding this channel of intercommunication, one of these lakes is of fresh water; the other brackish, and strongly impregnated with natron. It is noticeable that in this region all the valleys and all the mountain-chains run from north east to south-west, and the direction of the two lakes is the same. Their margin is fringed with papyrus, except that at the point where the water turns brackish the papyrus is succeeded by the kumba, the pith of which is edible. Dr. Barth's two attendants, born on the shores of the Tchad, immediately recognized this species of reed as growing in a similar manner at the point where that great inland sea touches the basins of nature that surround it. It is a curious circumstance that while the lake of fresh water is of a bright blue, and calm and smooth as a mirror, the other is green as the sea, and heaves to and fro in constant commotion, rolling its foamy waves to the beach, which they strew with marine weeds.

The town of Zindu is protected by a rampart and ditch. Its aspect is remarkable: a mass of rock rises in the western quarter; and outside the walls stony ridges run in all directions, throwing forth a myriad crystal streams, which fertilize the tobacco-fields, and secure for the immediate neighbourhood an exceptional fertility. The landscape is enlivened by frequent clumps of date-palms and by the huts of the Touaregs, who conduct a brisk trade in salt. To the south extends an immense piece of ground, utilized, at the time of Dr. Barth's visit, as a garden of acclimatization. It is easy, let us say, to define the ground-plan of Zindu, but not to depict the stir and movement of which it is the centre, limited as that activity may be, compared with the feverish and far-reaching life of the industrial centres of Europe. Zindu has no other manufacture than that of indigo; nevertheless, its commercial energy is so great that it may justly be termed "the port of the Soudan."

Here Dr. Barth received the welcome supply of a thousand dollars, which, not to excite suspicion, had been carefully concealed in a couple of sugar barrels. He was enabled, therefore, to purchase the articles necessary for barter or gifts in his expedition to Timbúktu, such as red, white, and yellow burnouses, turbans, cloves, cutlery, beads, and looking-glasses; and on the 30th of January, 1853, he resumed his march.

The country he had to traverse was the scene of incessant warfare between the Fulbi and the independent tribes. At the outset he met with some salt merchants from A'ir, whose picturesque encampments would have delighted an artist's eye, but did not add to the security of the roads. He arrived in safety, however, on the 5th of February, at Kátséna, and took up his quarters in a residence specially assigned to him. The house was spacious; but so full of ants, that, having rested himself for an hour on a bank of clay, he found that the freebooters had climbed the wall, constructed covered galleries right up to his person, and delivered a combined attack upon his shirt, in which they had eaten large holes.

The governor of Kátséna gave our traveller a courteous reception, and deigned to accept with evident satisfaction the burnouses, cafton, cup, two loaves of sugar, and pistol, which Dr. Barth offered him. The pistol gave him so much pleasure that he asked for a second; and, of course, a refusal was impossible. Thenceforth he ate and drank and walked and slept with his two pistols in his belt, and terrified everybody who approached him by snapping caps in their face. It happened that, at this time, the ghaladima of Sikoto, inspector of Kátséna, was in the town collecting tribute. He was a frank and simple-natured man, neither very generous nor very intelligent, but of benevolent disposition and sociable character. Dr. Barth purchased some silk and cotton stuffs from the looms of Mepè and Kanó, and being very anxious to pursue his journey, waited for the ghaladima to set out, in order to enjoy the advantage of his escort. It was on the 21st of March that this high official, accompanied by our traveller, took his departure. The governor attended them as far as the limits of his jurisdiction, and they had a numerous guard; while, as a further protection against mishaps, they steered to the south, instead of to the west, in which direction war was raging.

It was the happy time of spring; a bloom was on the earth, and a light and perfume in the air; nature put on her greenest attire; the alleluba, the parkia, the cucifera, the bombyx rose in masses of foliage. The country through which the travellers rode was fair and fertile, populous and well cultivated; the pastures echoed with the low of cattle; the fields rejoiced in profuse crops of yams and tobacco. In the district of Maja, cotton, indigo, potatoes were grown on a very large scale. Beyond Kuruyá, a town of 5000 to 6000 souls, the fertility of the land increased, if such increase were possible; the many-rooted banyan, or Indian fig-tree, displayed its colossal splendour:—

> "Irregularly spread,
> Fifty straight columns propped its lofty head;
>   And many a long depending shoot,
>   Seeking to strike its root,
> Straight, like a plummet, grew towards the ground;
> Some on the lower boughs, which curved their way,
>   Fixing their bearded fibres, round and round,
>   With many a ring and wild contortion wound;
>   Some to the passing wind, at times, with sway
>   Of gentle motion moving;
>   Others of younger growth, unmoved, were hung
> Like stone-drops from the cavern's fretted height."

Bassiaparkia, sorghum, and millet were abundant. But at Kulfi the travellers reached the limit which divides the Mohammedans from the heathens—civilization (imperfect and undeveloped, if you will, but not wholly without a respect for law and order) and barbarism. As Dr. Barth advanced, he seemed to pass from spring to winter; cultivation disappeared; villages ruined and silent bore witness to the desolating work of war; and it was only by the cattle browsing in the scanty pastures that he knew the land was not entirely deserted. At Zekka, a town of some importance, with wall and ditch, he separated from the ghaladima, and, through a dense forest, pushed forward to the ruins of Moniya. He had intended to halt there, but an armed force had encamped at Moniya on the preceding evening, and he retreated into the shelter of the forest until the morning. A day's march brought him to Zyrmi, a considerable town, the governor of which was formerly chief of the whole province of Zanfara.

On the 31st of March, he stood on the border of the Gúndúmi Desert, of the passage of which Major Clapperton has left so exciting a narrative. It is passable only by a forced march. Dr. Barth began by striking too far to the south, and lost valuable time in the midst of an impervious jungle. Recovering the direct track, he marched all that day, all that night, without seeing any sign of human life, and until the middle of the following day, when he met some horsemen who had been sent forward to meet him, with vessels of water. Two miles further, and he could see the village where the Emir Aliyú had pitched his camp; he was then at war with the people of Gober. For thirty hours he and his followers had marched without a halt; they were completely spent, and the men, in their absolute weariness, fell prostrate upon the ground. The intrepid Barth rallied his energies; his excitement dispelled the sense of fatigue; and he searched his baggage for some valuable gift to the Emir, who was to depart on the following day, for upon him and his favour the success of his enterprise wholly depended. The day glided by, and he had begun to despair of being admitted to an audience; but in the evening the Emir sent him an ox, four fat sheep, and four hundred parcels of rice, and a message to the effect that he awaited his visit. It must be owned that some of these barbaric potentates do things right royally!

Dr. Barth entered the august presence. The Emir immediately seized him by the hand, made him sit down, and interrupted him when he began to excuse himself for not having visited Sokotó before he went to Kúkáwa. His two requests, for the Emir's safe-conduct as far as Timbúktu, and a royal letter guaranteeing the lives and property of Englishmen visiting his territories, he received very favourably; affirming that his sole thought was for the welfare of humanity, and, consequently, he desired to promote the friendly intercourse of all nations. Next day Barth had another interview, and offered a second supply of presents. He describes the Emir as a strongly built man, of average stature, with a round, full, but not unpleasant face.

On the 4th of April, with the royal letter, of which he had dictated the terms, and a hundred thousand kurdis which the prince had generously sent to him to defray his expenses during his absence, he took up his residence at Vurno, the Emir's usual abode. The unsavoury condition of the town, which was traversed by a *cloaca* more disgusting even than those of Italy, surprised and shocked him. Outside the walls, the Gulbi-n-rima formed several basins of stagnant water in the middle of a plain, where the traveller's camels sadly pined for pasture. The frontiers of three provinces—Kebbi, Adar, and Gober—meet in this arid plain, which, however, after the rainy season, wears a completely different aspect.

The town became more and more deserted; daily its notables departed to join the Emir; though, as a rule, these warriors cared only for their own pleasure, and would sell their weapons for a dram of kola-nut wine. In no part of Negroland did Dr. Barth see less military ardour or more physical depression. Meanwhile, he amused himself by collecting topographical details, studying the history of the country, and making excursions in the neighbourhood; among others to Sokotó, on the river Bugga. It was not until the 23rd of April that the Emir returned to his capital, after an expedition which, if not glorious, had been at least successful. Always generous towards Dr. Barth, he had invited him to meet him, and king and traveller went together to the palace. On the same day, Barth made him a present of a musical box, which appears to be the prize most eagerly coveted by African potentates. The Emir, in his rapture, summoned his grand vizier to see and hear the marvel; but the mysterious box, affected by the climate and the length of the journey it had undergone, refused to pour forth its melodious treasures. However, after a day or two's labour, Dr. Barth succeeded in repairing it, and releasing its imprisoned streams of music. Who shall describe the Emir's excess of joy? He proved the sincerity of his gratitude by immediately giving Dr. Barth a commendatory letter to his nephew, the chief of Gando, and the long-expected permission to depart.

Leaving Vurno on the 8th of May, Dr. Barth reached Gando on the 17th. It was the capital of another Fulbi chief, scarcely less powerful than the Emir, whose protection was of the greatest importance to the traveller, because both banks of the Niger were within his territory. It was not obtained without persevering effort—and many gifts, besides frequent bribes to an Arab consul, who had contrived to make himself indispensable to the feeble prince.

On the 4th of June our indefatigable explorer entered the deep valleys of Kebbi, which, in the rainy season, are converted into extensive rice-fields. At Kombara, the governor hospitably sent him all the constituents of a first-class Soudanian repast, from the sheep to the grains of salt and the Dodua cake. Gaumaché, formerly a thriving town, is now a village of slaves. A similarly fatal change has passed over Yara; formerly rich and industrious, rank weeds now grow in its silent streets. But life and death lie cheek by jowl in these fertile regions; and to the ruined towns and deserted villages immediately succeed prolific rice-fields, shaded by clumps of trees.

The whole country was overshadowed by the thunder-clouds of war; yet the traveller passed continuously through plantations of yams, and cotton, and papyrus, whose fresh green foliage waved above the walls. He halted at Kola, where the governor could dispose of seventy matchlocks and the men who handled them; an important personage in the disturbed condition of the country, whom it was politic to visit. The sister of this lord of warriors presented Dr. Barth with a fine fat goose—an addition to his dietary which rejoiced him greatly. As he approached Jogirma, the three sons of its chief came forth to salute him in their father's name. It proved to be a much more considerable town than the traveller had expected, and the palace was a spacious and even imposing building, in its architecture recalling the characters of the Gothic style. The population numbered seven to eight thousand souls, whom civil discord had reduced to a pitiful extremity. It was with no little difficulty that Dr. Barth obtained even a supply of millet.

On the 10th he entered a beautiful forest, where the air was heavy with the sweet odours of flowering trees; but the place is noted for its insalubrity. Dr. Barth was compelled to remain there for twenty-four hours, one of his camels having gone astray; and this circumstance appeared so extraordinary, that the neighbouring peasants were in the habit of referring to him as "the man who passed a whole day in the deadly desert."

On a quadrangular eminence, about thirty feet high, in the valley of Fogha—an eminence built up of refuse—stands a village with some resemblance to the ancient town of Assyria. The inhabitants extract salt from the black mud out of which their little hillock rises. There are other villages of a similar character. The condition of the population is most wretched; they suffer continually from the forays of the robbers of Dendina.

After a march of two or three miles over a rocky soil, sprinkled with bushes and brushwood, Dr. Barth, with intense satisfaction, caught the glimmer of water, as if the sun were lighting up a broad mirror, and rapidly pushing forward, came, in an hour's time, to Say, a ferry on the great river of the Soudan—the river which has divided with the Nile the curiosity of geographers, and attracted the enterprise of the adventurous; the river which, perhaps, surpasses the Nile in its promise of future commercial industry; the river which we associate with the names of so many heroic travellers, from Mungo Park to Cameron,—the Niger.

III.

The Niger—all the various names of which (Joliba, Mayo, Eghirrau, Isa, Kuara, Baki-a-rua) signify one and the same thing, *the River*—is about seven hundred yards broad at the Say ferry, and flows from north-north-east to south-south-west with a velocity of three miles an hour. The left bank has an elevation of about thirty feet; the right bank is low, and crowned with a town of considerable size. The traffic is incessant; Fulbis and Sourays, with their asses and oxen, continually pass to and fro. The boats in use are constructed of two hollow trunks of trees, fastened together, and measure a length of forty feet and a breadth of four feet and a half. With feelings of a mingled character Dr. Barth crossed this stately river, the exploration of which has necessitated the sacrifice of so many noble lives, and entered the busy town of Say. Its walls form a quadrilateral of fourteen hundred yards; the houses of the inhabitants, all built of reeds except the governor's, are scattered in groups over the area they enclose. In the rainy season, a hollow or valley, which cuts across it from north to south, is filled with water, which impedes communication, and renders the place insalubrious. When the river is flooded, the town is entirely inundated, and all its inhabitants are compelled to migrate. The market of Say is not well provided: the supply of grain is small, of onions *nil*, of rice *nil*, though the soil is well adapted to their cultivation; of cotton, however, there is always a large quantity; and Say will prove an important position for Europeans as soon as the great river route of Western Africa begins to be utilized.

Dr. Barth was told by the governor—who had the manners of a Jew, but was evidently born of a slave-mother—that he should welcome with joy a European vessel bringing to the town the many articles its inhabitants needed. He was astonished to find that the traveller was not a trader; and believing that only some very powerful motive could induce any man to undertake such an expedition, he grew alarmed at the possibility of treacherous and insidious designs, and requested him to leave the place. Dr. Barth was by no means unwilling, and on the following day left behind him the Niger, which separates the explored regions of Negroland from the unexplored, and eagerly directed his course towards the mysterious zone which stretched before him.

He had crossed the low swampy island occupied by the town of Say, and the western branch of the river, at that season entirely dry, when a great storm of thunder and rain broke upon him, and his progress was arrested by the rolling clouds of sand which the wind accumulated in his path. After a halt of three hours his march was resumed, though the soil was flooded with water to a depth of several inches. The country through which he passed had been colonized by the Sourays; it is a dependency of the province of Guinea, and the natives were at war both with the colonists and the Fulbi. Thence he entered a well-cultivated district, where the Fulbi, who regard the cow as the most useful member of the animal world, breed large herds of cattle. The scenery was varied by thickets of mimosas, with here and there a baobab or a tamarisk. More attractive to the traveller, because more novel, were the numerous furnaces, six or seven feet high, used for casting iron.

The ground broke up into great irregularities; ridges of rock ran in all directions; formations of gneiss and mica schist predominated, with rare and beautiful varieties of granite. There, through banks of twenty feet in height, picturesque and rocky, flowed the deep waters of the Sirba. To effect the passage, Dr. Barth's followers could obtain only some bundles of reeds; the chief and all the inhabitants of the village sitting calmly on the bank, and watching their operations with lively interest. The men had expressive countenances, with effeminate features; long plaited hair, which fell upon the shoulders; a pipe in their mouths; and, for attire, a blue shirt and wide blue trousers. The women were dumpy and ill proportioned; they wore numerous collars, and pearls in their ears; their bosom and legs were naked.

Another storm overtook the travellers, and converted the jungles through which they wound their way into a wide expanse of water. The solitariness of the land was broken at one point by a village, charmingly enclosed within a quickset hedge; fields of maize were succeeded by a tract of forest; then they entered a populous district, where the loaded camels laboured heavily through the clayey soil. At Sibba, where the governor, standing at the gate, was explaining to his people certain verses of the Koran, Dr. Barth was handsomely lodged in a hut newly built, with walls excellently polished, and quite an attractive and refreshing appearance. But, in life, there is always a flavour of wormwood in the cup of joy; appearances are proverbially deceitful; and Dr. Barth's beautiful abode proved to be a nest of ants, which committed wholesale depredations on his baggage.

The day after his arrival chanced to be the last of the great Mohammedan feast of the Ramadan. That it was to be a day of festival was announced at earliest dawn by the sound of merry music; the Fulbi streamed forth from their houses, clad in white chemises, as a sign of the white purity of their faith; and the governor paraded through the town at the head of a *cortége* of forty horsemen. As the cadi showed an inclination to represent Dr. Barth in the unwelcome capacity of a sorcerer, he deemed it prudent to distribute a largess among the people of the procession.

He arrived at Doré, the chief town of Libtako, on the 12th of July. The soil is dry, and troops of gazelles frolic about the arid plain which borders on the market-place. The market, on the occasion of Dr. Barth's visit, was frequented by four or five hundred persons, who were buying or selling salt, and cotton stuffs, and copper vessels, and corn, and kola-nuts, and asses. The inhabitants of Doré are partial to ornaments made of copper;

and Dr. Barth noticed two young girls wearing in their hair a copper device of a horseman, sword in hand and pipe in mouth. The pipe, be it observed, is in great request among the Sourays, who seem to be of the opinion of Lord Lytton, that "he who doth not smoke hath either known no great griefs, or refused himself the softest consolation, next to that which comes from heaven."

Beyond Doré the country was a network of rivers and morasses. Buffaloes were exceedingly numerous. A venomous fly, very rare to the east of the Soudan, seriously annoyed Dr. Barth's cattle. It was the wet season; rain descended perpetually, as if the floodgates of heaven had been opened, and water was everywhere—in front, in rear, on either side; water, water, water! For quiet English gentlemen, living at home at ease, or occasionally indulging in a railway journey of a few hundred miles, in a comfortable carriage, through fields well cultivated and well drained, where rivers seldom break their bounds, or if they do, never accomplish greater injury than the overflowing of a green meadow or two, it is almost impossible to conceive the difficulty, and even danger, of traversing the African plains in the rainy season, of conveying heavy baggage through leagues upon leagues of swamps, which the unloaded camel finds it laborious to cross. More than once Dr. Barth was afraid that his horse, in spite of its robust vigour, would fail to extricate its limbs from the deep mud, and sink with its rider in the slough. So tremendous are the rains, that in a single night they have been known to sweep away the fourth part of a large village, and in one house eleven goats have perished.

Hitherto Dr. Barth had maintained his quality as a Christian; but on entering Dalla, a province belonging to the fanatical chief of Masina, who would never have permitted "an infidel" to traverse his territories, Dr. Barth thought it advisable to assume the character of an Arab. But a dispute which he had with his host, respecting a pack of dogs that showed a decided unwillingness to give place to a stranger, indicated no great religious fervour on the part of the population. Good Mohammedans have no liking for the canine race. The Fulbi will not employ them even as guides for their cattle, which they direct by the voice. All the dogs were black; the poultry were black and white. Dr. Barth observed that the crops suffered greatly from the ravages of a large black worm, which he had not met with since his expedition into Bagirmi.

On the 5th of August he entered into a region of swamp and morass, and he was glad when, to relieve the monotony of the landscape, he caught sight of the picturesque Souray villages and the fantastic outline of the chain of the Hombori mountains. The various forms of this singular range, none of the peaks of which rise more than eight hundred feet above the level of the plain, can hardly be imagined; they irresistibly attract the traveller's eye. On a gentle slope, composed of masses of rock, is built a perpendicular wall, the terraced summit of which is inhabited by a native race who have ever maintained their independence. That these heroic hillmen sometimes descend from their fastnesses is shown by their flocks of sheep and crops of millet. Starting from this point, a twofold range of remarkable crests extends along the plain, with a curious similitude to the ruins of mediæval castles.

Refused admission at Boná, and afraid to enter Nuggera, well known to be a hot-bed of fanaticism, Dr. Barth solicited the hospitality of some Towaregs, who were encamped in the neighbourhood. Their chief, a man of agreeable physiognomy, with fine features and a fair complexion, placed one of his huts at the traveller's disposal, and sent him some milk and a sheep ready cooked. Next day, his tents of canvas figured in the midst of those of his host, and he was besieged by a number of very stout ladies, all importunate for gifts. At Bambara, a considerable agricultural centre, surrounded by the canals and affluents of the Niger, he resided for several days. It is situated upon a backwater (mariyet) of the river, which, at the time of Barth's visit, was almost dry. In the ordinary course of things, it ought, in three weeks, to be crowded with boats, going to Timbuktú by Oálázo and Saráyamó, and to Dirá by Kanima. The prosperity of the town depends, therefore, on the rains; and as these had not begun, the whole population, with the Emir at their head, implored the pretended Arab doctor, whom they chose to regard as a great magician, to exercise his powers to obtain from the skies a copious benediction. Dr. Barth eluded the request for a formal ceremony, but expressed a hope that Heaven would listen to wishes so very reasonable. As it happened, there was a slight fall of rain next day, which drew from the inhabitants the sincerest gratitude; but, for all that, Dr. Barth was very glad to put some distance between himself and Bambara.

On the 1st of September, at Saráyamó, Dr. Barth embarked on one of the branches of the Niger, and sailed towards Timbuktú. The stream was about a hundred yards wide, and so thick with aquatic plants that the voyagers seemed to be gliding over a prairie. Moreover, in its bed the asses and horses obtained the chief part of their sustenance. In about two miles and a half they entered open water, and the boatmen, whose songs had rung the praises of the Julius Cæsar of Negroland, the Sultan Mohammed ben Abubakr, carried them, from winding to winding, between banks clothed with cucifers, tamarinds, and rich grasses, on which sometimes cattle were feeding, and sometimes the gazelle. The presence of alligators was a sign that they approached a broader water, and the channel suddenly widened to two hundred yards; its banks alive with pelicans and other water-birds, while men and horses went to and fro. The curves and bends of the stream increased, and the banks assumed a more defined and regular formation; wider and wider became the water-way, until it reached three hundred and forty yards. Some fires shone out against the evening shadows. At the bottom of a little creek clustered a little village. In no part of the course could any current be discerned; it was a kind of lagoon which the voyagers were crossing, and sometimes the wave flowed in one direction, sometimes in another. After two centuries of war, its shores, once so animated, have sunk into silence; and Gakovia, Sanyara, and many other villages have ceased to be. There, on the edge of the bank, towered aloft a clump of graceful trees, the haunt of numerous bees; here, a patch of greensward brightened with the colours of many blossoms. The river now flowed from south-west to north-east, with a noble expanse of six hundred yards; its majestic flood rolling like a volume of silver in the moonlight, with the reflection of stars sparkling thickly on the crests of its waves.

After a pilgrimage of eight months' duration, Dr. Barth arrived at Kabara, the river-port of Timbuktú; and was lodged in a house on the highest ground, which contained two large and several small rooms, and a first floor. The inner court was occupied by a numerous and varied assortment of sheep, ducks, pigeons, and poultry. At early dawn, on the day after his arrival, our traveller, almost suffocated, left his room; but he had scarcely begun his walk before a Towareg chief interrupted him, and demanded a present. Receiving a prompt refusal, he coolly announced that, in his quality as a bandit, he could do him a good deal of harm. Dr. Barth, in fact, was *hors la loi*, and the first wretch who suspected him of being a Christian might slay him with impunity. He succeeded, however, in getting rid of the Towareg. Meanwhile, the house was crowded with visitors from Timbuktú, some on foot, some on horseback, but all wearing blue robes, drawn close to the figure by a drapery, with short breeches and peaked straw hats. All carried lances, while some had swords and guns; they seated themselves in the courtyard, overflowed the chambers, staring at one another, and asking each other who this stranger might be. In the course of the day, Dr. Barth was "interviewed" by fully two hundred persons. In the evening, a messenger whom he had despatched to Timbuktú returned, accompanied by Sidi Alawat, one of the Sultan's brothers. Dr. Barth confided to him the secret of his Christian profession, but added that he was under the special protection of the sovereign of Stamboul. Unfortunately, he had no other proof of his assertion than an old firman dating from his former residence in Egypt; the interview, however, passed off very agreeably.

On the following day, they crossed the sand-hills in the rear of Kabara; the yellow barrenness of the country contrasting vividly with the fertility of the verdurous borders of the river. It is, indeed, a desert, infested by roving bands of murderous Towaregs. Such is the well-known insecurity of the route, that a thicket, situated midway, bears the significant name of "It does not hear"—that is, it is deaf to the cries of a victim. To the left stands the tree of Wely-Salah, a mimosa which the natives have covered with rags in the hope that the saint will replace them by new clothes. As they drew near Timbuktú, the sky clouded over, the atmosphere was full of sand, and the city could scarcely be seen through the rubbish surrounding it. A deputation of the inhabitants met Dr. Barth, and bade him welcome. One of them addressed him in Turkish. He had almost forgotten the language, which, of course, in his character of a Syrian, he ought to have known; but he recalled a few words with which to frame a reply, and then avoided awkward questions by spurring his horse and entering the city. The streets were so narrow, that not more than two horsemen could ride abreast; Dr. Barth was astonished, however, by the two-storied houses, with their ornamented façades. Turning to the west, and passing in front of the Sultan's palace, he arrived at the house which had been allotted for his accommodation.

He had attained the goal of his wishes; he had reached Timbuktú; but the anxieties and fatigue of his journey had exhausted him, and he was seized with an attack of fever. Yet never had he had greater need of his energy and coolness. A rumour had already got abroad that a Christian had obtained admission into the city. The Sultan was absent; and his brother, who had promised his support, was sulking because he had not received presents enough. On the following day, however, the fever having left him, Barth received the visits of some courteous people, and took the air on the terrace of his lodging, which commanded a view of the city. To the north could be seen the massive outlines of the great mosque of Sankora; to the east, the tawny surface of the desert; to the south, the habitations of the Ghadami merchants; while the picture gained variety from the presence of straw-roofed huts among houses built of clay, long rows of narrow winding streets, and a busy market-place on the slope of the sand-hills.

A day or two later, there were rumours of a meditated attack upon his residence, but his calm and intrepid aspect baffled hostile designs. The sheikh's brother made an attempt to convert him, and defied him to demonstrate the superiority of his religious principles. With the help of his pupils, he carried on an animated discussion; but Dr. Barth confuted him, and by his candour and good sense secured the esteem of the more intelligent inhabitants. A fresh attack of fever supervened on the 17th; his weakness increased daily; when, at three o'clock in the morning of the 26th, a blare of instruments and a din of voices announced the arrival of the sheikh, El Bakay, and his warm welcome to the stranger dispelled his pains and filled him with a new vigour. He strongly censured his brother's ungracious conduct; sent provisions to Barth, with a recommendation to partake of nothing that did not come from his palace; and offered him his choice between the various routes that led to the sea-coast. Could he have foreseen that he was fated to languish eight months at Timbuktú, Dr. Barth thinks that he could not have supported the idea; but, happily, man never knows the intensity or duration of the struggle in which he engages, and marches courageously through the shadows which hide from him the future.

Ahmed El Bakay was tall of stature and well proportioned, with an open countenance, an intelligent air, and the bearing and physiognomy of a European. His complexion was almost black. His costume consisted of a short black tunic, black pantaloons, and a shawl bound negligently round his head. Between him and Dr. Barth a cordial understanding was quickly formed and loyally maintained. He spoke frequently of Major Laing, the only Christian whom he had ever seen; for, thanks to the disguise assumed by the French traveller, Caillé, no one at Timbuktú was aware that he had at one time resided in their city.

Timbuktú is situated about six miles from the Niger, in lat. 18° N. Its shape is that of a triangle, the apex of which is turned towards the desert. Its circuit at the present time is about three miles and a half; but of old it extended over a much larger area. It is by no means the wealthy, powerful, and splendid city which was dreamed of in the fond imaginations of the early travellers. Its streets are unpaved, and most of them narrow. There are a thousand houses clay-built, and, in the northern and north-western suburbs, some two hundred huts of reeds. No traces exist of the ancient palace, nor of the Kasba; but the town has three large and three small mosques, and a chapel. It is divided into seven quarters, inhabited by a permanent population of thirty thousand souls, which is increased to thirty-five or forty thousand from November to January, the epoch of the caravans. Founded early in the twelfth century by the Towaregs, on one of their old pasture-grounds, Timbuktú belonged to the Souray in the first half of the fourteenth. Recovered, a century later, by its founders, it was snatched from them by Sami Ali, who sacked it, then rebuilt it, and drew thither the merchants of Ghadami. As early as 1373 it is marked upon the Spanish charts, not only as the entrepôt of the trade in salt and gold, but as the scientific and religious centre of the Western Soudan; and exciting the cupidity of Mulay Ahmed, it fell, in 1592, with the empire of the Askias, under the sway of Marocco. Down to 1826 it remained in the hands of the Ramas, or Maroccan soldiers settled in the country. Next came the Fulbi; then the Towaregs, who drove out the Fulbi in 1844. But this victory, by isolating Timbuktú on the border of the river, led to a famine. Through the intervention of El Bakay, however, a compromise was effected in 1848; the Towaregs recognized the nominal supremacy of the Fulbi, on condition that they should keep no garrison in the city; the taxes were to be collected by two cadis, a Souray and a Fulbi; and the administration, or rather the police, was entrusted to two Souray magistrates, controlled simultaneously by the Fulbi and the Towaregs, between whom was divided the religious authority, represented by the sheikh, a Rama by origin.

Dr. Barth's residence in Timbuktú was a source of intense dissatisfaction to some of the ruling spirits. Even in the sheikh's own family it led to grave dissensions; and many demanded that he should be expelled. El Bakay remained firm in his support, and, to protect the life of his visitor, moved him to Kabara. Dr. Barth speaks in high terms of this liberal and enlightened man, and of the happiness of his domestic circle. Europe itself could not produce a more affectionate father or husband; indeed, Dr. Barth hints that he yielded too much to the wishes of his august partner.

Week after week, the storms of war and civil discord raged more and more furious; the traveller's position became increasingly painful. His bitterest enemies were the Fulbi. They endeavoured to drag him from the sheikh's protection by force, and when this failed, had recourse to an artifice to get him into their power. The Welád Shinan, who assassinated Major Laing, swore they would kill him. On the 27th of February, 1854, the chief of the Fulbi again intimated to the sheikh his request that Barth should be driven from the country. The sheikh peremptorily refused. Then came a fresh demand, and a fresh refusal; a prolonged and angry struggle; a situation more and more intolerable; while commerce suffered and the people were disquieted by the quarrels of their rulers. So it came to pass that, on the night of the 17th of March, Sidi Mohammed, eldest brother of El Bakay, beat the drum, mounted his horse, and bade Dr. Barth follow him with two of his servants, while the Towaregs, who supported them, clashed their bucklers together, and shouted their shrill war-cry. He found the sheikh at the head of a numerous body of Arabs and Sourays, with some Fulbi, who were devoted to him. As might be expected, Dr. Barth begged that he might not be the cause of any bloodshed; and the sheikh promised the malcontents that he would conduct the obnoxious Christian beyond the town. He encamped on the frontier of the Oberay, where everybody suffered terribly from bad food and insects.

At length, after a residence of thirty-three days on the creek of Bosábango, it was decided that the march should be begun on the 19th of April. On the 25th, after having passed through various encampments of Towaregs, they followed the windings of the Niger, having on their left a well-wooded country, intersected by marshes, and enlivened by numerous pintados. Then they fell in with the valiant Wughduga, a sincere friend of El Bakay, and a magnificent Towareg warrior, nearly seven feet high, of prodigious strength, and the hero of deeds of prowess worthy of the most famous knight of the Table Round. Under his escort Dr. Barth reached Gogo—in the fifteenth century the flourishing and famous capital of the Souray empire, now a small and straggling town with a few hundred huts. Here he took leave of his kind and generous protector; and, with an escort of about twenty persons, recrossed to the right bank of the river, and descended it as far as Say, where he had passed it the year before. In this journey of one hundred and fifty leagues, he had seen everywhere the evidence of great fertility, and a peaceable population, in whose midst a European might travel in security; speaking to the people, as he did, of the sources and termination of their great fostering river—questions which interest those good negroes as much, perhaps, as they have perplexed the scientific societies of Europe, but of which they do not possess the most rudimentary knowledge.

Arriving at Sokotó and Vurno in the midst of the rainy season, Dr. Barth was warmly welcomed by the Emir; but, with strength exhausted and health broken, he could not profit by his kindness.

On the 17th of October he arrived at Kanó, where he had been long expected; but neither money nor despatches had been forwarded for him— no news from Europe had been received. Yet at Kanó he had arranged to pay his servants, discharge his debts, and renew his credits, long since exhausted. He pledged the little property remaining to him, including his revolver, until he could obtain the cutlery and four hundred dollars left at Zindu; but, alas! these had disappeared during recent intestine commotions. Kanó must always be unhealthy for Europeans; and Dr. Barth, in his enfeebled condition, acutely felt the ill effects of its climatic conditions. His horses and camels fell ill, and he lost, among others, the noble animal which for three years had shared all his fatigues.

Over every difficulty, every obstacle, that splendid energy which had carried the great explorer to the Niger and Timbuktú ultimately prevailed; and on the 24th of November he set out for Kúkáwa. In his absence it had been the theatre of a revolution. A new ruler held the reins of government, and Dr. Barth was doomed to encounter fresh embarrassments. It was not until after a delay of four months that he was able to resume the journey through the Fezzan. He followed this time the direct route, by Bilma—the route formerly taken by the travellers, Denham and Clapperton.

At the end of August he entered Tripoli, where he spent only four days. By way of Malta he proceeded to Marseilles; and thence to Paris; arriving in London on the 6th of September, 1855.

It may be doubted whether the English public have fully appreciated the labours of this persevering explorer. To us it seems that he occupies a high place in the very front rank of African travellers, in virtue not only of the work he did, but of the courage, perseverance, skill, and energy which he displayed. He failed in nothing that he undertook, though his resources were very limited, and the difficulties in his path of the gravest character. He explored Bornú, A'damáwa, and Bagirmi, where no European had ever before penetrated. He surveyed, over an area of six hundred miles, the region which lies between Katséna and Timbuktú, though even to the Arabs it is the least known portion of the Soudan. He formed friendly relations with the powerful princes on the banks of the Niger, from Sokotó to the famous city which shuts its gates upon the Christian. Five of his best years he dedicated to this astonishing enterprise, enduring the gravest privations, and braving the most pestilential climates, as well as the most implacable fanaticism. All this he did, without friends, without companions, without money. Of the five brave men who undertook this adventurous expedition, he alone returned; and returned loaded with treasure, with precious materials of all kinds for the use of the man of science or the merchant—with maps, drawings, chronologies, vocabularies, historical and ethnological notes, itineraries, botanical and geological data, and meteorological tables. Nothing escaped his attention; he was not only a traveller and an observer, but a scientific pioneer. Let us give due honour to a Livingstone, but let us not forget the debt we owe to a Barth. [156]

MR. THOMAS WITLAM ATKINSON,
AND HIS ADVENTURES IN SIBERIA
AND CENTRAL ASIA.

A.D. 1849–55.

I.

MR. THOMAS WITLAM ATKINSON among recent travellers is not one of the least distinguished. He ventured into what may be called "virgin country"—a region scarcely known to Europeans; carrying his life in his hand; animated by the desire of knowledge rather than the hope of fame; quick to observe, accurate in his observations, and intelligent in combining them into a distinct and satisfactory whole. For some years he lived among the wild races who inhabit Siberia and Mongolia, the Kirghiz steppes, Chinese Tartary, and the wilder districts of Central Asia; and he collected a vast amount of curious information in reference not only to their manners and customs and mode of life, but to the lands which they call their own. The broad and irresistible wave of Western civilization has reached the confines of their vast territories, before long will pour in upon them, and already is slowly, but surely, undermining many an ancient landmark. In the course of another fifty years its advance will have largely modified their characteristics, and swept away much that is now the most clearly and picturesquely defined. We need, therefore, to be grateful to Mr. Atkinson for the record he has supplied of their present condition; a record which to us is one of romantic interest, as to the future historian it will be one of authentic value.

In introducing that record to the reader, he says:—"Mine has been a tolerably wide field, extending from Kokhand on the west to the eastern end of the Baikal, and as far south as the Chinese town of Tchin-si; including that immense chain Syan-shan, never before seen by any European; as well as a large portion of the western part of the Gobi, over which Gonghiz Khan marched his wild hordes; comprising a distance traversed of about 32,000 versts in carriages, 7100 in boats, and 20,300 on horseback—in all, 59,400 versts (about 39,500 miles), in the course of seven years." Neither the old Venetian, Marco Polo, nor the Jesuit priests, could have visited these regions, their travels having been far to the south, even the recent travellers, Hue and Gobet, who visited "the land of grass" (the plains to the south of the great Desert of Gobi), did not penetrate into the country of the Kalkas. It is unnecessary to premise that in such a journey, prolonged over so many years, extended into so many countries, he suffered much both from hunger and thirst, was exposed to numerous tests of his courage and fortitude, and on several occasions placed in most critical situations with the tribes of Central Asia; that he more than once was called upon to confront an apparently inevitable death. Within the limits to which we are confined, it will be impossible for us to attempt a detailed narrative of his labours, but we shall hope to select those passages and incidents which will afford a fair idea of their value and enterprise.

Armed with a passport from the Czar of All the Russias, which in many a difficult conjuncture proved to its bearer as all-powerful as Ali Baba's "Open Sesame," Mr. Atkinson left Moscow on the 6th of March, intent upon the exploration of the wild regions of Siberia. A ten days' journey brought him to Ekaterineburg, the first Russian town in this direction, across the Asiatic boundary. Here he took boat on the river Tchoussowaia, which he descended as far as the pristan, or port, of Chaitanskoï. Thence he made an excursion to the house of an hospitable Russian, the director of the Outskinkoï iron-works, traversing a forest of pines, which deeply impressed him by its aspect of gloomy grandeur. Resuming his river-voyage, [159] he observed that the valley widened considerably as he advanced. On the west bank spread a large extent of meadow-land; on the eastern, the soil was partly cultivated, and bloomed with young crops of rye. The pastures shone with fresh strong verdure, were already starred with flowers, while the birch trees were hourly bursting into leaf. In this region the change from winter to summer is magically sudden, like that of a transformation scene. At night, you see the grass browned by frost, and the trees bare of buds; in twenty-four hours, the meadows are covered with fresh greenness, and the woods spread over you a thick canopy of vigorous foliage. But if you come from a temperate clime, you miss that sweet and gradual development of bud and bloom, of leaf and flower, which is the charm and privilege of spring. You miss the rare pleasure of watching the opening violet, the first primrose, the early tinge of green upon the hedgerow and in the coppice, which you recognize as the heralds and pledges of happy days to come.

At Oslanskoï Mr. Atkinson took his leave of the Tchoussowaia, and prepared to cross the Ural Mountains. But while staying at Nijne-Toura, he resolved upon ascending the great peak of the Katchkanar. The road led through a tract of deep forest, which spread over high hills, and down into deep valleys, filled with white vapour, through which the branches of lightning-stricken pines loomed ghastly like the shivered masts of a wreck through the ocean mist. Towards noon a thunder-storm came on, accompanied by heavy rain. Portions of the forest were so thick as completely to exclude the daylight; and Mr. Atkinson and his companions frequently found it necessary to cut their way through the intertangled growth.

Though bears and other beasts of prey frequent these wilds, Mr. Atkinson met with none; the chief danger was a fall in the midst of rocks and prostrate trees, which might have been attended with painful consequences. At last they emerged from the forest gloom, at the foot of a steep ascent overlaid with huge blocks of stones. As their horses slowly clambered up the rugged acclivity, the sound was heard of the roar of water, indicating a cataract close at hand. It proved to be the outcome of a small stream, which tumbled down a steep and rocky bed in a succession of shining falls. Crossing this stream, the riders pursued their upward course until at eight o'clock they reached the Katchkanar, after a tedious journey of eleven hours. The guide, a veteran hunter, proposed to halt for the night at the foot of some high rocks—a proposition readily accepted. All hands set to work, and soon a great fire was blazing, not only for the purpose of warmth, but as a protection against the clouds of mosquitoes which swarmed around, and threatened to murder sleep.

At three o'clock, Mr. Atkinson was up and about. The dawn was swiftly advancing over the interminable Siberian forest. Above the vast horizon stretched long lines of pale yellow clouds, which every minute became more luminous, until they seemed like so many waves of golden light rolling and breaking on the far celestial shore. As the sun gradually rose into the heavens, every mountain-top blazed with fire, like gigantic altars, and the pines were transformed into columns of gold. The adventurers were soon afoot, and, crossing a little grassy valley, began the real ascent.

It was a chaotic mass of loose huge rocks, with snow filling up many of the cavities; in other places they passed under colossal blocks, over which it would have been no easy task to climb. Further up they stretched across large patches of frozen snow, and reached the foot of the high crags of the Katchkanar; many of which stand out like huge crystals, not less than one hundred feet in height, and are composed of regular courses, with pure magnetic iron ore between their beds, varying from one inch to four inches thick. In some places cubes or crystals of iron project from the solid rock, three and four inches square; and in others the whole mass seems to be of iron, or some other mineral substance. Climbing one of the highest pinnacles, Mr. Atkinson enjoyed a glorious prospect, such as it is difficult for the dweller in plains, with their always limited horizons, to form even an idea of. For hundreds of miles the view to the east extended into Siberia, until all disappeared in fine blue vapour. "There is something truly grand," says Mr. Atkinson, "in looking over these black and apparently interminable forests, in which no trace of a human habitation, not even a wreath of smoke, can be seen to assure us that man is there. Turning to the north, and about one hundred versts distant, Pardinsky Kanem rises out of the dark forest (this is one of the highest points in the Ural chain); it is partly covered with snow, and shines like frosted silver in the bright sun. All the mountains near are blue, purple, and misty, with a rugged foreground of rocks of great height, broken into all shapes and forms. In fact, the summit of the Katchkanar is evidently a mountain in ruins, the softer parts having been removed or torn away by the hand of time, leaving the barren portion, or vertebræ of the mountain, standing like a huge skeleton, which, seen at a distance, often assumed the most fantastic and picturesque shapes."

After a brief rest, Mr. Atkinson and his friends began the descent of the mountain, taking, however, a circuitous route which secured them a variety of scenes, and about seven o'clock in the evening they reached the site of their encampment on the preceding night. There they slept until dawn, when they made the best of their way back to Nijne-Toura—a long day's journey.

While at Nijne Mr. Atkinson had an opportunity of seeing something of the pastimes popular among the iron-workers of the district. It was the occasion of a popular festival, and the workmen and their families were all holiday-making. Females and children were riding merrily in the boxes of the large swings that had been temporarily constructed. The men were wrestling, just as they might do in Devonshire or Cornwall. Stripping off his coat, each man tied his long sash firmly round his waist; this his antagonist gripped with the right hand, while the left was placed on his shoulder; then the struggle began. One of the athletes was so conspicuously superior to the rest in skill and prowess, that at length no one would respond to his repeated challenges to try a fall. Assuming the honours of championship, he was on the point of quitting the arena when a slim-built, but well-proportioned, young man suddenly stepped forward as a competitor. He was evidently a stranger, and his appearance was greeted with a good deal of laughter, in which the champion readily joined. The latter acted as if assured of an easy victory, but, to the general surprise, a sharp and prolonged contention ensued. The wrestler, angry at the prospect of losing his laurels, exerted all his dexterity to throw his daring opponent, and when that failed, endeavoured to overcome him by superior strength. In vain: he was flung prostrate on the ground. Red with shame, he sprang to his feet and repeated his challenge. A second combat followed, and the would-be champion, by a second defeat and a heavy fall, was taught a lesson in modesty, which it is to be hoped he long remembered.

Meanwhile, the young girls, in their best and brightest costumes, shone like a bed of many-coloured tulips. Some, with hands clasped together, walked to and fro, singing simple songs to those plaintive Russian melodies which, in their sweet minor keys, are often so beautiful. Others joined in a game which resembles our English see-saw. A plank, about seven feet long, was placed on a centre block, six inches high. At each end stood a player, who, by springing up and alighting again on the board, caused her companion at the other end to rise higher every time. The players in this way would sometimes bound as high as three feet or three feet and a half.

From Nijne Mr. Atkinson made several excursions into the mining districts of the Ural, and afterwards returned to Ekaterineburg, to complete the preparations for his Siberian expedition. He took with him a young man, about twenty-four years old, who spoke German fluently, and bidding adieu to his friends, started on his journey. In spite of every effort, he says, a feeling of deep sadness overtook him when his gaze rested for the last time on the lofty mountain crest which forms the boundary of Europe. But the die was cast; he gave the word "Forward!" and away dashed the horses into Asia. Kamenskoï was the first stage; beyond which he entered the valley of the Issetz, and rapidly approached the great monastery of St. Tolometz. It stands on the left bank of the Issetz, near its junction with the river Teleta, and in external appearance resembles the Kremlin of Moscow. The walls are strengthened by towers at the angles, and close to the east end stands the church, an elegant and a spacious edifice. The road from this point still lay along the high bank of the Issetz, which here flows through a well-wooded country and teeming fields of wheat and rye. There are no fences in the fields; but every village has its ring-fence of posts and rails, enclosing an area of from two to three miles in diameter, with gates on the high-road, and a watchman to open and shut them. Passing station after station, Atkinson crossed the Issetz and the Tobol, and struck into the steppes of Ischim—a flat, uninteresting tract of country between the rivers Tobol and Ischim. It is watered by several lakes, and the small sandy ridges—they can scarcely be called hills—are often covered with pine-woods.

Here he fell in with a large party of convicts, marching, under a strong guard, into Eastern Siberia. There were ninety-seven in the gang, the van of which was led by seventeen men and three women, in chains, destined for Nertchinsk, more than four thousand versts further. The journey would occupy them eight months. The others followed in pairs, on their way to the government of Irkutsk; they had three thousand versts to travel, or a march of six months. Behind them came telagas [166] with baggage, and eleven women riding; some of whom were accompanying their husbands into their miserable exile. In front and on each side rode mounted Cossacks, who strictly guarded the prisoners; but what were they to do if they escaped? There was no prospect before them but death by starvation.

At the various posting-stations barracks are built, the front buildings of which are occupied by the officers, guards, and attendants. From each end, to the distance of about forty or fifty feet, stretches a high stockade, which returns at right angles, and runs about sixty feet. It is then carried along the back so as to enclose in all an area of two hundred feet by sixty; in the middle are the buildings for the prisoners. The stockade is formed of trunks of trees, twelve inches in diameter, standing fifteen feet above the ground, and cut to a sharp point at the top; placed close together, they form a very strong barrier. The prisoners, moreover, are placed under continual supervision. They march two days, at a rate of twenty to twenty-five versts daily, and rest one. A gang leaves Ekaterineburg every Monday morning.

After leaving Kiansk, which Mr. Atkinson anathematizes as "the worst town in all Siberia," he travelled directly south, with the view of visiting Lakes Sartian and Tchany, the remains of a great inland sea. From Lake Tchany a chain of lakes, some of which are fifty or sixty versts broad, extends south-west for nearly two hundred and fifty versts. The country was low and swampy, but rose occasionally in slight undulations, clothed with long coarse grass, and frequently relieved by extensive clumps of birch and aspen, or a thick underwood of bushes. The lakes proved to be surrounded by so dense a growth of reeds that the water was visible only at a few points. Beyond, the country was thickly wooded, with large pieces of cultivated land, on which were fine crops of wheat and rye growing. The villages were well-built and clean; the inmates looked comfortable and cleanly; and large herds of cattle grazed in the village pastures. Speeding onward in his tarantass, as fast as six horses could carry him, our traveller crossed the Barabinsky steppe—a region curiously unlike that dreariness of monotony, or monotony of dreariness, which is generally associated with the name. The traveller might have been excused for thinking himself in some fair district of England, when he looked around on hills of gentle slope, covered with noble trees, which formed the boundaries of considerable plains, and saw the deer nimbly bounding through the fresh green glades. The view was brightened here and there with plantations of large timber; at other points rose sheltered belts of young trees; the effect being in each case so picturesque as to induce the fancy that art had thus arranged them. The ground teemed with flowers, as if Proserpine's fertile feet had consecrated it—with the bright geranium, pale blue and deep blue delphinium, white and dark rich crimson dianthus, peony, and purple crocus. The lakes that studded the expanse, like silver gems in an emerald setting, bore expanded on their tremulous wave the blooms of the white and yellow *Nymphoea*. The whole scene was exquisitely sweet and tranquil.

But in Siberia changes are frequent and sudden, and to this Eden bit quickly succeeded a Slough of Despond. Crossing a morass in a heavy vehicle, drawn by six or seven horses, is not a pleasant sensation; happily, the traject was accomplished without accident. Another and another followed; and through each, with hard struggling on the part of the horses, and much yelling on the part of the yemtschick, or driver, the traveller was carried successfully. He was thankful, however, when the country again improved, and his road once more lay among the hills and pastures. At Krontikha, he was greeted with a noble view of the valley of the Ob, one of the great rivers of Siberia. From one high ridge to the other, twelve or fifteen versts is the width of the valley; in the middle, with constant undulations, first to one side and then to the other, like a coquette between two suitors, the shining stream pursues its capricious way, sometimes breaking off into several channels, divided by green little patches of island. Looking to the north-east, the traveller discerns, at a distance of one hundred and fifty versts, Kolyvan, formerly the chief town of the government—a rank now assigned to Tomsk, which lies one hundred and fifty versts further in the same direction. To the north and east the eye rests on a vast level, dark with the heavy shadows of forests of pine.

At Barnaoul, the chief town in the mining district of the Altai, Mr. Atkinson found himself 4527 versts from St. Petersburg. After a night's rest he resumed his forward course, and the character of the country soon warned him that he was approaching the steppes which extend westward to the banks of the Irtisch. These dreary wildernesses were the home and haunt of the Kirghiz, before the Russians drove them across the river, and built a line of forts along its bank from Omsk to the mouth of the Bouchtarma. The frontier to the Kirghiz steppe is guarded by a line of barracks; the whole length of the line (about 2500 versts) stretching far up into the Altai mountain range, and along the boundary of China. Dull beyond description is the landscape here. The chief product is wormwood; and around the fords and watercourses grow only a few bushes and stunted willows.

Kolyvan Lake lies at the foot of some offshoots of the Altai chain. The masses of rocks which strew its shores, broken and fantastic of outline, present all the appearance of a ruined city. The granite seems to have been forced up in a soft or liquid state; then to have flowed over and cooled; after which it has been forced up again and again, with the result that it has assumed, in hardening, the most extraordinary forms. The rocks on the heights of the Altai are not less remarkable: some mock you with the aspect of ruined battlements and feudal keeps; others might be mistaken for human heads of a size so colossal that even the magic helmet in "The Castle of Otranto" would have been a world too small for them.

It is at Oubinskoï, a small town or village on the broad, deep, willow-fringed Ouba, that the ascent of the Altai really begins. Thence you cross the Oulba, and ascend a valley full of charming bits for the artist, to the silver mines of Riddersk. About fifteen versts beyond rises the snow-crowned height of Ivanoffsky-Belock, the source of the Gromotooka, or stream of thunder ("grom"), one of the wildest rivers in the Altai. With a roar like that of thunder it hurls its foaming waters down the rugged steep, frequently tearing off and whirling along with it huge fragments of rock, and filling the startled air with a din and clang which are audible for miles. At Riddersk Mr. Atkinson was compelled to abandon his tarantass; he engaged twenty horses to accompany him, and an escort of fifteen men, five of whom carried rifles, while the rest were equipped with axes. A ride of twenty versts, and he reached Poperetchwaia, the last village in this part of the Altai. It is occupied by only eighteen families, who live there in the solitude of the mountain valley, with the great white peaks around them, ignorant of all the events that daily help to make up the history of the age into which they have been born—ignorant of the intellectual movements that are agitating the minds and filling the thoughts of men. A strange, apparently a useless, life! A life without action, without hope, without purpose! Surely ten years of our free, busy, progressive English life are preferable to a hundred years in this lonely Siberian wild. Each family, we are told, have their horses and cows, and around the village is pasture sufficient for large herds. The stags on the mountains are also theirs, and the deer on the hills, and the fish that teem in the rivers. Wild fruit is plentiful; and the bees in their hives produce abundance of honey. It is a Siberian Arcady; but an Arcady without its poetic romance.

The patriarch of the village is described by Mr. Atkinson as a fine old man, with a head and countenance which would have furnished an artist with a model for one of the Evangelists. Health and happiness shone in his face, the ruddy glow of which was set off by his silver-white beard. He wore a plain white shirt, hanging over trousers of thin linen, and fastened round his waist with a red sash; the trousers were tucked into a pair of boots which reached almost to the knee. In winter, a wolf or sheep skin coat is added to this picturesque costume.

In ascending the Altai our traveller plunged into a glorious forest of cedars, which, with their gnarled and twisted branches, formed an arched roof almost impervious to the sun. The scene afterwards changed to a silvery lake, the Keksa, which slept peacefully in the deep shadows of the mountains. Then came woods of larch, and pine, and birch, all freshly green, and breathing a pungent aromatic odour; and grassy glades, fit haunts for the Oreads of the Greek, or the fairies of the Teutonic mythology, with high cedar-crowned mountains rising on either hand.

There were no birds; but on the crags stood numerous graceful stags, watching suspiciously the passage of the strangers, and from bough to bough the black squirrel leaped in his mirth. Less pleasant inhabitants were the flies and mosquitoes, which infested the valley depths and lower levels. Still continuing to ascend, Mr. Atkinson entered a rocky gorge that crossed the shoulder of the mountain ridge. Here the crags presented their most savage grandeur. Time had hewn them into various imposing forms: some like turreted battlements and massive towers; others like enormous buttresses thrown up to support the huge sides of the mountain. While threading the defile, the travellers were overtaken by a terrible storm; the wind raged over the heights and through the ravines with a cruel and sudden fury; the lightning like blood-streaks wound across the darkened sky; the thunder broke in peal after peal, which the echoes caught up and repeated until the air rang as with the din of battle. They sheltered themselves behind a crag until the tempest was past, and then began the descent of the other side of the mountain.

Glad were they to find themselves in the more genial lowlands; and leaving behind them the Chelsoun chain of the Altai, which they had just crossed, they rode at a rapid rate towards Zirianovsky, a mining station at the foot of the Eagle Mountains. The silver mines here are the most valuable in the Altai. Some of the ores, which are exceedingly rich, lie at a depth of two hundred and eighty feet; others have been followed to a depth of four hundred and ninety feet. In working them the great difficulty to be confronted by the miners is the vast quantity of water that almost inundates the mines; but this might be obviated by the employment of a steam-engine. To carry the ore to the smelting-works upwards of two hundred horses are employed. First, it is conveyed in small carts, drawn by one horse, to Werchnayan pristan, on the Irtisch, a distance of more than one hundred versts; thence it is sent down the river in boats to Oust-Kamenogorsk pristan; and from the last place it is removed again in carts to Barnaoul, Pavlovsky, and other zavods; making a traject of nine hundred versts in all from the mines to the smelting-works.

Skirting the base of the Kourt-Choum mountains, which form the boundary between the Russian and Chinese empires, Mr. Atkinson turned his face southward, and before long arrived at Little Narym—a small outpost of Cossacks, stationed on a plain within a few versts of the Russian frontier. He was then on the military road, which extends only about twenty versts further, to the last outpost from Western Siberia. Having obtained horses, two telagas, and Cossack drivers, he started down the valley of the Narym, which opens into that of the Irtisch, and at nightfall entered Great Narym. To the officer in command he explained his project of crossing the Chinese frontier; but was warned that, as winter had already set in, and the snow lay deep in the Kourt-Chume chain, he would probably be lost or frozen to death if he attempted that route. He was advised to go through the Kirghiz steppe; and the officer courteously offered to forward him from one Cossack post to another, until he reached the fortress at Kochbouchta. Mr. Atkinson gladly accepted the offer, and arranged to meet his new friend in Ust-Kamenogorsk, on the Irtisch, hiring a boat and men to convey him thither. The boat consisted of two small canoes lashed together, five feet apart, with beams placed across, and the whole boarded over so as to provide a platform, or deck, about fifteen feet by ten. In the head and stern of each canoe sat a strong, sturdy fellow, with a small paddle, not much larger than a child's garden spade; this was used only to guide the bark, its progress being sufficiently provided for by the rapidity of the current. Paddling out into the middle of the river, which was more than a thousand yards broad, the boatmen soon got into the swing of the current, and the voyage began. "I was watching the changes in the scene," says Mr. Atkinson, "as one mountain peak after another came in view; when suddenly, and without any previous intimation, two of the men called out that their canoe was filling fast, and that they must make for the shore without a minute's delay! Before we got halfway to the bank she was nearly full of water, and when within about a hundred yards, the men cried out that she was sinking; this brought our broad deck down to the water on one side, and helped to float her. The men paddled with all their might, and at last we reached a thick bed of reeds, which assisted in keeping us afloat, till we succeeded in getting near enough to the bank to throw our luggage ashore; and then we landed."

After some trouble, Mr. Atkinson was able to hire a good boat, used for transporting the ore; and the luggage was transferred to it. Then a new difficulty arose; one of the men deserted. But with great promptitude Mr. Atkinson seized a bystander, and kept him prisoner until the deserter was given up. At last, a fresh start was effected. The sun was setting; a keen cutting wind blew up the river; and there was no shelter to be obtained, nor wood for a fire, for many versts. Fast over the valley crept the cold shades of night, and swiftly did they steal up the mountain sides. No signs of any resting-place could be discovered, and the scenery grew more and more gloomy. Turning a rocky headland, they beheld at a great distance the glimmer of a fire, though whether it was in a dwelling, or on the river bank, they could not determine. Bending vigorously to their oars, the boatmen shot forward rapidly; and after a long pull arrived at a small Cossack station, where Mr. Atkinson readily obtained shelter.

Asia, he remarks, is the land for tea; there it is that a man learns to appreciate the herb at its full and proper value. After refreshing himself with the popular beverage, he took a long walk alone on the bank of the

Irtisch. The fine, picturesque scenery was seen with impressive effect under the influence of a splendid moonlight, which cast the lower mountains into deep shade, while a silver lustre rested on the snow-crowned peaks, contrasting vividly with the gloom of the valleys. "How infinitely small," says Mr. Atkinson, "the sight of these mighty masses made me feel, as I wandered on in my solitary ramble! Excepting myself, I could not see one living thing—all was silent as the grave. I had passed some high rocks that shut out the Cossack post from my view, and had entered a valley, running up into the mountains, which lay shrouded in dusky shadow. Two white peaks rose far into the cold, grey sky; the full light of the moon shining upon one of them, and aiding much in giving a most solemn grandeur to the gloomy scene. Fancy began to people this place with phantoms, ghosts, and goblins of horrible aspect. It required but the howling of the wolves to give a seeming reality to the creations of the imagination."

Passing the mouth of the Bouchtarma, Mr. Atkinson descended the river to Mount Kamenogorsk. There he found his friend, the Cossack colonel, who provided him with an escort of two stalwart Cossacks, armed with sabre, gun, pistol, and long lance. His party also included an unarmed Cossack driver, and his own attendant. He set out in a light telaga, drawn by three horses, and plunged into the solitude of the Kirghiz steppe, which extends eastward to Nor-Zaisan and southward to the Tarbogatni Mountains. There are many undulations on this vast plain, which in summer affords pasturage for immense herds of horses. While halting on the bank of a dried-up stream to dine, Mr. Atkinson observed in the distance a small column of white smoke, which he supposed to proceed from a Kirghiz aul, or village; but a guide whom he had hired assured him there were no encampments in that direction, and that the smoke issued from burning reeds on the shores of Lake Nor-Zaisan. Thitherward the traveller immediately proceeded; sometimes over rich pastures, at others over a rough tract of ground and stones almost bare of vegetation. After riding a couple of hours, they were able to make out that the steppe was on fire, and that all the reeds were feeding the flame; and in due time they came upon a miserable Kirghiz yourt, or dwelling, inhabited by a dirty Kirghiz woman and four children, three of whom were very ill. She received the stranger, however, with simple hospitality, kindled the fire, and set his kettle on it. In return he made tea for himself and the children, who were lying on a voilock, covered up with skins. He then walked to the summit of a neighbouring hill to gain a view of the burning steppe. The fire was still about ten versts to the east, but was travelling west, and across Mr. Atkinson's track, extending in breadth some miles across the plain—a great wave of flame, which, accompanied by rolling clouds of smoke, ran swiftly along the ground, consuming the long grass, and reddening the horizon with a lurid glow.

Next morning Mr. Atkinson resumed his journey, passed a Kirghiz aul, and reached the margin of the Nor-Zaisan, but was unable to obtain a glimpse of its waters, owing to the dense masses of tall reeds which completely encircled it. He rode across to the Irtisch, but there too the view was similarly blocked up. There was nothing to be done but to return as quickly as possible to Kochbouchta, and prepare for the expedition into Chinese Tartary, which he had long had in contemplation. A man of irrepressible energy and singularly firm resolution, Mr. Atkinson, when his plans were once formed, lost no time in carrying them into execution. But while the necessary arrangements were being made, he found time to accomplish some short but interesting excursions in the neighbourhood of Kochbouchta, visiting the gold mines, and sketching the romantic scenery of the valley of the Isilksou. At length he was ready for his departure, and with an escort of three Cossacks, his servant, and his own Cossack attendant, he once more crossed the Irtisch, and began his journey across the Kirghiz steppe. All the party were well armed and well mounted, and Mr. Atkinson felt competent to encounter, if need be, half a hundred of the nomadic bandits, if they should attempt to plunder him. His servant, however, manifested so lively a dread of the robbers of the steppes, and so strong a disinclination to a close acquaintance with the Kirghiz, that Mr. Atkinson ordered him back to Ust-Kamenogorsk to await his return, rightly judging that his fears would render him an incumbrance and an impediment rather than a useful auxiliary.

II.

The tribes of the Kirghiz nation spread over the Asiatic steppes from the Aral river to the Ala-Tau Mountains. From time immemorial they have been divided into the Great, the Middle, and the Little Hordes. The Great Horde occupies the territory north of the Ala-Tau, extending into China and Tartary. The Middle Horde inhabits the countries lying between the Ischim, the Irtisch, Lake Balkash, and Khokand. The Little, which is by far the most numerous Horde, wanders over the undulating plains bounded by the Yamba and the Ural, over Turkistan (now under Russian rule), and into Siberia. As a whole, the Kirghiz population may be assumed to number about 1,250,000 souls. They are of Turco-Tartaric origin; and, according to Max Müller, Southern Siberia was their mother country. Nominally, they own the supremacy of the Great White Czar on the one side, and of the Chinese Emperor on the other; but their nomadic habits secure their virtual independence. Each tribe is governed by its sultan or chief. Quarrels and blood feuds between the different tribes are of constant occurrence. Many live wholly by brigandage; swooping down suddenly, under cover of night, on the richer auls, or villages, they carry off horses, cattle, and other objects of value, besides men, women, and children, whom they sell into slavery. These nocturnal raids are called barantas.

The yourt, or tent, of the Kirghiz bears a close resemblance to the kibitka of the Kalmucks. One of the better class is thus described: It was formed of willow trellis-work, put together with untanned strips of skin, made into compartments which fold up. It represented a circle of thirty-four feet in diameter, five feet high to the springing of the dome, and twelve feet in the centre. This dome is formed of bent rods of willow, an inch and a quarter in diameter, put into the mortice-holes of a ring about four feet across, which secures the top of the dome, admits light, and lets out the smoke. The lower ends of the willow rods are tied with leathern thongs to the top of the trellis-work at the sides, which renders it quite strong and secure. The whole is then covered with large sheets of voilock, made of wool and camel's hair, fitting close, so that it is both warm and water-tight. The doorway is formed of a small aperture in the trellis-work, over which hangs a piece of voilock, and closes it. In the daytime this is rolled up and fastened on the roof of the yourt.

The reader will not be surprised to learn that the furniture and fittings of the yourt are remarkable for their simplicity; the Kirghiz having none of the ingenuity of a Robinson Crusoe or the inventiveness of an American backwoodsman. The fire is kindled on the ground in the centre of the yourt. Directly opposite to the door, voilocks are spread; on these stand sundry boxes containing the clothing of the family, pieces of Chinese silk, tea, dried fruits, and ambas of silver (small squares, about two inches and a half long, an inch and a half wide, and three-tenths of an inch thick). Some of the Kirghiz possess large quantities of these ambas, which are carefully hoarded up. Above the boxes are bales of Bokharian and Persian carpets, often of great beauty and value. In another part of the yourt lies the large sack of koumis, or mare's milk, completely covered up with voilock to keep it warm and promote the fermentation. And near this bag stands a large leathern bottle, sometimes holding four gallons, and frequently enriched with much ornament; as are the small bottles which the horseman carries on his saddle. In another place may be seen the large iron caldron, and the trivet on which it rests when used for cooking in the yourt. There are usually half a dozen Chinese wooden bowls, often beautifully painted and japanned, from which the koumis is drunk; some of them hold three pints, others are still larger. On entering a Kirghiz yourt in summer, each guest is presented with one of these Chinese bowls full of koumis. To return the vessel with any koumis in it is considered impolite, and the rudeness is one of which a good Kirghiz is assuredly never guilty.

The saddles are deposited on the bales of carpets. As the wealthy Kirghiz greatly esteem rich horse trappings, many of these are beautiful and costly. If of Kirghiz workmanship, they are decorated with silver inlaid on iron, in chaste ornamental designs, and are padded with velvet cushions; the bridles, and other parts of the equipment, are covered with small iron plates, similarly inlaid.

Leathern thongs, ropes made of camel's hair, common saddles, saddle-cloths, and leathern tchimbar hang suspended from the trellis-work. The tchimbar, or trousers, however, are not infrequently made of black velvet, richly embroidered with silk, more especially the back elevation; and they are so large and loose that a Kirghiz, when he rides, can tuck into them the laps of his three or four khalats. As he ties them round his waist with a leathern strap, he presents a most grotesque appearance with the centre part of his person bulging like a great globe, out of which the very diminutive head and legs protrude.

The national dress of the Kirghiz is the khalat, a kind of pelisse, very long and very full, with large sleeves, made of cashmere or silk, and in the most dazzling colours; but the poorer nomad substitutes for this state dress a horse-skin jacket. Breeches fastened below the hips by a girdle of wool or cashmere, high-heeled madder-coloured boots, and a fox-skin cap, rising into a cone on the top, and lined inside with crimson cloth, complete his costume. His weapons are the spear, gun, and axe. The last is a long formidable weapon; the iron head is moderately heavy and sharp; the handle, about four and a half feet long, is secured by a leathern thong round the wrist. It is often richly inlaid with silver. The women wear a high calico head-dress, a part of which falls over the shoulders and covers up the neck; boots of the same make and colour as the men's, and a long and ample khalat, with, sometimes, a shawl tied round the waist.

The Kirghiz begin to make koumis in April. The mares are milked at five o'clock in the morning and about the same time in the evening, into large leathern pails, which are immediately taken to the yourt, and emptied into the koumis bag. The latter is five to six feet long, with a leathern tube, about four inches in diameter, at one corner, through which the milk is poured into the bag, and the koumis drawn out of it. A wooden instrument, not unlike a churning-staff, is introduced into the bag, for the purpose of frequently agitating the koumis, which is not considered in good condition until after the lapse of twelve to fourteen days. It is drunk in large quantities by such of the Kirghiz as are wealthy enough to keep up a considerable stud of brood mares; and every Kirghiz, rich or poor, slings his koumis bottle to his saddle in summer, and loses no opportunity of replenishing it at the different auls he visits.

In crossing the steppe, Mr. Atkinson fell in with the aul of Mahomed, a Kirghiz chief, who was reputed to be very wealthy. Mahomed was a fine robust man, about sixty years old, stout and square-built, with broad features, a fine flowing grey beard, a pair of small piercing eyes, and a fairly pleasant countenance. He wore on his head a closely fitting silk cap, handsomely embroidered in silver; his dress consisting of a large robe, or khalat, of pink and yellow striped silk, tied round the waist with a white shawl. His boots were of reddish-brown leather, small, with very high heels, causing a real or apparent difficulty in walking. His wife, much younger than himself, and probably not more than thirty or thirty-five years of age, had a broad face, high cheek-bones, twinkling black bead-like eyes, a small nose, a wide mouth; she was neither pretty nor prepossessing; but decidedly in want of a hot bath. Attired in a black kaufa (Chinese satin) khalat, with a red shawl round the waist; reddish-brown high-heeled boots, like her husband's; she also wore a rather pointed white muslin cap, the lappets of which, finely wrought on the edge with red silk, hung down nearly to her hips. This couple were rich in the world's goods from a Kirghiz point of view. Not only was their yourt well stocked with voilocks and carpets, and richly ornamented weapons, and costly caparisonings, but they owned an amount of live stock which would astonish the most opulent English farmer. The noise in and around the aul was deafening. It was a babel of sounds: the sharp cry of the camels, the neighing of the horses, the bellowing of the bulls, the bleating of the sheep and goats, and the barking of the dogs, all combining in one hideous, ear-shattering chorus. Mr. Atkinson counted no fewer than 106 camels, including their young; besides more than 2000 horses, 1000 oxen and cows, and 6000 sheep and goats. Yet even these large totals did not represent all the wealth of the Kirghiz chief; for he had two other auls, and at each were 1000 horses and numerous cattle. It was a picturesque and interesting sight to see the women busily milking the cows, and the men conducting the vast herds to their pastures. The horses and camels are driven to the greatest distance, as far as ten and fifteen versts; the oxen come next; the sheep remain nearest the aul, but still at a distance of five or six versts.

While Mr. Atkinson was sojourning in Mahomed's aul, a night attack was made upon it. He was aroused, about two hours after midnight, by a tremendous noise, which to him, sleeping on the ground, seemed as if it issued from some subterranean hollow. At first he thought it was the rumbling of an earthquake, and immediately sat upright. But the sound rolled on, drew nearer and nearer; presently it passed, so that the whole earth shook. Then he knew that the herd of horses was dashing onward at full gallop; and when he caught the shrieks of women and the shouts of men, he understood that an assault had been made upon the aul by robbers. In a moment he seized his rifle, and sallied forth from the yourt, to behold the Kirghiz, battle-axe in hand, leap on their horses, and gallop towards the point of attack. The herds were rushing wildly round the aul; the Cossacks, with their muskets loaded, were ready for the fray; all was confusion and disorder. Presently the sound of horses swiftly approaching could be heard; they came nearer and nearer; in less than two minutes a dark troop swept past like a whirlwind at twenty paces distant, making the air ring with loud, defiant shouts. Five bullets whistled after them; there was a scream from a horse, but on they dashed. The Kirghiz followed quickly in pursuit, accompanied by two of the Cossacks, who had rapidly mounted. After riding about a verst they came up with the robbers, to find they were three times their number, and prepared to fight for their booty. Against such odds no success could be hoped for, and accordingly the Kirghiz retired to the aul. When day dawned it was ascertained that this daring razzia had cost Mahomed a hundred horses.

This was not the only adventure that befell Mr. Atkinson while he made Mahomed's aul his headquarters. One day, he was returning from an excursion to some finely coloured porphyry rocks, when the wind begun to blow across the steppe in strong and frequent gusts, and his Kirghiz guides announced that a storm was at hand. Their prediction was confirmed by the clouds that gathered about the lower peaks of the Altai, and soon a dense mass of blackness, extending for a long distance from north to south, rolled rapidly in the direction of the travellers. Not a tree or a rock offered the slightest shelter. Spurring their horses briskly, they galloped over the plain, pursued by the storm, as, in Goethe's ballad, the father and his doomed child are pursued by the Erl King. The gusts of wind ceased, and for a short time a deadly calm prevailed. Meanwhile, the clouds were painfully agitated, as if by some internal force, and streams of vapour issuing from their blackness whirled rapidly round. A low murmur stole through the air; gradually it deepened and strengthened, until, as the storm broke upon the steppe, it swelled into a roar like that of a thousand cannon. The grasses and low bushes were rooted up, and sent flying into the air with fearful velocity. The terrified horses stopped suddenly; nor could they be induced to move until the whirlwind had passed by. Fortunately the travellers had not been caught in its vortex, and no serious accident occurred.

Leaving the hospitable Mahomed, Mr. Atkinson continued his explorations of the steppe, and rode onward to the next aul, which lay to the northward, and was reached in two days' journey. Here, after the usual entertainment, he found himself free to write up his journal—much to the astonishment of his companions, the three R's being unknown in the steppe to any but the mullahs, or priests, of the various tribes. The manuscript was a wonder to the children of the wilderness, and they regarded its owner as a very wealthy mullah, possessed of the priceless treasure of a book full of amulets. For the mullah sells his amulets, or charms, at the rate of a sheep for each scrap of paper, which he has covered with unmeaning characters. Mr. Atkinson's ring was examined; also his knife; also a piece of red sealing-wax. On a piece of thick paper from his sketch-book he took impressions of his seal, and presented them to the women of the yourt, who doubtlessly long wore them in their caps as talismans or ornaments of special value and importance. His watch was likewise an object of curiosity. He held it to the ear of a woman sitting near him. Evidently she thought it was alive and talking, for she communicated the fact to her companions, and they all expressed a wish to hear it speak.

By way of Mount Kamenogorsk, his old quarters, Mr. Atkinson proceeded to Barnaoul, which he reached on the 1st of November. This town is built at the junction of the small river Barnaulka with the Ob. The streets are wide, laid out in parallel lines, and intersected by others at right angles. There are three ugly brick churches, and one large hospital. Its silver smelting works are on an extensive scale, producing annually about nine thousand pounds. Almost all the gold found in Siberia is also smelted here, and cast into bars; and every year six caravans leave with the precious metals for St. Petersburg—four in winter by the sledge roads, and two in summer. Barnaoul is the centre for the administration of the mines of the Altai, and the residence of the Natchalink, or director, as well as of the heads of the principal departments.

The public museum at Barnaoul contains a very good collection of minerals, some Siberian antiquities, a few Siberian animals and birds, and four tiger-skins. The wearers of these skins were killed in different parts of Siberia; in two instances their capture proving fatal to some of the peasants engaged in it, for pea-rifles and hay-forks are scarcely fit weapons with which to encounter the fiercest of the beasts of prey. They are seldom found in Siberia; only when driven by hunger do they cross the Irtisch, and many peasants do not know them even by name. The last of the Barnaoul company, now reposing peacefully in a glass case, was discovered, early one morning, prone on the top of a small hay-rick, near the village. The peasant, who had come for some hay for his horses, beheld with surprise and terror the strange and formidable creature, and shrank from his glaring eyeballs, which seemed to sparkle with fire. At the same moment the peasant's dog caught sight of him, and, with a loud bark, bravely dashed towards the rick. Growling terribly, the tiger sprung to the ground. The dog met him intrepidly,—to be crushed in a moment beneath his heavy paw. Hastening towards the village, the man gave the alarm, and quickly returned with a valiant company; some armed with pea-rifles, others with hay-forks and axes. Several dogs followed them. On approaching the rick, they were apprised of the enemy's position by a furious growl. The dogs made a brilliant charge; but the tiger crouched sullenly, and did not spring. A small shot through his hide roused him, and at a bound he was in among the dogs, killing a couple of them instantly with his terrible paws, and scattering the rest in ignominious flight. He received two more balls, but they served only to inflame his fury, and leaping in among his assailants, he felled one of them to the ground, dead. Again the dogs charged him, while the peasants with their hay-forks stabbed him in the back and sides. At last he withdrew slowly towards a bank covered with brushwood, followed by the dogs and their masters; but on reaching the bank he halted, faced round, growled angrily, and prepared for another spring. His enemies halted, and poured in shot upon him; the dogs barked furiously; but he held his ground, and could not be induced to move. After a while, encouraged by his inaction, the dogs began to close in upon him, and finally it was discovered that a ball had pierced him in a vital part, and the beast was dead.

The river Ob, which flows past Barnaoul, is described as a magnificent stream, running in a valley twelve versts broad; its numerous small branches divide this valley into islands, on which large trees are growing. In May the melting of the snow swells the stream into a great flood, which inundates much of the valley, and gradually widens from one bank to the other, with the tops of the trees rising above the swirl of waters like islands. At this time many of the scenes along the Ob are very grand, especially if seen at sunrise or sunset, when the various colouring of the luminous sky is mirrored in the mighty stream, which, flashing with golden and crimson lights, rolls through the deep purple masses of the forest, to terminate its course in the Arctic Ocean.

The neighbourhood seems to be an attractive one for the sportsman; snipe abound in June and July, blackcock in August, and rebchicks, or tree partridges, in September. Wild hen are also plentiful, and in winter, hares. Or if the hunter care for more venturous sport, he may sally out against the wolves and bears.

The bears are dangerous antagonists. A very large one was seen by some woodcutters about fifteen versts from the gold mine; and two men, one of whom was known as a bold, skilful, and veteran hunter, started in pursuit. They found the beast's track quite fresh in the long dewy grass, and cautiously followed it up, until a low growl warned them of his presence. He sprang out of a thicket, about thirty-five paces distant, and confronted his pursuers. The hunter fired, and his shot told, but not in a vital part. The wounded animal charged immediately, the other man reserving his shot until he was within twenty paces. Then, unfortunately, his rifle missed fire. The bear at once stood on his hind legs, and sprang forward against his first assailant, striking him to the earth with a blow that stripped his scalp and turned it over his face; then, seizing his arm, he began to gnaw and crush it to the bone, gradually ascending to the shoulder. The sufferer called to his companion to load and fire; but, losing heart when he saw his friend so terribly mangled, the craven took to flight.

Returning to the gold mine, he related what had happened; but it was then too late to despatch a party in search of the unfortunate hunter. At daylight next morning, however, they set out, with the craven as guide. On arriving at the scene of the affray, no remains of the victim could be found but some torn clothing and his rifle; and the trampled grass showed that he had been carried off into the thick covert. The trail was pursued with the utmost diligence, and at length, under a heap of branches, in a dense thicket of trees and bushes, the hunter's body was discovered, and, strange to say, though grievously mutilated, it still throbbed with life. With tender care the miserable victim was conveyed to the gold mine and taken to the hospital, where he was treated with the utmost kindness, and all was done that medical skill could do. For a long time he remained unconscious; but at the end of two months a slight improvement was noticeable, and he recovered his reason. His first question was about the bear; his next, about his own defeat. In truth, his conversation turned only upon these subjects: he seemed possessed by a monomania; was continually asking for his rifle, that he might go and kill "Michael Ivanitch" (the bear). As his strength returned, it was thought necessary to place him under restraint, lest his desire to contend with his fierce and powerful enemy should lead him into some dangerous enterprise.

But when autumn arrived, and laid its magical finger on the forest, the monomaniac seemed to have forgotten his hate, so that he was watched with less rigour. He took advantage of his comparative freedom to steal from the hospital, gain his own cottage, and, in the absence of his family, arm himself with his rifle and axe, and stow away in his wallet a loaf of black bread. Then, as the shades of evening began to fall, he started for the forest, and soon disappeared in the gathering gloom.

As soon as his absence from the hospital was known, a close search for him was instituted; but in vain. A week passed by, and it was supposed that he had perished, when one day he strode into the hospital, carrying on his shoulders the skin of a huge black bear. Throwing it down, he exclaimed, "I told you I would have him." Thenceforward he rapidly recovered; both his physical and mental health were re-established, and he lived to bring down many another "Michael Ivanitch" with his deadly rifle.

A curious incident befell a Cossack officer in the woods of Barnaoul.

Alone and unarmed, he was sauntering through the forest glades, gathering specimen plants, when, at a distance of about eight versts from the gold mine, he emerged into an open space, where stood a few isolated trees; and the same moment he descried, not more than two hundred yards off, a she-bear and her two cubs gambolling together. She, too, recognized his presence; and, with a fierce growl, drove her young ones into a tree as an asylum, and, resolute to defend them, mounted guard at its foot.

To carry off the cubs as trophies was the Cossack's resolve, but he wanted a weapon. Retiring into the wood a few steps, he came to a place where the woodmen had felled several young birch trees, and from one of these he selected four feet of a stout, strong, but manageable stem, with which he returned to the scene of action. At his approach the old bear resumed her growling, and moved uneasily to and fro in front of the tree, but carefully keeping within a few feet of it. He continued his advance. She growled more savagely, and plainly suspected his hostile intentions. Still he moved forward, with his eyes steadfastly fixed upon her. When he was within about fifty paces, she made a fierce rush that would have put most men to flight. He held his ground, and as the cubs began to whine, she trotted back towards the tree, in a mood of uncontrolled rage. The Cossack followed; she turned; the two antagonists stood face to face at a distance of twenty yards.

Retreat was now impossible; and there they stood, gazing keenly on each other, and each waiting for an opportunity to attack. The bear, with fiery eyeballs, made a second rush, and at a few paces from her daring enemy, rose on her hind legs, either to fell him with her heavy paws or crush him in her cruel embrace; but, with wonderful coolness, he brought down his club and toppled her over. In a second she sprang to her feet, and prepared to renew the charge; another tremendous stroke laid her on the ground. The combat assumed a desperate and deadly character, and several "rounds" were determinedly fought. Eventually, the Cossack's well-directed blows subdued her courage, and when she could neither charge him in front nor get in his rear, she fell back towards the tree, still fighting desperately. Under the tree a fresh spirit was infused into the affray, and every time she heard her cubs whine, she returned with increased fury to the assault. She was received, however, with such a shower of blows, that, at last dispirited and exhausted, she retreated hastily towards the forest, and entered its shades; contriving, nevertheless, whenever the gallant Cossack moved towards the refuge of her cubs, to make a rush in that direction.

All this time the cubs remained perched among the branches, and the officer, considering himself victorious, longed to take possession of his prize. But he could devise no plan of getting at them, and it was evident they would not come down at his call. Luckily, a woodman, on his way to the gold mine, rode into the arena. The Cossack hailed him; ordered him to dismount, to take from his saddle the zumka, or leather saddle-bags, and, climbing the tree, to thrust the cubs into them, while he himself kept watch over the mother bear. This was done, though not without several sharp encounters between the she-bear and the officer; and, finally, the peasant threw his heavy bags across his horse, and led the way to the ravine, the Cossack covering the rear. In this fashion they marched into Barnaoul; first, the woodman and his horse, next the Cossack officer, and behind him the bear. The march occupied two hours, and the unfortunate mother persevered to the very last, not abandoning her young ones until their captor had reached the cottages. Then she hastily returned into the forest, and was seen no more.

III.

There is much to attract and impress in the scenery of the lakes of the Altai. Lake scenery in a mountainous country is always picturesque, always striking, from the variety of forms which it presents, and its endless contrasts of light and shade, and its magical combinations of colours. Moreover, it passes so rapidly from the calmly beautiful to the sublime! for at one moment the silver waters sleep as profoundly as a babe on its mother's breast; at another, the storm-wind issues from the savage glen, and lashes them into a white wrath. In the genial days of summer it shines and sparkles with a peculiar radiance; a golden glory seems to hang upon the mountain sides, and a purple light rests on the bosom of the lake. In the dreary winter, nothing can be grander in its gloom; the hollows and the glens are heavy with an eery darkness, through which the white peaks show like sheeted phantoms. In truth, it appeals to us by its twofold features of the mountain and the water. The former awakens our awe, lifts us out of our commonplace lives, and fills us with a sense of the wonder and mystery of God's work; it is an embodiment of majesty and power, a noble and sublime architecture, the study of which awakens the higher and purer impulses of the soul. Beauty of colour, perfection of form, an endless change in the midst of what seems to us an everlasting permanency—all those are the mountain's; all these belong to that great cathedral of the earth, with its "gates of rock," its "pavements of cloud," its snow-white altars, and its airy roof, traversed by the stars. Then as to water; has it not a wonder and a beauty of its own? "If we think of it," says Ruskin, "as the source of all the changefulness and beauty which we have seen in clouds; then as the instrument by which the earth we have contemplated was modelled into symmetry, and its crags chiselled into grace; then as, in the form of snow, it robes the mountains it has made, with that transcendent light which we could not have conceived if we had not seen; then as it exists in the foam of the torrent, in the iris which spans it, in the morning mist which rises from it, in the deep crystalline peaks which mirror its hanging shore, in the broad lake and glowing river; finally, in that which is to all human minds the best emblem of unwearied, unconquerable power, the wild, various, fantastic, tameless unity of the sea; what shall we compare to this mighty, this universal element, for glory and for beauty? or how shall we follow its eternal changefulness of feeling?" Bring the two together, the water and the mountain, and the landscape attains its highest character; the picture is then as consummate in its mingled beauty and grandeur as Nature can make it; and hence it is, I think, that lake scenery has always such a power over the imagination.

The Altin-Kool, or Golden Lake, measuring about one hundred versts in length, and from three to twelve in breadth, lies in an enormous chasm, with peaks and precipices all around it, some of them two thousand feet in height, and so perpendicular as to afford no footing even for a chamois. On the west side of the lake, the mountain pinnacles rise to 10,500 feet, and on the south several are even loftier. On the east side their elevation is less, but still they reach far above the line of vegetation into the region of perpetual snow. Having engaged some Kalmucks, or boatmen, Mr. Atkinson and his companions set out in canoes to explore the lake, beginning on the east. For the first ten versts the mountains do not rise very abruptly; they slope to the north, and green cedar forests cover them to the very summit, while the banks on the opposite side are almost treeless. Winding round a small headland, the lake expands into a splendid basin, with picturesque mountains grouped on either shore. Early in the evening the voyagers stopped near a torrent, which poured its foam and din down a narrow gorge, and the Kalmucks recommended it as a favourable site for an encampment. A bed of clean white sand, about fifteen feet wide, sloped gradually to the water-side. Between the upper rim of the sand and the rocks, large cedars were growing, and under these a bulayan, or wigwam, was constructed. Though consisting only of a few bare poles, covered with birch bark, open in front, and the ends filled up with branches, it was warm, and it kept out the mosquitoes; and within its welcome covert Mr. Atkinson and his party contentedly passed the night.

At daybreak, a fresh wind was blowing, and until this subsided the Kalmucks could not be induced to move. Satisfied at last with the promise both of sky and mountains, they pushed off, and doubling round a rocky point, entered a broad and beautiful bay, curving gracefully in the shadow of snow-capped mountains. At Tasck-tash, a bold headland, the lake turns directly south. Climbing to its summit, Mr. Atkinson enjoyed a noble view of the expanse of shining waters—one of those views which rests in the memory for ever, and is at all times a beauty and a joy. The general character of the landscape is boldness. Along the west shore the rocks dip to the east, at a very sharp angle, while upon their foundations the crags rise perpendicularly, and, above all, a snow-crowned summit shines like silver against the sapphire sky. On the east, as already stated, the mountains are less abrupt; but one, a conspicuous peak, rears a lofty and rounded crest far into the clouds, with white vaporous billows clinging to its rugged sides, and the eternal snow whitening its remote crest.

As the voyage progressed, the voyagers came upon such mysteries of colour as filled them with delight. Out of the chinks and clefts in the deep red granite bloomed bright plants and flowers with tropical luxuriance. Some slate rocks, grey, purple, and orange, intervened; the bright yellow of the birches lighted up the distant rocks; and the background was filled in with the deep purple mountains. The whole was a wonder of rich harmonious colouring, like a symphony of Beethoven's. At another point a gleaming waterfall leaped boldly over a succession of picturesque rocky terraces, the colours of which were bright as those of the rainbow, green, yellow, purple, and glowing red. There was also a white marble, spotted with purple; another, white, with veins of bluish purple; and a mass of exquisite, deep plum-coloured jasper. On the third day of their exploration, the voyagers entered one of the wildest parts of the lake—a deep circular recess in the Karakorum Mountains, into which three streams fling their heedless waters, uniting near the brink of a mighty precipice, and then tumbling down from ledge to ledge, to pass through a natural arch and fall into the lake. Prom the summit of the cliff, where the water takes its first leap, to the level of the lake, is not less than two thousand feet. "Avalanches must sometimes sweep over this place, and large trees are bent down and stripped of their branches. Huge rocks are torn up and hurled along, crushing and grinding everything in their course, as they rush on into the lake. No man can conceive the chaotic confusion into which the mass of ice and rocks has been heaped. One enormous stone, weighing not less than a hundred and fifty tons, had been placed on its end, on the edge of the rock, in an overhanging position towards the lake."

Various rivers flow into the Altin-Kool, such as the Tchoulishman, the Kamga, and the Karbou. They are navigated by the Kalmucks in light canoes, each constructed from the trunk of a single tree. The poplar is much used for this purpose; but, notwithstanding the softness of its wood, the labour of canoe-building is very great, owing to the rude character of the tools employed. The sides are cut down to a thickness of about three-quarters of an inch; but the bottom, which is usually made flat and without a keel, is nearly double the thickness.

Having completed his circumnavigation of the Altin-Kool, Mr. Atkinson, with his thirst for new scenes unquenched, started on a visit to the source of the river Katounaia. His route lay past Kolyvan, a town where the population is principally employed in cutting and polishing jasper and porphyry, and across the river Tchenish. He then crossed into the valley of the Koksa, and descended upon the Yabagan steppe, where he met with some Kalmuck auls, and was present at a curious pseudo-religious ceremony, the offering up of an annual sacrifice to the Kalmuck deity. A ram was presented by its owner, who desired a large increase to his herds and flocks. It was handed to an assistant of the priest, who duly killed it. Meanwhile, the priest, looking eastward, chanted a prayer, and beat on a large tambourine to attract the attention of his god, while he petitioned for multitudes of sheep and cattle. When the ram had been flayed, the skin was hoisted on a pole above the framework of the bulayan, and placed with its head to the east. The tambourine was loudly beaten, and the wild chant continued. Then the flesh was cooked in the large caldron, and all the tribe partook of the dainty—"there was a sound of revelry by night."

The Kalmuck priest wears a leather coat, over the laps of which impend hundreds of strips, with leather tassels on the breast. He fastens a girdle round his waist; and an assortment of brass balls on his back, and scraps of iron in front, produces a continuous jingle. His crimson velvet cap is ornamented over the forehead with brass beads and glass drops, and at the back with feathers from the tail of the crane.

The Kalmucks who inhabit these steppes own large herds of horses and oxen, and flocks of sheep. Some of the men are sturdy fellows and perfect Nimrods; they live by the chase, and spend months alone in the mountain wilds. Mr. Atkinson speaks of them as brave, honest, and faithful. "I have slept at their bulayan, and partaken of their venison. A City alderman would be horrified to see the haunch of a fine buck cut into small pieces an inch square and half an inch thick, through twenty of which a sharp-pointed stick is run, and the thick end stuck into the ground in a leaning position near the fire. Every man here is his own cook, and attends to the roast. The upper piece is first done, when it is slipped off, dipped in salt, and eaten quite hot—without currant jelly."

At Ouemonia Lake, the last village in the Altai, Mr. Atkinson halted in order to obtain a sufficient number of men and horses for his ascent to the source of the Katounaia, and the Bielouka, the highest point in the Altai chain. He was provided by the chief official, or magistrate, with an escort of six Kalmucks and two Russians (one of them a veteran hunter), and at seven o'clock on Wednesday morning sprang into his saddle and rode away. Including himself and his attendant, the party consisted of ten men, with sixteen horses and one dog. Crossing a little steppe, about six versts long, they entered the forest belt which surrounds the lower declivities of the forest-range, and through groves of pine, cedar, birch, and poplar, began their ascent of the first chain. Emerging from the thick leafy covert, they came upon the bare mountain-side, with a storm of rain and sleet beating in their faces, and pursued their way to the foot of a lofty acclivity, across which lay their track. Here they rested, in a "cedarn shade," until the gale had subsided: then *en avant!* Through masses of fallen granite and jasper, interspersed with a few giant cedars, they slowly made their way, until they began in earnest to climb the great steep; a slow operation and a dangerous, for great crags, hurled from the upper heights, hung here and there so insecurely as, apparently, to need but a breath to send them crashing downwards in an avalanche, and at other places the ledges along which they rode were so narrow, that the slightest stumble on the part of their patient horses must have precipitated them into destruction! A painful ride of two hours brought them to the summit, which commanded a noble view of the Katounaia valley and the mountains to the north.

Their ride was continued over a high plateau, on which huge rocks, rugged and curiously wrought, the remains of shattered peaks, stood in their awful grandeur; carrying back the imagination through the dim shadows of the past to a period long before the present forms of life existed, and speaking eloquently of the vast changes which earth has undergone. Their aspect was often that of colossal castles, grim with tower and battlement, which fancy peopled with the demons of the mountain and the wilderness. But the travellers could not stay to study them; signs of a terrible tempest were visible, and they dashed forward at a hard gallop to seek shelter in the valley of the Tschugash. A group of cedars, with a patch of smooth turf, was found on the river bank, and there they bivouacked. The night passed without accident or adventure; and early next morning they were again on horseback, and across ridge and valley, through scenes of the strangest picturesqueness, pursued their track. Across ridge and valley, but in a lofty region always—just below the line of perpetual snow, but above the region of vegetation; the eye unrelieved by branch of moss or blade of grass; until, towards evening, they descended into the valley of the Arriga. Then they wound over a low wooded ridge, and struck into a rugged pass, at the head of which they encamped for the night. The tents were pitched; a huge fire blazed; and the hunter having shot a very fine deer, a savour of venison speedily perfumed the cool night air. What with venison and wodky, the travellers feasted gloriously, and the echoes rang with the wild songs of the Kalmucks.

The morning came, and with it the signal "Forward!" They ascended the bank of the Arriga to its source—a small circular basin of about thirty feet diameter, at the foot of a precipice seven or eight hundred feet in height.

The basin was deep, with a bed of white pebbles; the water, clear as crystal, issuing forth in a copious stream, rolled downward in a series of small and shining cascades. The path, from this point, lay across a high mountain, the upper part of which was deep shrouded in snow, and it toiled up to the summit in about a hundred bends and curves; a summit like a razor-back, not more than twenty-five feet wide. The ascent was arduous and perilous, but still worse the descent on the other side, owing to the exceeding steepness. Accomplishing it in safety, Mr. Atkinson found himself in the valley of the Mein. The river rises at the foot of a precipice which reaches far above the snow line, and winds its course through a morass which, in the old time, has been a lake, shut in by a barrier of rocks, except at one narrow gap, where the little stream finds an exit in a fall of about fifty feet deep. At the head of the lake is another cataract, which throws its "sheeted silver's perpendicular" down the precipice in one grand leap of full five hundred feet.

Crossing another chain, and still ascending, the explorers reached another little lake, the Kara-goll, or "Black Lake," with its waters shining a deep emerald green. This effect, however, is not produced by any surrounding verdure, for the lake is almost encompassed by high mountains, and crags of red and yellowish granite, that rise up into the region of eternal snow. At the upper end a huge mass of basaltic rocks, of a deep grey colour, forms a fine contrast to the yellow castellated forms at their base. On the opposite side of the lake high precipices of granite are backed by grand mountain summits, white with the snows of uncounted ages.

Fording the Kara-sou, or "black water"—a stream issuing from the lake—and crossing a beautiful valley, the riders entered a thickly wooded region which stretches over the lower mountain range down to the Katounaia, and arrived on the bank of the river Bitchuatoo. Thrice had they changed from summer to winter in the course of a day's ride. Turning to the south, they ascended a steep and lofty summit, from which it was supposed the Bielouka would be visible. It proved to be a rocky height that towered above all the mountains to the west of the Katounaia, even above the loftiest crests of the Chelsoun; and vast and magnificent was the panorama which it commanded. In the foreground, a ridge of huge granite crags, tinted with mosses of almost every hue. In all directions rolled chains of snowy peaks, like the storm-tossed waves of a suddenly frozen sea; and as they rolled, they gradually ebbed, so to speak, down to the far steppes of Chinese Tartary, and were lost in a vapour-shrouded horizon.

But the Bielouka was not to be seen, and Mr. Atkinson resumed his ride, keeping along the crest of the mountain for about two versts, and then striking into a little valley, watered by several lakelets. A dreary place! There were neither shrubs nor trees; and the barrenness of desolation was relieved only by a few patches of short mossy grass. Sharp edges of slate, projecting above the surface, showed that the upheaval of the strata had been effected perpendicularly. To the south rose "half a mountain" in a precipice of not less than 2500 feet above the lakes; while a similarly strange combination of cliffs faced it on the north. Between these precipices, at the head of the valley, towered what might be taken for a colossal dome; beyond which a forest of white peaks were sharply defined against the blue serene.

The travellers reached the head of the valley, and examined from a near point the enormous dome. From a distance the curve on its sides had appeared as regular as if wrought by human skill; but they now found that it was piled up with huge blocks of slate and granite, over which it would be impossible to take the horses. A steep ascent to the north brought them, however, to its summit. There the scene was sufficiently remarkable: you might have thought that the Titans had been at play, with great fragments of slate, granite, jasper, and porphyry for their counters. The horses and most of the men were sent round by the base of the cliffs, while Mr. Atkinson, with his servant and the village-hunter, scrambled through the chaos to the edge of a vast circular hollow, which proved to be a vast volcanic crater, not less than nine to twelve hundred feet in diameter, and fully fifty feet in depth. It was heaped up with blocks and boulders and fragments of all sizes, from a cube of twelve inches to a mass weighing half a hundred tons. It is a belief of the Kalmucks that this gloomy spot is inhabited by Shaitan, and they regard it with superstitious dread. Certainly, it is eery enough to be haunted by many a ghostly legend.

Next day, taking a different track, Mr. Atkinson descended the valley of the Tourgau, listening to the music of the stream as it raced over its rocky bed with the speed of a "swift Camilla." At a point where it suddenly swept round the base of some cliffs of slate, the Kalmuck guide said that it might be forded, though the passage was very difficult. "We stood on the high bank a few minutes," says Mr. Atkinson, "and surveyed the boiling and rushing water beneath, while immediately above were a succession of small falls, varying from six to ten feet in height. At the bottom of the last there was a rapid, extending about twenty paces down the river; then came another fall of greater depth; after which the torrent rushes onward over large stones until it joins the Katounaia. Across this rapid, between the falls, we had to make our passage—not one at a time, but five abreast, otherwise we should be swept away As we could only descend the rocky bank in single file, and scarcely find room at the bottom for our horses to stand upon, it was no easy matter to form our party before plunging into the foaming water. Zepta was the first to descend; I followed; then came three others, with two led horses. To go straight across was impossible; we could only land on some shelving rocks a few paces above the lower fall. The brave Zepta gave the word, and we rode into the rushing waters, knee to knee. Our horses walked slowly and steadily on, as the water dashed up their sides; instinct making them aware of the danger, they kept their heads straight across the stream. The distance we forded was not more than twenty paces, but we were at least five minutes doing it; and it was with no small satisfaction that we found ourselves standing on the rocks, some twenty feet above the water, wishing as safe a passage to our friends. When I saw them drawn up on the little bank, and then dash into the stream, I felt the danger of their position more than when crossing myself. Their horses breasted the torrent bravely, and all were safely landed; the dog was placed on one of the pack-horses, where he lay between the bags in perfect security. I am certain that every man felt a relief when the enterprise was accomplished, which would have been impossible had the water been three inches deeper."

Continuing their ride down the valley, in about ten hours the party reached the river Katounaia and the grassy valley through which it foams and flows. Their route lay up its banks, and speedily brought them to the broad swift stream of the Tourgau, which reflects in its water groups of cedars and birches, with rows of tall poplars decked in foliage of the richest colours. Fording the Tourgau, they soon afterwards came again upon the Katounaia, and crossing it, reached a bend in the valley, which presented to them the monarch of the Altai chain, the magnificent Bielouka. Its stupendous mass uplifts two enormous peaks, buttressed by huge rocks, which enclose a number of valleys or ravines filled with glaciers; these roll their frozen floods to the brink of the imposing precipices which overhang the valley of the Katounaia.

Mr. Atkinson determined on attempting the ascent of this regal height. It was a bright morning when he started, and the two white peaks shone grandly in the early sunshine, which gradually dipped down into the valley, and with its fringes of gold touched the sombre cedars. An hour's ride carried him and his followers to the bifurcation of the Katounaia, and then they ascended the north-eastern arm, which rises among the glaciers of the Bielouka. When they had got beyond the last tree that struggled up the mountain's side, they dismounted; and Mr. Atkinson, with the hunter, Zepta, and three Kalmucks, pressed forward on foot, leaving the others in charge of the horses. At first they clambered over the ruins of a mighty avalanche, which in the preceding summer had cloven its way down the precipices, until they reached the glacier, stretching far up the mountain, whence wells the Katounaia in two little ice-cold, transparent streams. There they halted for their mid-day meal. Turning to the west, they toiled up a terrific gorge, filled with fallen rocks and ice, and then climbed a rugged acclivity that, like an inclined plane, reached to the very base of one of the peaks of the Bielouka. Step after step they wearily but persistently ascended, until they reached the frozen snow, scaling which for about three hundred paces they reached the base of the peak, already at such a height as to overlook every summit of the Altai. Far away to the west the vast steppes of the Kirghiz were lost in the blue distance. To the west many a mountain-ridge descended towards the steppes on the east of Nor-Zaisan, and to the Desert of Gobi. The shimmer of a lake was visible at several points; while innumerable rivers, like threads of silver, traced their fantastic broidery through the dark green valleys.

About a hundred paces further, the adventurers found themselves at the head of another glacier, which stretched westward through a deep ravine. Beyond it lay the great hollow between the two peaks. This, in Mr. Atkinson's opinion, it was possible for them to reach, though they could not hope to ascend either peak. They are cones, he says, from eight hundred to a thousand feet high, covered with hard frozen snow, with a few points of the green slate jutting through. We imagine, however, that to a member of the Alpine Club, to any one who has conquered the Matterhorn or the Jungfrau, they would offer no insuperable difficulties.

Mr. Atkinson retraced his steps in safety, gained the spot where the Kalmucks were waiting with the horses, and rode rapidly towards the place which he had selected for a camp. Next morning he proceeded to cross the mountains by a new route to the mouth of the river Koksa; it proved to be the most arduous of his many enterprises. Hour after hour, his Kalmuck guide led him through a wilderness of rocks and sand, and he rejoiced greatly when at last they descended towards the wooded region, and caught sight of the dark Katounaia winding in a deep valley three thousand feet below. They followed downwards a track made by animals, but, though easy for stags and deer, it was difficult for horses. In many places the only traject was a narrow ledge, with deep precipices beneath, and often steep, rugged acclivities above. In one place they had to ride over what the Kalmucks call a "Bomb"—a narrow ridge of rocks, passable only by one horse at a time. Should two persons meet on any part of these "Bombs," one of the horses must be thrown over, as it is as impossible to turn round as to pass. On reaching the track by which the Kalmuck hunters ascend the mountains, Zepta called a halt, and sent one of his companions on foot to the other end of the fearful ridge, hidden from view by some high crags, round which the party had to ride. In less than half an hour he returned, but without his cap, which had been left as a signal to any hunters who might follow, that travellers were crossing the "Bomb."

And now we shall allow Mr. Atkinson to speak himself:—

"Zepta and the hunter told me to drop the reins on my horse's neck, and he would go over with perfect safety. The former led the van; I followed, as desired, at three or four paces behind him. For the first twenty yards the sensation was not agreeable. After that I felt perfect confidence in the animal, and was sure, if left to himself, he would carry me safely over. The whole distance was about five hundred paces, and occupied about a quarter of an hour in crossing. In some places it was fearful to look down—on one side the rocks were nearly perpendicular for five or six hundred feet; and on the other, so steep, that no man could stand upon them. When over, I turned round and watched the others thread their way across; it was truly terrific to look at them on the narrow and stony path—one false step, and both horse and rider must be hurled into the valley a thousand feet below! These are the perils over which the daring sable-hunters often ride. With them it is a necessity; they risk it to obtain food, and not for bravado, or from foolhardy recklessness—like that of some men who ride their horses up and down a staircase. Kalmuck and Kirghiz would laugh at such feats. I have seen men who would ride their horses along the roof of the highest cathedral in Europe, if a plank, eighteen inches wide, were secured along the ridge. Nor would they require a great wager to induce them to do it; theirs is a continual life of danger and hardships; and they never seek it unnecessarily."

This ridge carried them across the valley, and they descended through a dense cedar forest to the bank of the river, where they supped splendidly on a fine fat buck that had fallen to the guns of Zepta and Mr. Atkinson. Next morning, they were again in the saddle *en route* for Ouemonia, where their safe return excited much popular enthusiasm. Bidding adieu to his faithful companions, he crossed the Katounaia, and with a new escort rode on towards the Koksa. Leaving it to the south, he struck the river Tschugash, encamped for the night in a clump of pines on its bank, and in a day or two arrived at his old quarters on the Tchenish.

Mr. Atkinson's next expedition was to the great Desert of Gobi, sometimes called *Scha-ho*, or the Sandy River. Beginning upon the confines of Chinese Tartary, its vast expanse of sterile wilderness stretches over some twelve hundred and fifty miles towards the coasts of the Pacific. It consists in the main of bare rock, shingle, and loose sand, alternating with fine sand, and sparsely clothed with vegetation. But a very considerable area, though for a great part of the year not less monotonously barren, assumes in the spring the appearance of an immense sea of verdure, and supplies abundant pasturage to the flocks and herds of the Mongolian nomads; who wander at will over the wide "prairie-grounds," encamping wherever they find a sheltering crag or a stream of water. The general elevation of the Gobi above the sea is about 3500 feet.

It must be owned that the Gobi is not as black as it is painted. There are fertile nooks and oases, where the sedentary Mongols, and especially the Artous, sow and reap their annual crops of hemp, millet, and buckwheat. The largest is that of Kami. The gloomy picture of "a barren plain of shifting sand, blown into high ridges when the summer sun is scorching, no rain falls, and when thick fog occurs it is only the precursor of fierce winds," [211] is true only of the eastern districts, such as the Han-hai, or "Dry Sea," or the Sarkha Desert, where, for instance, you meet with scarcely any other vegetation than the *Salsoloe*, or salt-worts, which flourish round the small saline pools. "In spring and summer," says Malte Brun, "when there is no rain, the vegetation withers, and the sun-burnt soil inspires the traveller with sentiments of horror and melancholy; the heat is of short duration, the winter long and cold. The wild animals met with are the camel, the horse, the ass, the djiggetai, and troops of antelopes."

It has been observed, and not without reason, that the great Asiatic desert has exercised a fatal influence on the destinies of the human race; that it has arrested the extension of the Semitic civilization. The primitive peoples of India and Tibet were early civilized; but the immense wilderness which lay to the westward interposed an impassable barrier between them and the barbarous tribes of Northern Asia. More surely even than the Himalaya, more than the snow-crowned summits of Srinagur and Gorkha, these desert steppes have prevented all communication, all fusion between the inhabitants of the north and those of the south of Asia; and thus it is that Tibet and India have remained the only regions of this part of the world which have enjoyed the benefits of civilization, of the refinement of manners, and the genius of the Aryan race.

The barbarians who, when the darkness of ruin hung over the Roman Empire, invaded and convulsed Europe, issued from the steppes and table-lands of Mongolia. As Humboldt says [212]:—"If intellectual culture has directed its course from the east to the west, like the vivifying light of the sun, barbarism at a later period followed the same route, when it threatened to plunge Europe again in darkness. A tawny race of shepherds—of Thon-Khiu, that is to say, Turkish origin—the Hiounguou, inhabited under sheep-skin tents the elevated table-land of Gobi. Long formidable to the Chinese power, a portion of the Hiounguou were driven south in Central Asia. The impulse thus given uninterruptedly propagated itself to the primitive country of the Fins, lying on the banks of the Ural, and thence a torrent of Huns, Avars, Chasars, and divers mixtures of Asiatic races, poured towards the west and south. The armies of the Huns first appeared on the banks of the Volga, then in Pannonia, finally on the borders of the

Marne and the Po, ravaging the beautiful plains where, from the time of Antenor, the genius of man had accumulated monuments upon monuments. Thus blew from the Mongolian deserts a pestilential wind which blighted even in the Cisalpine plains the delicate flower of art, the object of cares so tender and so constant."

IV.

With three Cossacks, seven Kalmucks, eight rifles, and a store of powder and lead, Mr. Atkinson passed into the Gobi. His Kalmucks had their hair cut close, except a tuft growing on the top of the head, which was plaited into a long tail, and hung far down their back. The chief was named Tchuck-a-bir, a stalwart, powerful fellow, with a fine manly countenance, large black eyes, and massive forehead. He wore a horse-skin cloak, fastened round his waist with a blood-red scarf. In warm weather he drew his arms from the sleeves, which were then tucked into his girdle, and the cloak draped around him in graceful folds, adding to the dignity of his tall and robust form.

Across the Kourt-Choum mountains the travellers took their way, directing their course towards the Tanguor chain, many of the peaks of which soar above the line of eternal snow. Ascending one of these summits, they enjoyed a noble prospect: immediately beneath them lay the Oubsa-Noor; to the south-west were visible the Oulan-Koum Desert and the Aral-Noor; to the south lay Tchagan Tala, and the ridges descending down to the Gobi; to the south-east the white crests of the Khangai Mountains. This was such a view of Central Asia as never before had European enjoyed.

Keeping far away to the east, they approached the sources of the Selenga and Djabakan, in the neighbourhood of which he hoped to meet with the Kalka tribes. In a rich green valley they came upon one of their auls, and were hospitably received by Arabdan, the chief, who, according to the custom of the desert, at once handed to Mr. Atkinson a bowl of tea. Not, indeed, tea as we English understand it, the clear thin fluid, sweetened with sugar and tempered with cream; but a thick "slab" mixture of tea, milk, butter, salt, and flour—tea-soup it might appropriately be called. Arabdan was tall and thin, between fifty and sixty years of age, dark-complexioned, with high cheek-bones, small black eyes, a prominent nose, and a scanty beard. His meagre figure was wrapped in a long dark-blue silk khalat, buttoned across his chest; in a leather girdle, adorned with a silver buckle, he carried his knife, flint, and steel. His helmet-shaped black silk cap was trimmed with black velvet, and looked very gay with its two broad red ribbons hanging down behind. This brave costume was completed by a pair of high-heeled, madder-coloured boots. As for the women, one wore a robe of black velvet, the other a khalat of red and green silk; the waist of each was defined by a broad red sash. Their hair was fantastically coiffured, falling upon their shoulders in a hundred small plaits, some of which glittered with coral beads, the principal toilette ornament of the Mongolian women. Their red leather boots were very short and high at the heels, so that they walked as badly and awkwardly as English ladies. The children wore little more than nature had provided them with; except that, by rolling in the mud, they contrived to coat their bodies with reddish ochre, in striking contrast to their elfin locks of jet black.

Externally the yourts of the Kalkas resemble those of the Kalmucks, but they differ in the arrangements of the interior. A small low table is placed opposite the doorway, and upon it the upper idols, or household gods, and several small metal vases, are set out. In some are kept grains of millet; in others, butter, milk, and koumis—offerings to the aforesaid deities. On the left side of this altar stand the boxes which contain the family property, and near them various domestic utensils and the indispensable koumis bag. Opposite lie several piles of voilock, on which the family take their rest.

Immediately on Mr. Atkinson's arrival a sheep was slain to do him honour, and it was soon steaming in the iron caldron, with the exception of a portion broiled for his special delectation. Supper, however, was not served in the chief's yourt, but in another; to which everybody repaired with appetites which suggested that they had fasted for weeks. When the completest possible justice had been done to the mutton, men, women, and children retired to their rude couches.

Next morning our indefatigable traveller was once more in the saddle. We cannot follow him in all the details of his daily journeyings, which necessarily bore a close resemblance to one another; but we may accompany him on a visit to the great Kalkas chief, Darma Tsyren. On entering his yourt, Mr. Atkinson was entertained with tea-soup as usual. Then, he says—

"The chief sat down in front of me, and the two young men who had conducted me sat near him—they were his sons. Beyond these sat ten or twelve other Kalkas, watching my movements with intense interest. I was undoubtedly the first European they had ever seen. My large felt hat, shooting jacket, and long boots, will be remembered for years to come— not that I think they admired the costume; theirs is far more picturesque. Presently a number of women came into the yourt, and at their head the wife of the chief. She sat down near him, and was joined by her daughter; the others got places where they could; but the gaze of all was upon me. No doubt it would have been highly amusing could I have understood their remarks, as they kept up an incessant talking.

"At this moment a Cossack brought my samovar into the yourt; and these people were much astonished to see the steam puffing out, with no fire under it. One man placed his hand on the top, and got his fingers burnt, to the great amusement of his friends. My dinner of broiled venison was brought in on a bright tin plate; this and the knife and fork excited their curiosity—such articles being quite new to them. They watched me eat my dinner, and nothing could induce them to move till the plates were taken away. Darma Tsyren had ordered a sheep to be killed, which had now been some time in the caldron. When the announcement was made that it was ready, I was soon left to myself; the whole aul, men, women, and children, were shortly enjoying the feast."

From Darma Tsyren Mr. Atkinson obtained the loan of four Kalkas and twelve horses, and taking also two of his Kalmucks and two Cossacks, he started on a journey to the river Toss. In the evening he and his party encamped in a pretty valley, watered by a small lake, which supplied them with some snipes and ducks for supper. During the night a pack of wolves visited the encampment. On receiving warning of their approach by a distant howl, Mr. Atkinson loaded his double-barrelled gun and distributed ammunition among his people, in order to give the unwelcome visitors a warm reception. The horses were collected, and picketed in a spot between the camp and the lake. Nearer and nearer came the enemy; the tramp of their feet could be heard as they galloped forward. They reached the camp, and through the night air rang their ferocious howl. Some dry bushes flung on the fire kindled a sudden flame, which revealed their gaunt figures, with eyes flashing and ears and tails erect; and immediately a deadly volley crashed into their midst. With a yell of pain and terror they turned tail; and Mr. Atkinson and his party hastened to reload their guns, feeling certain they would return.

The fire flickered down among its embers, and for a time all was silent. Then arose a stir and an alarm among the horses; and it was discovered that the pack had divided, one division stealing upon the animals from the water side, the other interposing between them and the camp. A rush and a shout of the Kalmucks and Kalkas drove them back; and a Cossack and a Kalmuck wore posted on each flank, to guard the approaches and give the alarm. Moreover, the fire was replenished, and its glare lighted up the scene for miles around. A hush, and a moment of expectation! Then might you see the hungry pack advancing once more to the assault, with eyeballs glaring like red-hot iron. A crack of rifles on the right was followed by Mr. Atkinson's two barrels, one of which brought down its victim, while the other, discharged into the midst of the pack, wounded two or three. Gradually the growling ceased; the wolves again retired; but both

Kalkas and Kalmucks advised that a close watch should be kept, as they would certainly make a third effort.

There was little fuel left, and it was necessary, therefore, to be doubly vigilant. The night was one of deep darkness, without moon or stars, and nothing could be seen, even at a short distance, except towards the lake, where a shimmer of dubious light rested on the waters. Keen ears and eyes were on the alert, but no sight or sound of wolf rewarded their watchfulness. The Kalkas said the wolves were simply waiting until all was silent in the camp to make another dash at the horses. For a long time, however, no movement was made, when two of the horses grew uneasy, tugging at the thongs and snorting loudly. At the same time, the clouds cleared from the sky, and the stars peering forth threw more light upon the lake. Howling was heard in the distance, and Tchuck-a-bir declared that another pack of wolves was approaching. As they drew near, the former pack, still lurking in the shades, began to growl, and it seemed possible that a combined attack would be delivered. In order to renew the fire, four of the men, two being armed, crept along the margin of the lake, returning in about ten minutes, each with an armful of fuel. The embers were stirred into life, and the brushwood placed ready to be blown into a flame when wanted. Suddenly a great tumult arose; the other wolves had come on the scene, and the echoes rang with a medley of discordant sounds. Again the watchers waited; and after their patience had been tested for half an hour, the horses began to pull and plunge in frenzied terror. The bushes were lighted, and by their blaze Mr. Atkinson saw a group of eight to ten wolves within fifteen paces. He fired both barrels at them; his men also fired; and the herd, with a frightful howl, ignominiously fled. At daylight Mr. Atkinson examined the scene of action, and found the carcases of eight wolves. With their skins as trophies, he returned to Darma Tsyren's aul.

A day or two later, Mr. Atkinson had an adventure with boars. Leaving four men to guard the camp, he had ridden out, with five followers, in search of sport. Plunging into a thick copse of long grass and low bushes, they started more than one boar from his lair, and tracing them by their motion in the herbage, galloped in hot pursuit. As they emerged into the open, they could see two large dark grizzly boars about a couple of hundred yards ahead, and spurred after them with might and main. Rapidly they gained upon the panting brutes, and when within about fifty yards, Mr. Atkinson and a Cossack sprang from their horses, fired, and wounded one of the boars. While they reloaded, the rest of the party galloped on, and presently other shots were fired. The boars had separated: one, dashing across the valley, was followed up by two of the men; the other was pursued by Mr. Atkinson and his Cossack. After a splendid chase, they drew near enough to see the foam on his mouth, and his large tusks gnashing with rage. The Cossack fired; the ball hit him, but did not check his wild, impetuous course. Swiftly Mr. Atkinson urged on his horse, got abreast of the animal at about twenty paces distant, and lodged a bullet in his shoulder. This stopped him, but it took two more shots to kill him. He proved to be a noble fellow, weighing nine poods, or about 324 lbs., with long, sharp tusks, which would have been formidable weapons in a close encounter.

Leaving the Cossack and a Kalmuck to dress the prize and convey it to the camp, Mr. Atkinson, after reloading his arms, hastened to join the rest of his party, who were in full chase on the other side of the river, at a distance of about three versts. He rode briskly forward, but the hunt was at an end before he reached the river. His followers, on joining him, announced that they had killed a large boar, though not the one first started. He had escaped, and while they were searching for his trail amid some reeds and bushes, a large boar sprang in among them, and charged at a Cossack's horse. When within three or four paces of his intended victim he was stopped by a bullet from Tchuck-a-bir's rifle; but he got away before a second shot could be fired, and an animated chase began. He received several balls, but they seemed to have no effect on his impenetrable hide. Rushing into the river, he swam across, at a point where it expanded into a deep broad pool; the men followed him, and a ball from one of the Kalmucks inflicted a severe wound. Furious with rage and pain, he dashed full at the man who had wounded him; the Kalmuck dexterously wheeled his horse aside, and a ball from Tchuck-a-bir laid the monster dead. With two large boars as the spoils of their prowess, Mr. Atkinson and his "merry men" returned to camp triumphant.

Mr. Atkinson next travelled in a southerly direction for two days; after which he turned to the west, and struck upon the river Ouremjour; his object being to enter the Gobi to the north of the great chain of the Thian-Chan, or, as he calls them, Syan-Shan Mountains. These are the highest in Central Asia, and amongst them rises that stupendous mass, Bogda Oöla, with the volcanoes Pe-shan and Hothaou, to see which was his leading purpose and aim. He gives an animated description of his approach to the Syan-Shan. A bright sun was rising behind the wayfarer, but its rays had not yet gilded the snowy peaks in his front. As he rode onward he watched for the first bright gleam that lighted up the ice and snow on Bogda Oöla; presently the great crest reddened with a magical glow, which gradually spread over the rugged sides, and as it descended, changed into yellow and then into silvery white. For many minutes Bogda Oöla was bathed in sunshine before the rays touched any of the lower peaks. But in due time summit after summit shot rapidly into the brave red light, and at last the whole chain shone in huge waves of molten silver, though a hazy gloom still clothed the inferior ranges. In these atmospheric effects we cannot but recognize a marvellous grandeur and impressiveness; there is something sublimely weird in the sudden changes they work among the stupendous mountain masses. Onward fared the traveller, obtaining a still finer view of Bogda Oöla, and of some of the other peaks to the west; but, as the day advanced, the clouds began to fold around its head, and the huge peak was soon clothed with thick surging wreaths of vapour. The lower range of the Syan-Shan is picturesque in the extreme; jagged peaks stand out in bold relief against the snow-shrouded masses, which tower up some eight to ten thousand feet above them, while the latter are clothed with a luminous purple mist that seems not to belong to this world. Mr. Atkinson continued his route in a north-westerly direction, towards one of the lower chains which run nearly parallel with the Syan-Shan. Thence he could see the Bogda Oöla in all its grand sublimity, and the volcanic peak Pe-shan, with black crags outlined against the snow, still further to the west; while beyond these a long line of snow-capped summits melted into the vaporous distance.

In the course of his wanderings in Chinese Tartary, our traveller saw much of the Kirghiz chiefs, the Sultans of the steppes. On one occasion, while riding in the sterile desert, he fell in with the aul of Sultan Ishonac Khan—a stoutly built man, with strong-marked Kalmuck features, who, in right of his descent from the famous Genghiz Khan, wore an owl's feather suspended from the top of his cap. His costume was gallant and gay; Chinese silk, richly embroidered.

About fifty versts to the south of Sultan Ishonac's aul, lie the Barluck Mountains, situated between the Tarbagatai and the Alatou Mountains, and eastward of the small rocky chain of the Ala-Kool, which extends some sixty versts from east to west, and measures about twenty-five in breadth. The highest summit is not more than three thousand feet above the plain. Vegetation thrives on the lower slopes, but the upper parts are gloomily bare. From Sultan Ishonac Khan Mr. Atkinson obtained a loan of fresh horses, and of eight of his Kirghiz to escort him to the Tarbagatai. A dreary ride it was,—over sandy hills, through sandy valleys, where not even a blade of grass was green. In many places the ground was thickly covered with a saline incrustation, which the horses' feet churned up into a pungent dust, that filled every mouth and caused intolerable thirst. Welcome was the glimmer of a lake that relieved by its sparkle the dulness of the landscape; but when horse and man rushed forward to drink of its waters, to their intense disappointment they found them bitter as those of Marah. Not till the evening of the fifth day, when they reached the river Eremil, did they enjoy the luxury of fresh water.

Next day they reached the Tarbagatai, in the neighbourhood of the Chinese town of Tchoubuchack, and encamped for the night at the foot of a great tumulus or barrow, about one hundred and fifty feet high, which is surrounded by many smaller barrows. They are the last resting-places of a Kirghiz chief and his people, who belonged to a remote generation, and to a race of which these tumuli are the only memorials. Another day's ride, and they arrived at the aul of Sultan Iamantuck, of whom and his family Mr. Atkinson speaks as by far the most intelligent people he met with in this part of Asia. The aul was pitched among high conical tombs of sun-burnt bricks, the cemetery of the Sultan's ancestors; and it appears that once a year it was regularly visited by their pious descendant and representative. With another relay of horses and a fresh Kirghiz escort, Mr. Atkinson dashed onward, undeterred by the dreariness of the sandy level, where neither water nor grass was to be found, and the only living things were tarantulas and scorpions. His course lay direct for the Alatou ("Variegated Mountains"), and he could see the shining peaks of the Actou ("White Mountain"), which forms its highest crest, and raises its summits fourteen to fifteen thousand feet above the sea. After fording the broad deep stream of the Yeljen-sa-gash, he arrived on the shore of Lake Ala-kool, measuring about sixty-five versts in length by twenty in width, with a rocky island near the north shore, erroneously described by Humboldt as the site of a volcano. It has no outlet, yet it receives the tribute of eight rivers; the water is carried off by evaporation.

Here Mr. Atkinson struck westward to find the aul of Sultan Bak, the Rothschild of the steppes; a man who owns ten thousand horses, and a proportionate number of camels, sheep, and oxen. Wealthy men are not always well disposed towards stranger guests, and Sultan Bak evinced his dislike of intrusion by sending Mr. Atkinson a diseased sheep! This was immediately returned, with an intimation that Mr. Atkinson wanted neither his company nor his gifts; he was the first Sultan who had shown himself so discourteous, and though he had a large body, it was clear his heart was that of a mouse. It is not surprising that a message of this kind provoked him to wrath. He ordered the intruders to quit his aul; if they did not, his men should drive them into the lake. But when he found that they were well armed, that discretion which is the better part of valour enabled him to subdue his temper; he sent one of his finest sheep as a peace-offering, with an assurance that they might stay as long as they liked, and should have men and horses when they left. Evidently the Kirghiz patriarch knew how to make the best of a bad situation.

Accompanied by his poet, he paid a visit to Mr. Atkinson's camp, supped heartily off his own mutton, and exchanged the warmest professions of friendship. The minstrel, at his master's bidding, sang wild songs to wilder tunes in glorification of the prowess and freebooting expeditions of the Sultan and his ancestors, to the great edification of the listening Kirghiz. So the evening passed peacefully, and the Sultan and the white man parted on cordial terms. Next day, Mr. Atkinson was riding towards the Karatou, a mountainous chain of dark purple slate; and six days later he visited Sultan Boubania, on the river Lepson. In the neighbourhood were many large tumuli, the largest being the most ancient. One of these was built up of stone, and formed a circle of 364 feet in diameter, with a dome-like mound thirty-three feet in height. Tradition has not preserved the name of the dead honoured with so extraordinary a memorial; the Kirghiz attribute it to demons working under the direction of Shaitan. Another kind of tumulus, of more recent construction, was circular in plan, but carried up to the height of fifty-four feet, in the shape of "a blast furnace," with an aperture at the top, and lateral opening two feet square and four feet from the ground. In the interior were two graves covered with large blocks of stone. According to the Kirghiz, these tombs were built by the people who inhabited the country before the Kalmucks. A third kind, of sunburnt bricks, and Mohammedan in design, are ascribed to Timour Khan and his race.

Through the rocky gorge of the Balütz, Mr. Atkinson commenced his ascent of the Alatou. His eye rested with pleasure on the richly coloured rocks that composed the cliffs on either side—deep red porphyry, flecked with veins of white; slate, jasper, and basalt. He explored several of the valleys that break up the lower mass of the mountain chain, and rode along many of its elevated ridges. Sometimes the roar of torrents filled his ears; sometimes bright streams and sources sparkled in the sunshine; sometimes he saw before him a fair mosaic of wild flowers; sometimes the landscape was ennobled by the conspicuous figures of white mountain peaks, relieved by a background of deep blue sky; sometimes the distant vapours hovered wraith-like above the calm surface of Lake Tengiz. From a plateau not far beneath the line of perpetual snow he obtained a noble view of the Actou, and, to the south, of the lofty and picturesque peaks of the Alatou; while, nearer at hand, the river Ara poured its thunderous waters into a gorge some thousand feet in depth. The plateau was covered with tumuli; one of which, measuring two hundred feet in diameter and forty feet in height, was enclosed within a trench, twelve feet wide and six feet deep. On the west side stood four masses of large stones in circles; the altars, perhaps, on which, long ago, victims were sacrificed to appease some sanguinary deity. It is a tradition of the Kirghiz that these antiquities belonged to a native who, for some unknown cause, determined on a great act of murder and self-destruction, and that they were constructed before the terrible work was begun. They say that the father killed his wife and all his children, excepting the eldest son, on whom devolved the duty of killing, first his father, and then himself.

Mr. Atkinson visited, near the river Kopal, the Arasan, or warm spring, which wells up in the centre Of a ravine formed of yellow and purple marbles. Its temperature, all round the year, is 29' R. or 97° F. Here, in a remote past, the Kalmucks built a bath, which is still frequented by Tartars, Kirghiz, and Chinese. The waters, it is said, are wonderfully beneficial for scurvy and other cutaneous disorders.

Another route carried him to the Tamchi-Boulac, or "Dropping Spring," at the foot of the Alatou. The water oozes out of columnar cliffs in myriads of tiny streams that glitter like showers of diamonds; while in some parts they seem changed to drops of liquid fire by the reflected colouring of the rocks, which vary in colour from a bright yellow to a deep red.

For one hundred and three days Mr. Atkinson wandered among the Alatou Mountains, exploring peak, precipice, valley, and ravine; surveying torrent and river and waterfall; now ascending far above the line of perpetual snow, now descending into warm and sheltered woods, where the greensward was enamelled with blossoms. From the eastern end of the Alatou, a seventeen days' ride over hill and steppe brought him to the Russian frontier and the comforts of civilization at Semipalatinsk. But, almost as strongly possessed with the spirit of continuous motion as the Wandering Jew in the grim old legend, he next set forth on a journey across Siberia, from its western boundary on the Irtisch, to its Oriental capital, Irkutsk. In the course of his long journey he visited the Saian Mountains; ascended the valley of the Oka; explored a bed of lava and a volcanic crater in the valley of the Ojem-a-louk; rode across the rugged shoulder of Nouk-a-Daban; and descended the little river Koultouk to Lake Baikal, or, as the natives call it, the Holy Sea. Hiring a small boat, with a crew of seven men, he crossed the lake to the mouth of the river Angara. Baikal is the third largest lake in Asia— about four hundred miles in length, and varying in breadth from nineteen miles to seventy. Though fed by numerous streams, it has only one outlet, the Angara, a tributary of the Yenisei. Lying deep among the Baikal Mountains, an off-shoot of the Altai, it presents some vividly coloured and striking scenery. Its fisheries are valuable. In the great chain of communication between Russia and China it holds an important place, and of late years its navigation has been conducted by steamboats. The native peoples inhabiting its borders are the Buriats and Tungusians.

Mr. Atkinson spent eight and twenty days in exploring this Alpine sea, and afterwards proceeded to Irkutsk. [228]

ALEXINA TINNÉ
AND HER WANDERINGS IN THE SOUDAN.

ABOUT 1862, letters from Khartûm, the capital of Nubia, stimulated the curiosity of European geographers by announcing that three courageous ladies had undertaken a journey into Central Africa, with the view of reaching those mysterious Sources of the Nile which, for generations, had been the object of Western research. At first the news was received with suspicion; many persons did not hesitate to speak of it as a hoax; but incredulity vanished as the information grew more copious and more precise, and it became known that the guiding spirit of the adventure was a certain Miss Alexandrina or Alexina Tinné, a lady of great personal charms and very wealthy. It was then unanimously agreed that she was one of those brave daughters of England who, in the Continental belief, will go anywhere and do anything that is hazardous or eccentric. And though of Dutch extraction she really did owe something to English influences. Her father was a Dutch merchant who, after acquiring an ample fortune in Demerara, was naturalised in England, and finally settled at Liverpool. He died while Alexina (born in October, 1835) was still a child, but the wealthy heiress was brought up by her mother as befitted her social position. What impelled her, in her young maidenhood, to plunge into the dangers of African exploration—whether her action was due to a love of adventure, a thirst after knowledge, a spirit rebelling against the conventionalisms of society, or to baffled hope and slighted affection—does not seem to be known. But it is certain that about 1859 she set out from the Hague, accompanied by her mother and aunt, and visited various parts of Egypt and Syria. For some months she resided at Beirut and Tripoli; next she repaired to Damascus; afterwards, to the ruins of Palmyra, haunted by the memory of Zenobia; and, finally, she dreamed of imitating the romantic career of Lady Hester Stanhope, and installing herself as Queen of the Lebanon. Her mood, however, changed suddenly; she returned to Europe, not to resume the monotonous habits of social life, but to make preparations for an expedition in search of the Sources of the Nile.

In this daring project she appears to have been encouraged partly by her own fearlessness of nature; partly by the example of Mrs. Petherick, wife of the English consul at Khartûm, whose fame had spread far and wide; and partly by the flattering thought that it might be reserved for her, a woman, to succeed where so many brave men had failed, and to be the first to solve the great enigma of the Nilotic sphynx. What immortality would be hers if she triumphed over every danger and difficulty, and stood, where no

European as yet had stood, on the margin of the remote well-head, the long secret spring, whence issued the waters of Egypt's historic river! It must be owned that in this ambitious hope there was nothing mean or unworthy, and that it could have been possible only to a high and courageous nature.

She set out in the month of July, 1861, still accompanied by her mother and her aunt, two ladies of mediocre character, who readily yielded to the influence of a stronger mind. A part of the winter was spent in a pleasant country house in one of the suburbs of Cairo—a kind of palace of white marble, situated in the midst of odorous gardens, and looking out upon the ample Nile and the giant forms of the Pyramids. There they made extensive preparations for the contemplated journey; while Alexina spent many thoughtful hours in studying the map of Africa, in tracing the sinuosities of the White Nile above its point of junction with the Blue, in laying down the route which should carry her and her companions into the regions of the great lakes.

It was on the 9th of January, 1862, that she and her companions directed their course towards Upper Egypt, voyaging in three boats, attended by a numerous train of guides, guards, and servants. In the largest and most commodious "dahabeeyah" were installed the three ladies, with four European servants and a Syrian cook. Alexina's journal, it is said, preserves many curious details in unconscious illustration of the mixed character of the expedition, which might almost have been that of a new Cleopatra going to meet a new Mark Antony; we see the Beauty there as well as the Heroine—the handsome woman who is mindful of her toilette appliances, as well as the courageous explorer, who does not forget her rifle and cartridges.

Passing in safety the first cataract, Miss Tinné's expedition duly arrived at Kousko; where she and her companions took a temporary leave of the Nile, tourists, and civilization, and struck across the sandy desert of Kousko to Abu-Hammed, in order to avoid the wide curve which the river there makes to the westward. The caravan, besides Miss Tinné's domestics, included six guides and twenty-five armed men. Of camels loaded with baggage and provisions, and dromedaries which carried the members of her suite, there were a hundred and ten. The desert did not prove so dreary as it had been painted; sand and rock were often relieved by patches of blooming vegetation; the monotony of the plains was often broken by ridges of swelling hills. The camels every evening browsed contentedly on the herbage, and quenched their thirst in the basins of water that sparkled in the rocky hollows.

The time usually required for crossing the desert is eight to nine days; but as Alexina advanced very leisurely, by daily stages not exceeding seven or eight hours, she occupied nearly three weeks. In spite of this easy mode of travelling, her mother was so fatigued that, on arriving at Abu-Hammed, on the banks of the Nile, she insisted they should again take to the river. A dahabeeyah was accordingly hired, along with six stalwart boatmen, who swore on the Koran to keep pace with the swiftest dromedaries. So while the caravan tramped onwards through the burning, shifting sand, Alexina and her companions voyaged up the Nile; but the rowers soon proved false to their promises, slackened their oars, and allowed the caravan to outstrip them. When reproached with their lethargy, they excused themselves on the score of the arduousness of their work and the great heat of the sun.

Meanwhile, the caravan had made considerable progress, and at nightfall tents were pitched and fires lighted. As no dahabeeyah could be seen, men were sent in search of it; but in vain. No news of it was obtained until the following day, when it was ascertained that the Egyptian boatmen had at last laid down their oars in sullen indolence, and that Miss Tinné and her companions had been compelled to spend the night in a Nubian village. The misadventure taught them the lesson that in Eastern countries it is generally wiser to trust to brutes than to men; the boatmen were dismissed, and the travellers once more joined the caravan.

But the heat proved insupportable, driving them to make a second experiment of the river traject. A boat was again hired; again they embarked on the glittering Nile; and again an evil fortune attended them. Instead of reaching Berber, as they should have done, in four days, the voyage was extended to over a week; but it was some compensation for their fatigue when, at two hours' march from the city, they were received by some thirty chiefs, mounted upon camels, and attended by janizaries in splendid attire, who, with much pomp and circumstance, escorted them to the gates of Berber. There they were received by the governor with every detail of Oriental etiquette, installed in pavilions in his gardens, and waited upon in a spirit of the most courteous hospitality. No longer in need of a complete caravan, Miss Tinné dismissed her camel-drivers; but, desirous of leaving upon their minds an enduring impression, she rewarded them with almost prodigal liberality. Her gold coins were so lavishly distributed, that the Arabs, in surprise and delight, broke out into unaccustomed salutations; and to this very day, remembering her largesses, they sing of her glory, as if she had revived the splendour of Palmyra.

There was a policy in this apparently thoughtless profusion. As a natural result, her reputation everywhere preceded her; hospitality was pressed upon her with an eagerness which may have been dictated by selfish motives, but was not the less acceptable to her and her companions. Women, gathering round her, prostrated themselves at her feet. The young girls danced merrily at her approach; they took her for a princess, or, at least, they saluted her as such.

After a residence of some weeks at Berber, the adventurous ladies hired three boats, and ascended the Nile to Khartûm, the capital of the Egyptian Soudan. Situated at the confluence of the White and Blue Nile, it is the centre of an important commerce, and the rendezvous of almost all the caravans of Nubia and the Upper Nile. Unfortunately, it is one of the world's *cloacinæ*, a kind of moral cesspool, into which the filth and uncleanness of many nations pours—Italians, Germans, Frenchmen, Englishmen, whom their own countries have repudiated; political gamblers, who have played their best card and failed; fraudulent bankrupts, unscrupulous speculators, men who have nothing to hope, nothing to lose, and are too callous to fear. The great scourge of the place, down to a very recent date, was the cruel slave-traffic, at that time carried on with the connivance of the Egyptian Government. Recently the energetic measures of Colonel Gordon have done much towards the extirpation of this cancerous growth, and even the moral atmosphere of the town has been greatly purified. To Alexina Tinné the place was sufficiently loathsome; but a residence of some weeks' duration, while preparations were made for the advance into Central Africa, was imperative. She did what she could to avoid coming into contact with the "society" of Khartûm, and exerted all her energies to stimulate the labours of her subordinates, so that she might depart at the earliest possible moment. At length, provisions were collected, and a supply of trinkets to be used as gifts or in barter; an escort of thirty-eight men, including ten soldiers fully armed, and all bearing a good character for trustworthiness, was engaged; and, finally, she hired for the heavy sum of ten thousand francs, a small steamboat, belonging to Prince Halim. With a glad heart she quitted Khartûm, and resumed the ascent of the White Nile, passing through a succession of landscapes fair and fertile. As for the river, its quiet beauty charmed her; and she compared it to Virginia Lake, the pretty basin of water that sparkles in the leafy shades of Windsor Forest. Its banks are richly clothed with trees, chiefly gumtrees, which frequently attain the dimensions of the oak. But the graceful tamarisk is also abundant, and myriads of shrubs furnish the blue ape with a refuge and a home. The air glitters with the many-coloured wings of swarms of birds. On the bright surface of the stream spread the broad leaves and white petals of colossal lilies, among which the hippopotamus and the crocodile pursue their unwieldy gambols.

How marvellous the effects of colour when this magical scene is bathed in the hot rays of the sunshine! Through the transparent air every object is seen with a distinct outline, and the sense of distance is overcome. Where a shadow falls it is defined as sharply as on canvas; there is no softening or confusing mist; you see everything as in a mirror. In the noontide heats all nature is as silent here as in a virgin forest; but when the cool breath of evening begins to be felt, and that luminous darkness, which is the glory of a summer night in Central Africa, spreads softly over the picture, the multiform life of earth swiftly re-awakens; birds and butterflies hover in the air, the monkeys chatter merrily, and leap from bough to bough. The sounds which then break forth—song and hum and murmur, the roll of the river, the din of insects, the cries of the wild beasts—seem all to mingle in one grand vesper hymn, proclaiming the might and majesty of the Creator. These are generally hushed as the night wears on; and then myriads of fireflies and glow-worms light their tiny torches and illuminate the dark with a magical display; while the air is charged with sweet and subtle odours exhaled from the corollas of the plants which open only during the cool and tranquil hours.

While slowly making her way up the river, Alexina encountered an Egyptian pasha, who was returning with a booty of slaves from a recent razzia. She eagerly implored him to set the unhappy captives free, and when her solicitations failed, purchased eight of the poor creatures, to whom she immediately gave their liberty, supplying them also with provisions. This has been termed an act of Quixotism; it was rather one of generous womanly enthusiasm, and to our thinking redeems the failings of Alexina Tinné's character—compensates for the follies and frivolities which encumbered her enterprise. Her heart was true to every gentle impulse, and she ceased not to suffer keenly at the sight of the wretched condition of the poor negroes who fell victims to an unholy traffic.

This traffic had aroused such feelings of hatred and revenge in the breasts of the riverine tribes of the Nile, that the passage of the river had become very dangerous, and the journey by land almost impossible. The natives looked upon every white man as a Turk and a slave-dealer; and when a boat appeared on the horizon, mothers cried with terror to their children, "The Tourké, the Tourké are coming!" The scarlet tarbouch, or fez, added to the repulsion. "It is the colour of blood just spilled," said a negro to his family. "It never fades," they said; "the Turk renews it constantly in the blood of the poor black men."

Fortunately, they were able to distinguish between the boats of the slave-dealers and Alexina Tinné's steamer. Twice or thrice they approached the latter; at first not without fear, but afterwards with good courage. "Is the young lady who commands," they asked, "the Sultan's sister? Does she come to assist or to persecute us?" When fully informed of the object of her pacific expedition, they rapidly grew familiar and ventured on board her boat. "Since you mean no evil against us," they cried, "we will do *you* no harm; we will love you!" They accepted from her hands a cup of tea, and courteously drank it without manifesting their repugnance; and they explained to her their usages and manners, and supplied her with interesting information respecting the surrounding country. Her reception was so much to her mind, that she would have remained for some time among this kindly people, had she not felt bound to prosecute her journey to the south.

Once more the sails were unfurled, the fires lighted, and the steamer ploughed its steady course towards the land of the Derikas. Two or three villages were seen on the river banks, but the landscape was bare and bland, and the adventurous Alexina pursued her voyage until she reached Mount Hunaya. There she landed and pitched her tents. When it was known to be her design to remain in this encampment during the rainy season, her followers raised a vehement opposition, protesting that they would be devoured by lions or trampled to death by elephants. Their mistress, however, remained firm in her intention; but as the steamer was in need of repair, she sent it back to Khartûm in charge of her aunt.

It was during this lady's enforced residence at Khartûm that she made the acquaintance of an Englishman and his wife, whose names have become household words in every civilized nation—Sir Samuel and Lady Baker. Sir Samuel, who belongs to the illustrious company of African explorers, began his career of adventure by founding an agricultural colony at Nuvera Ellia—that is, six thousand feet above the sea, among the breezy mountain peaks of Ceylon. In 1855 he visited the Crimea, and afterwards he was engaged in superintending in Turkey the organization of its first railway. In 1861 he started with his wife on a journey of discovery in Central Africa, with the design of meeting the Government expedition, which, under Captain Speke, had been despatched in search of the Nile sources. In nearly a year he and his wife explored the Abyssinian highlands, which form the cradle of the Blue Nile, arriving at Khartûm in June, 1862. There he collected a large company to ascend the Upper Nile, and setting out in December, 1862, he reached Gondokoro in February, 1863, in time to meet Captain Speke and Grant returning victoriously from their discovery of the Victoria Nyanza. Baker furnished them with the means of transport to Khartûm, and then pushed forward across a district infested by slave-hunters, until he fell in with a great fresh-water basin, the Luta N'zize, which he christened the Albert Lake, or Nyanza, and ascertained to be one of the chief reservoirs or feeders of the Nile. He returned to England in 1866. Three years later, he accepted from the Khedive of Egypt the command of a military force, with unlimited powers, for the purpose of annexing savage Africa to the civilized world, and opening up its fertile lake-regions to the enterprise of legitimate commerce. The work, which was well done, occupied him until 1873, and was afterwards carried on by Colonel Gordon.

In all his adventures, which, as we shall see, were often of a most critical character, Sir Samuel was accompanied by his wife, whose sympathy consoled, while her example inspired him. This brave and chivalrous lady gave abundant proof of her heroic courage, her devoted affection, and her indomitable resolution.

When the repairs of her vessel were completed, Alexina Tinné returned to Gebel Hunaya. She was received with shouts of joy, and with a salute of several pieces of artillery, which awakened the greatest trepidation among the natives. Some few incidents had occurred during her absence, but none of a very notable character. One morning, Alexina was reading at a short distance from the camp. Feeling thirsty, she turned towards a rivulet which sparkled among the herbage close at hand; but as she approached it, the dog which accompanied her barked loudly with affright, and showed a manifest unwillingness to draw nearer to the rocks impending over the stream. Accepting this intimation of danger, Alexina stepped forward very cautiously, and soon discovered a young panther lurking behind the rugged boulders. She had the presence of mind to stand perfectly still, while she summoned her soldiers and servants to her assistance. They speedily came up, and, drawing a cordon round the animal, succeeded in capturing it alive. On another occasion, her men killed, before her eyes, a huge crocodile, which was duly stuffed as a trophy. They also caught a great ape, whose head was covered with long hair, mixed black and white. The animal would have been a valuable specimen of the African fauna, but, unfortunately, it died within a few months of its capture.

On the 7th of July, the steamer, which was heavily loaded and towed two boats, left Hunaya, to continue its course up the river. Between Hunaya and the confluence of the Bahr-el-Ghazal (the Gazelle river) the scenery is far from being attractive; the river banks are arid, and sunburnt. Here and there, however, grow clumps of whispering reeds and aquatic plants; while, at other points, the river overflows its limits for two or three thousand yards, creating, on each side, an inaccessible swamp.

The voyagers did not pause until they reached the settlement of an Arab chief, named Mohammed-Cher, who by his audacity had subjected the neighbouring tribes, and ruled supreme over this part of the Soudan. When, as frequently happened, he was in want of money, he exercised the right of the strong hand, and, at the head of his freebooters, sallied forth; destroying villages, slaying the male inhabitants, seizing upon the women and children, and carrying off the cattle. He loved to surround himself with barbaric pomp, and paraded upon a magnificent horse, the saddle of which was embroidered with gold and silver, and sparkled with precious stones. But when our voyagers arrived at his village, this great warrior showed signs of recreancy; he was terrified by the Turkish soldiers who occupied the steamer's deck. It was supposed to be owing to this spasm of alarm that he received the ladies with royal honours, sending them sheep, oxen, fruit, vegetables, dancers, archæological curiosities; in short, he seemed anxious to offer them all he possessed. Afterwards, however, the secret of his ready liberality came out; the swarthy chieftain thought he was doing honour to the favourite daughter of the Grand Turk—in his zeal, he was anxious to proclaim her Queen of the Soudan.

When his visitors were taking leave, he strongly advised them not to advance further to the south. "Take care," said he, "you do not come into collision with the Shillooks, who are our sworn enemies, and the enemies of all who cross their frontiers. Take care that they do not set fire to your boats, as they have already done to all vessels coming from Khartûm."

In spite of these warnings, Alexina Tinné resolutely continued her voyage, and, a few days later, anchored off a Shillook village. The sailors, frightened by Mohammed's story, would not approach it; she therefore landed with only an interpreter, an officer, and an escort of ten soldiers. But the news of the arrival of a daughter of the Sultan had preceded her, and instead of being received as an enemy, she was welcomed with every demonstration of respect. The Shillooks, as is the case with savage tribes in all parts of the world, endeavour to engage every stranger in their personal enmities; and they now hoped to secure the assistance of the expedition against that terrible Mohammed-Cher, who, only a few days before, had shown so much anxiety to proclaim the European lady Queen of the Soudan. When she refused to join in their campaign, their disappointment was extreme. All travellers speak warmly of this unfortunate tribe, who suffer scarcely less from Europeans than from Arabs. The conditions under which they live are very pitiful; wherever they turn, they are met by enemies. Constantly falling victims to the cruelty of the slave-hunters, it is no wonder that they regard with suspicion, and too often treat with ferocity, the strangers who come among them; naturally implicating them in the traffic by which they suffer so severely. The slave-hunting abomination is, we must repeat, the mortal wound of Central Africa; it impedes commercial enterprise, and paralyzes the efforts of the pioneers of Christian civilization. Let us hope that, in the lake regions, the vigorous action of Colonel Gordon has greatly diminished, if it has not absolutely rooted out, the evil.

Pressing southward with unshaken resolution, Alexina Tinné reached at length the junction of the Sobat with the Nile. She resolved to ascend that tributary as far as it was navigable, calculating that the *excursus*, going and returning, would occupy seven or eight days. The valley of the Sobat is more interesting in character than much of the course of the White Nile. Its broad pastures, stretching away to the distant horizon, teem with flocks of ostriches and herds of giraffes. The river banks are thickly indented by the heavy hoofs of elephants, and the colossal animals themselves wander freely over the uplands. For some weeks the voyagers lingered in the Sobat, well pleased with its succession of striking scenes; and then they steamed up the Nile again, until they reached the mouth of the Bahr-el-Ghazal, the majestic stream which, with slow current, traverses Lake Nû.

Here the Nile strikes sharply towards the south, forming a complete right angle; and broadens into an imposing expanse of shining waters.

The flora of the surrounding country is very picturesque: tamarinds, mimosas, climbing plants, the papyruses, and the euphorbias thrive in unchecked luxuriance, as they have thriven for countless centuries, and blend together their thick growth of various foliage. The colouring of the flowers is often so intense that the eye aches in contemplating it. It should be added that the euphorbia, which is very common in this region, yields a poisonous milky juice, in which the natives dip their arrows. A scratch from one of these envenomed weapons will rapidly prove mortal.

Beyond Lake Nû, the White Nile breaks into an intricate series of curves and meanders, pouring its waters downwards with violent swiftness. Such, indeed, was the strength of the flood, that the steamer was compelled to throw off the towing-rope of the two dahabiehs, and the sailors and servants landed in order to haul them against the stream. But in the greatest stress of the current the rope broke, and the boats, drifting away, were threatened with destruction. Osman Aga, a resolute and courageous soldier, who was on the deck of the steamer, seized another rope and leaped instantly into the river. With vigorous strokes he made for the shore. He had almost gained it, and had flung the rope to his expectant comrades, when he suddenly disappeared. After a while his dead body was found, and immediate preparations were made to give it an honourable burial. Wrapped round, according to the custom of the country, with twenty yards of calico, it was interred, in the presence of the whole crew, at the foot of a patriarchal tree, on the trunk of which was cut a commemorative inscription.

Some days after this melancholy event, the expedition ascended the river to Heiligenkreuz, where some Austrian Catholic missionaries have founded a settlement. Remaining there until the 15th of September, Alexina Tinné made a short excursion into the interior, crossing rivers, traversing forests, and meeting with numerous villages, half hidden in leafiness.

As the voyagers approached Gondokoro, they observed that the panoramas assumed a grander character; that the landscapes were on a loftier scale. Tropical forests extended their deep shades along the river banks; and sometimes in their recesses it was possible to catch sight of the remains of ancient buildings, at one time, perhaps, inhabited by a busy race. Gondokoro, long regarded as the *Ultima Thule* of the Nile Valley, was reached on the 30th of September. It proved to be the extreme southward limit of Alexina Tinné's explorations. She ardently longed to advance—to share some of the glory resting upon the names of Speke and Grant, Baker and Petherick—to see with her own eyes the immense basin of the Victorian Sea—to trace to its well-head the course of the Nile; but the obstacles thrown in her way proved insurmountable. Moreover, most of her followers were seized with malarious fever, and she herself had an attack, which for some days held her life in danger. When she recovered, she began to study the habits and manners of the native tribes residing in the neighbourhood of Gondokoro. They are all Baris, and very ignorant and superstitious, but not naturally cruel. No trade flourishes among them like that of the sorcerer, who is also the medicine-man. When a Bari falls ill, he hastens to consult the Punok, who gives him some absurd but infallible recipe, and the cure is effected! One of these magicians succeeded in persuading the negroes that he was invulnerable. Oxen, sheep, and presents of all kinds were poured into his willing hands; but unluckily he declaimed against the expeditions of the Egyptians, who, not having any sense of humour, put him to death. His dupes, gathering round his dead body, waited patiently for his resurrection; and only began to doubt when the corpse putrefied.

Among the Bari sorcerers a high rank is held by the "rain-maker"—a personage of great repute, to whom the villagers bring oxen, fruits, and trinkets, in days of drought, to bribe him to invoke the clouds and their treasures of fertilizing rain. But his position is not without its inconveniences; if, after the performance of his rites, the drought continues, the people assemble at his house, drag him forth, and without more ado, cut open the stomach of the unfortunate Kodjour, on the plea that the storms must be shut up in it, as they make no external manifestation. Few are the years in which one of these rain-makers does not perish, unless he has the wit to escape out of danger before his deception is discovered.

From Gondokoro Alexina Tinné returned without delay to Khartûm, where she received the congratulations of the European community; but her rest was not of long duration. She had nothing of the lotos-eater in her temperament, and could find contentment only in action. Hers was the true traveller's character—energetic, active, daring, tenacious, with an insatiable thirst for new scenes. Thwarted in her first design, she immediately took up another. She would ascend the great western tributary of the Nile, the Bahr-el-Ghazal, explore the streams which feed it, and penetrate into the land of the Nyam-nyam, of whom Doctor Heughlin has furnished so interesting an account. Her preparations were soon completed. This time she and her mother—her aunt remained at Khartûm—did not travel alone; their expedition was reinforced by three experienced travellers, Doctor Heughlin, the naturalist, Doctor Steudner, and Baron d'Ablaing. The first two started in advance, so as to open up the route for the adventurous Alexina, who, with her mother and Baron d'Ablaing, quitted Khartûm at the end of February, 1863, in command of a flotilla composed of a steamer, a sailing-vessel, and several small boats.

Heughlin, who had set out some days before, passed, on the 31st of January, the Gebel Tefafan, a lofty mountain which rises at no great distance from the river. He reached Lake Nû—a point from which the voyager has more than two hundred miles to accomplish across the Bahr-el-Ghazal. At that time of the year the river in many places is as narrow as a canal, though on both sides bordered by a swampy plain, which stretches further than the eye can see, and bears a thick growth of gigantic reeds. At other places it deepens into considerable lakes.

The natives navigate it in light canoes, which they manage with much dexterity. They sit astride the stem, with their legs hanging down in the water; and if they fall in with no branches capable of being converted into oars, they row with their hands. The Nouers, who inhabit this land of marsh and morass, furnish an apparent exemplification of the Darwinian theory: by a process of natural selection they have become thoroughly adapted to the conditions of a soil and climate which would rapidly kill off an unaccustomed population. Their muscular strength is remarkable; and they are a race of Anaks, averaging from six to seven feet in height. Alexina Tinné records that, in spite of the heat of a tropical sun, and the attacks of swarms of insects, they would stand erect, with lance in hand, on the summit of the mounds thrown up by termites, anxiously watching the steamer and the boats in tow as they passed by swiftly and steadily, against wave and current—a type, shall we say? of the irresistible progress of civilization.

While Doctor Heughlin, in the true scientific spirit, industriously explored the banks of the Bahr-el-Ghazal, Alexina Tinné was making a persistent effort to rejoin him. Innumerable difficulties assailed her. When only a few miles from Khartûm, her captain came to tell her, with signs of the utmost terror, that the steamer was leaking, and would shortly sink. Her alarm may easily be imagined; but fortunately she was never wanting in presence of mind. She gave orders that the cargo should be immediately unloaded; the leak was repaired, and the voyage resumed. A few hours later, and the vessel was again in danger, the water rushing in with greater violence than before. A close investigation was made, and then it was discovered that the pilot and captain had each agreed to bore a hole in the ship's hull, with the view of putting a stop to a voyage which they, as well as the crew, dreaded. But our heroine was not to be conquered. She at once dismissed a part of the crew, and sent away both the captain and the pilot; then, with men pledged to be true to her, she sailed away resolutely for the Bahr-el-Ghazal.

At first, she made but slow progress, on account of the mass of tall dense grasses and aquatic plants that choked up the stream. In many places it was necessary to clear a way for the steamer with knife and axe. In the sun-baked mud grisly crocodiles swarmed; the snort of the hippopotamus rose from amid the reedy tangle; the elephant with calm eyes watched the movements of the strangers. The swamps of the Bahr-el-Ghazal are a paradise of wild beasts, and Mademoiselle Tinné saw thousands of them wandering to and fro. But though game is so abundant, to hunt it is very difficult. The sportsman cannot penetrate into the midst of the dry and withered vegetation without a crackling of leaves and a snapping of stems, which give instant alarm to vigilant and suspicious ears. No sooner does he set foot in the jungle, than, as if warned by some secret telegraphic agency, all its denizens take to flight. But while Mademoiselle Tinné's followers were vainly attempting to pursue the trail of the great pachyderms, a huge elephant, which had probably entered too far into the river in the keenness of his thirst, was caught up in the current, and driven against one of the boats. The opportunity was not neglected; the boatmen immediately assailed the unfortunate animal, killed it, and cut it in pieces.

Lake Reg is the highest navigable point of the Ghazal. [249] Our heroine found here a fleet of five and twenty craft, some with cargoes of ivory, others with cargoes of dourra or millet. She was received with enthusiasm, which specially manifested itself in the discharge of three volleys of musketry—a compliment to which Alexina Tinné replied by hoisting the Dutch flag.

As soon as her little flotilla was safely moored among the trading craft, the enterprising lady prepared to undertake a journey into the interior. But as it was found impossible to collect a sufficient number of porters to carry the baggage, she arranged that Doctors Heuglin and Steudner should start in search of suitable winter-quarters. The two travellers set out, but the malarious climate broke down their health, and both were seized with a dangerous marsh fever. They suffered greatly; but, sustained by their strong will, they pushed forward, crossing, on the 2nd of April, the river Djur, and arriving, the same evening, at the village of Wau. Here Doctor

Steudner rapidly grew worse. Before long he was unable to walk; he fell into a profound stupor, and passed away, almost without pain, on the 10th of April. Doctor Heughlin describes, with much pathos, the feelings of grief and melancholy which overpowered him when he buried his friend. The body was wrapped in Abyssinian cloth and covered with leaves; then interred in a deep trench dug at the foot of a clump of trees.

On the 17th of April, Doctor Heughlin quitted the lonely shades of Wau, and, having lured a large number of porters, returned to Lake Reg. Then, to complete the necessary arrangements for the projected expedition to the country of the Nyam-nyam, Baron d'Ablaing went on a trip to Khartûm, whence he brought back an abundant supply of provisions. During his absence, Alexina Tinné was visited by Mrs. Petherick, the wife of the English consul—a woman not less courageous than herself, who had accompanied her husband in most of his explorations. She claims the honour of having added numerous places to the map of Africa, and of having been the first European lady who had penetrated into those remote regions.

While Alexina Tinné represents Holland, and Mrs. Petherick England, Germany is represented by the wife of Sir Samuel Baker, to whom allusion has already been made. A woman of delicate and even feeble appearance, with a countenance of remarkable amiability of expression; she possesses, as Queen Elizabeth said of herself, "the heart of a man," and of a brave and chivalrous man. Deeds worthy of the most famous knights have been accomplished by this lady, who, it might have been thought, would have sunk before the first breath of the Simoom. One may here be recorded. While out hunting, Sir Samuel Baker was attacked by a buffalo, which had sprung upon him unperceived through the high thick grasses, and was on the point of impaling him on its horns, when Lady Baker, with cool and steady aim, raised her rifle, and lodging a bullet between the animal's eyes, stretched it dead on the ground. A moment's hesitation, the slightest wavering or nervousness, and Sir Samuel would have been lost.

Alexina Tinné, with Mr. and Mrs. Petherick, made numerous excursions in the neighbourhood of Lake Reg, in one of which they were surprised by a terrible storm. In the memory of living man no such hurricane had been known; and it seemed to spend its worst fury upon the traveller's caravan, which it threatened every moment to sweep from the earth. When it had somewhat subsided, other difficulties arose. The soldiers who formed the escort were not only inveterately idle, but irrepressibly dishonest; while as for the negroes, they were contumacious, and refused to follow the route indicated by their employer. A serious disturbance was on the point of breaking out, when the gale returned with fresh violence, tore down at least half of the encampment, and almost suffocated Alexina Tinné amidst the wreckage of her hut. While it lasted, terror prevented her followers from resorting to acts of open insubordination; but they regained their audacity as the tempest passed away, and, declaring that their supply of food was insufficient, demanded larger rations. A general mutiny seemed imminent; but the fair leader of the expedition was equal to the occasion. Though suffering from bodily pain and weakness, she boldly confronted the insurgents; with flashing eye, and in a fierce voice, addressed to them a severe reprimand, and ordered them to lay down their arms. Her intrepid demeanour awed them into submission, and the encounter ended in their humbly supplicating her forgiveness.

The crisis over, her overwrought system gave way. So serious was her illness that at one time recovery seemed impossible, and the deepest sorrow was manifested by the whole camp. Quinine, however, which is the sheet-anchor (so to speak) of African travellers, saved her. A gradual improvement took place, and by the 30th of May all danger had disappeared.

As soon as she was able to move, she gave orders for the expedition to advance. It travelled by short stages; and when, towards night, Miss Tinné came upon a village which promised convenient quarters, she sent for the sheikh, and the gift of a few beads was sufficient to make him expel from their huts the native families. Without striking a blow, the travellers got possession of the place, and in a few hours had settled themselves comfortably, while taking due care of their camels and cattle. As for the dispossessed inhabitants, they were left to find what shelter or accommodation they could, consoling themselves with the promise of ample compensation on the morrow.

The African villages are sometimes of considerable size. They are nearly always surrounded by a belt of cultivated ground, where dourra, sesamum, and culinary vegetables grow in profusion. The flocks scattered over the pastures often include some thousands of sheep, though they are never killed by the natives for purposes of food. Miss Tinné purchased several; but as soon as it was known that she slaughtered them for provision, their owners refused to sell. The natives apparently make the sheep the object of a superstitious *cultus*, as the Lapps do the hare. It is true, however, that their scruples vanished at the sight of Alexina Tinné's trinkets; their religion proved unable to withstand the temptation of a bright ring or glittering bracelet. Yet who shall blame them when Christians have been known to forswear their faith for equally small bribes? It is a curious fact that each tribe has its favourite colour—that while one swears by blue beads, another has eyes only for green; so that a tribe which will violate its conscience for a handful of blue beads or yellow, will preserve it intact if tested by beads of any other colour. But no bribe is so powerful, will prevail over so many vows, will appease so many scruples, as a piece of blue or red cotton. This, however, was reserved as a gratification for the chiefs alone; and it was a sight to make you laugh or weep, according as your philosophy is that of Democritus or Heraclitus, to see them strutting through their villages, proud as peacocks in their gaudy attire, haughtier than a mayor with his official chain round his portly chest, happier than a Frenchman with the ribbon of the Legion of Honour in his button-hole.

The countries of Djur and Dör, traversed by our caravan, offered a succession of the most varied panoramas. For several days it passed through marshy lowlands, covered with a coarse hard grass: the herbage was besprinkled with rare flowers, many of which belonged to species unknown to European botanists. As they advanced trees became more numerous; groves developed into woods, and woods expanded into a luxurious forest, where the eye surveyed with delight a rich network of climbing plants and wild vines, spreading from tree to tree, while the dense cloud of verdure was lighted up profusely with starry blossoms. In this happy land the mosquito was never found; nor were there any injurious insects, except the termites or white ants.

The picture suddenly changed as the travellers penetrated further into the interior; immense plains stretched away to a remote horizon, where earth and heaven seemed to mingle. Occasionally, however, the monotonous level was broken pleasantly by clumps of graceful trees, forming so many isles of greenery, in which the calm bland air was perfumed by the sweet odours that rose, like a breath, from magnificent cactuses, orchids, and irises. Thousands of birds, surprised among the tall grasses by the passing caravan, sprang aloft and filled the air with the whir of winnowing wings.

Enraptured by the beauty of this fortunate and favoured region, Alexina forgot the sufferings she had endured, and, giving a free rein to her womanly enthusiasm, exclaimed—"This is a delightful country, a marvellous land, which compensates us for all our fatigue; yes, and for all our outlay!" These last words may be considered as a striking example of bathos, or "the art of sinking," considering the circumstances under which they were pronounced; but it would appear that the enormous expenses of the expedition had by this time made a serious inroad even on Miss Tinné's large fortune.

As for some years a marked diminution had taken place in the number of elephants inhabiting the valley of the White Nile, the ivory dealers pushed forward into the countries watered by the Bahr-el-Ghazal and the Djur. There they found themselves in a virgin region, which hitherto had not been contaminated by the influences of a corrupt civilization. It was a mine to be worked with the happiest results, and accordingly they established a series of stations, each in charge of a vakil or manager. In the month of November these were visited in person by the traders, who loaded their boats with ivory, too frequently adding to their cargoes of elephants' tusks the unfortunate negroes who had served them as guides and hunters. As time went on, they extended their relations, and gave free course to their ambition. They armed the tribes one against another, promoted internecine contests, and in this way consolidated their cruel and unscrupulous despotism.

Our travellers nearly fell victims to one of these infamous speculators in the blood of the feeble and defenceless. Yielding to his repeated pressure, Alexina and her followers advanced to Bongo, where he exercised authority. They were received with a splendid welcome. On their arrival volleys of musketry woke all the surrounding echoes. Biselli (such was the name of their self-appointed host) met them at the entrance to the village, and conducted them into a spacious and convenient habitation, where, with the most courteous attention, they were served with sherbet, coffee, and other refreshing drinks. No one was forgotten in his profuse hospitality; masters and servants were entertained with equal liberality. The abrek, the delicious beer of the country, was freely circulated among the people, and generously distributed to the very porters.

As Biselli was absolute master in the village and its neighbourhood, and owned almost everything, Alexina Tinné requested him to sell some corn and oxen. He answered, like a true gentleman, that for twenty-four hours he was her host; that he had abdicated his position as a trader, and had no thought but her comfort, and to give her an honourable reception. His profuseness, far from diminishing, largely increased; and his European guests were almost ashamed to be the recipients of an hospitality so cordial, so unlimited, and so unexpected.

But unfortunately a change came over the spirit of the dream. Next day, clouds gathered on the horizon which had previously been so fair. The travellers wished to hire a small zoriba, or plantation, comprising two tents. Biselli named thirty thalers as the price. No objection was offered, and Miss Tinné's people began to store the baggage, when he suddenly made a demand for two hundred thalers. This exorbitant sum was promptly and firmly refused; he then reduced it to forty thalers, which was paid. Soon afterwards the caravan was in need of dourra, and there was no help for it but to apply to Biselli. Well aware of their necessity, the scoundrel charged forty times more than they would have had to pay at Khartûm, and on every other article he put in like manner a tax of forty or fifty per cent. The ex-gentleman had resumed his old character as an unprincipled speculator.

Our travellers, however, felt that they could no longer endure his impositions, and abandoning Bongo and Biselli, returned to Lake Reg. Here Alexina's mother was seized with an illness which carried her off in a few days (July 23rd). Two European servants were also attacked by fever, and succumbed to its fatal influence. Overwhelmed with grief, Miss Tinné abandoned her schemes of African exploration, and slowly and with difficulty made her way back to Khartûm, to find that her aunt, the Baroness van Capellan, had died during her absence (in May, 1864). As soon as she had recruited her strength, she removed to Cairo, where she took up her residence, and for four years made a conspicuous figure in its brilliant European circle.

The love of new scenes, however, had not been quenched by her adventures, and in her yacht she made frequent visits to Naples and Rome, Smyrna and Jaffa, Algiers and Tripoli. While at the latter port, a caravan arrived from the Sahara, with the products of the rich lands that lie beyond that famous desert. The incident suggested to her bold imagination the idea of an expedition which in romance and interest should eclipse her previous enterprise, and she traced the plan of a journey across Tripoli to the capital of Fezzan, thence to Kuka, and westward, by way of Wadai, Darfur, and Kordofan, to the Nile. As this route would carry her into the territory of the brave but treacherous Towaregs, a race to whom plunder and rapine seem the breath of life, she took care to provide herself with a sufficient escort, and on the 29th of January, 1869, set out from Tripoli at the head of a troop of fifty armed men. At Sokna, in Fezzan, which she reached on the 1st of March, she engaged the services of a Towareg chief, one Ik-nu-ken; but at the last moment he failed her, and she accepted as guides two chiefs of the same tribe, who professed to have been sent by Ik-nu-ken. These men, in conjunction with her attendant, Mohammed, a Tunisian, resolved upon murdering her in order to gain possession of her money and valuables. Soon after her departure from Sokna (it was on the 1st of August) they excited a quarrel among the camel-drivers, and when Alexina quitted her tent to ascertain the cause, one of the Towaregs shot her with a rifle-bullet, mortally wounding her. For four and twenty hours she lay dying at the door of her tent, no one venturing to offer assistance or consolation.

Such was the melancholy fate of Alexina Tinné! It is satisfactory to know that the murderers who, with their plunder, had escaped into the interior, were eventually captured, tried, and sentenced to imprisonment for life. [259]

MR. J. A. MACGAHAN,
AND CAMPAIGNING ON THE OXUS.

I.

MR. J. A. MACGAHAN, as special correspondent for the *New York Herald*, a journal well known by the liberality and boldness of its management, accompanied the Russian army, under General Kauffmann, in its campaigns in Central Asia in 1873 and 1874.

Bound for the seat of war, he made his way, in company with Mr. Eugene Schuyler, the American *chargé d'affaires* at St. Petersburg, who desired to see something of Central Asia, to Kasala, a Russian town on the Syr-Daria (the ancient *Jaxartes*), where he arrived in April, 1873. He describes this town, or fort, as the entering wedge of the Russians into Central Asia. Its population, exclusive of Russian soldiers and civilians, consists of Sarts, or Tadjiks, Bokhariots, Kirghiz, and Kara-Kalpaks; all being Tartar tribes, in whom an infusion of Aryan blood has more or less modified the old Mongolian type. As for the town, it is picturesque enough to a European eye—its low mud houses, with flat roofs, windowless, and almost doorless; its bazár, where long-bearded men, in bright-coloured robes, gravely drink tea among the wares that crowd their little shops; and the strings of laden camels that stalk through its streets, presenting a novel combination. As soon as he had obtained all the information he could with respect to the movements of the Russian force, Mr. MacGahan resolved on making a dash for the Oxus, hoping to reach that river before General Kauffmann's army had crossed it. But when the Russian authorities learned his design, they at once interfered, declaring that the journey was dangerous, if not impracticable, and must not be undertaken without leave from the Governor-General. Mr. MacGahan then resolved on pushing forward to Fort Perovsky, as if going only to Tashkent; trusting to find there an officer in command who would not be troubled by such conscientious scruples about his personal safety. No objection was made to a journey to Tashkent; Mr. MacGahan and Mr. Schuyler therefore hurried their preparations, stowed their baggage in a waggon, and themselves in a tarantass, and shaking the dust off their feet at inhospitable and suspicious Kasala, took their course along the banks of the Syr-Daria.

This, the ancient Jaxartes, is one of the most eccentric of rivers. It is continually changing its bed, like a restless traveller; "here to-day, and gone to-morrow," and gone a distance of some eight to ten miles. To adapt it to the purposes of navigation seems almost impossible, or, at all events, would be unprofitable; and the best use that could be made of its waters would be to irrigate with them the thirsty sands of the desert of Kyzil-Kum.

On Mr. MacGahan's arrival at Fort Perovsky, he proceeded to engage a guide and horses, having fully resolved to carry out his bold enterprise. From the commandant he was fortunate enough to obtain a passport, and on the 30th of April he bade farewell to Mr. Schuyler, and set out. His *cortége* consisted of Ak-Mamatoff, his Tartar servant, Mushuf, the guide, and a young Kirghiz attendant, all mounted, with ten horses to carry the baggage and forage. As a man of peace, he says, he went but lightly armed. Yet a heavy double-barrelled hunting rifle, a double-barrelled shot gun (both being breech-loaders), an eighteen-shooter Winchester rifle, three heavy revolvers, and one ordinary muzzle-loading shot gun throwing slugs, together with a few knives and sabres, would seem to make up a tolerable arsenal! Mr. MacGahan, however, assures us that he did not contemplate fighting, and that he encumbered himself with these "lethal weapons" only that he might be able to discuss with becoming dignity questions concerning the rights of way and of property, on which his opinions might differ from those of the nomads of the desert, who hold to Rob Roy's good old rule, that

> "They should take who have the power,
> And they should keep who can."

That night our traveller accepted the hospitality of a Kirghiz. Next morning he and his men were in the saddle by sunrise, riding merrily away to the south-west, across a country innocent of road or path. Sometimes their course lay through tangled brushwood, sometimes through tall reeds which completely concealed each rider from his companions, sometimes over low sandy dunes, and sometimes across a bare and most desolate plain. Occasionally they heard the loud sharp cry of the golden pheasant of Turkistan; then they would pass large flocks and herds of sheep, cattle, and horses, quietly grazing; and again they would meet and salute a Kirghiz shepherd on horseback. To eyes that have been trained to *see* no desert can be utterly barren of interest; the vigilant observer will discover, in the most sterile waste, something of fresh and novel character, something suggestive of thick-coming fancies. For example, Mr. MacGahan noted the remarkable difference between the wide stretches of the sandy plain and the occasional streaks of ground that had been under recent cultivation; and he perceived that the desert had the advantage. Parched and sun-scorched, and without a trace of vegetation, was the land that had been irrigated only the year before; while the desert assumed a delicate tint of green, with its budding brushwood and thin grass, which always springs into life as soon as the snow melts, to flourish until stricken sore by the heats of summer.

At nightfall the travellers, weary with eleven hours' ride, drew up at a Kara-Kalpak aul, or encampment, consisting of a dozen kibitkas, pitched near a little pond in the centre of a delightful oasis. The owner of one of the kibitkas proved to be the guide's brother, and gave the party a cordial welcome. The Kara-Kalpaks are nomads like the Kirghiz, but though they live side by side with them, and frequently intermarry, they seem to belong to a different race of men. They are taller than the Kirghiz, and well-made; their skin is almost as white as that of a European; and instead of the small eyes, high cheek-bones, flat noses, thick lips, and round beardless faces of the Kirghiz, they have long faces, high noses, large open eyes, and are bearded "like the pard."

"After supper," says Mr. MacGahan, "I stepped outside the tent to take a look on the surrounding scene, and enjoy the cool air of the evening. The new moon was just setting; lights were gleaming in every direction over the plain, showing that ours was not the only aul in the vicinity. The bleating of sheep and the lowing of cattle could be heard, mingled with the playful bark of dogs and the laughing voices of children, which came to us on the still evening air like music. In places the weeds and grass of last year had been fired to clear the ground for the new growth, and broad sheets of fire crawled slowly forward over the plain, while huge volumes of dense smoke, that caught the light of the flames below, rolled along the sky in grotesque fantastic shapes like clouds of fire."

The kibitka, according to our traveller, is made up of numerous thin strips of wood, six feet long, which are fastened loosely together like a vine trellis, and can be opened out or folded up compactly, as necessity requires. As the strips are slightly curved in the middle, the framework, when expanded, naturally takes the form of a segment of a circle. Four of these frames constitute the skeleton sides of the tent; and on their tops are placed some twenty or thirty rafters, properly curved, with their upper ends inserted in the hoop, three or four feet in diameter, that serves as a roof-tree. The method of pitching a kibitka may be thus described:—As soon as the camel with the felt and framework reaches the chosen site, he is made to kneel down, and a couple of women seize the framework, which they straightway set up on end, and extend in the form of a circle. Next the doorposts are planted, and the whole bound firmly together with a camel's-hair rope. Then one of the women takes the afore-mentioned wooden hoop, and raising it above her head on a pole, the other proceeds to insert in their proper holes the twenty or thirty rafters, fastening their basis to the lower framework by means of hoops. When a thick fold of felt has been let down over the framework, the kibitka, which measures about fifteen feet in diameter, and eight feet in length, is complete. In appearance it is not unlike a magnified beehive of the old pattern.

The Kirghiz nomads are fierce, crafty, often cruel, but they hold the life of a guest sacred. For his property, however, they have no such high consideration, and they are not above the temptation of plundering him of any article that attracts their fancy. Their chief amusements are horse exercises and falconry. They love the chase with a true sportsman's passion; loving it for itself, rather than for the game it procures, as they can conceive of nothing daintier than a dish of mutton—a dish which they prepare with touching simplicity. For, a sheep having been skinned, they cut it into quarters, which they plunge into a large caldron of water, and boil for a couple of hours. Generally, on a principle of severe economy, they cook the intestines with the meat, not taking the trouble even to separate them. The guests arrange themselves in a circle on carpets of felt; the men, as recognized lords of the creation, occupying the foremost places, the women and children sitting in the rear. The smoking quarters of mutton are removed from the pot; each man draws his knife, slashes off a cantle, eats until satisfied, and passes what is left to his wife and children, who speedily effect a clearance. The dogs come in for the bones. Afterwards, bowls of the liquor in which the meat has been boiled are handed round, and not a Kirghiz but swallows the greasy potion with as much zest as an epicure takes his glass of dry champagne. This broth, koumis (fermented mare's milk), and tea, are his customary liquors; but the tea, instead of being prepared in the European fashion, is made into a kind of soup with milk, flour, butter, and salt. In every respectable Kirghiz kibitka the women keep constantly upon the fire a vessel of this beverage, which they offer to visitors, just as a Turk serves up coffee, and a Spaniard chocolate.

In their mode of life the Kirghiz display a certain originality. They spend the three winter months in mud huts on the bank of a river or a small stream, and resume their annual migrations as soon as the snow begins to melt. During these migrations they live in tents, and never halt in one spot for longer than three days. Their march is often continued until they have travelled three or four hundred miles; then they turn round, and retrace the same route, so as to reach their place of hibernation before the snow falls. In their selection of quarters they seem guided by some traditions handed down in the different auls; and not unfrequently a body of Kirghiz will pass over much excellent grazing ground, and travel many a league to inferior pasturage. The hardships they undergo are so many, their pleasures so few and mean, their objects so commonplace, that one is tempted to wonder what kind of answer an intelligent Kirghiz would return to the question not long ago put with some emphasis before the reading public, "Is life worth living?" Those higher motives, those purer aspirations which the cultivated European mind delights to recognize, are unknown to the wild nomad, and he spends day after day, and month after month, in what would seem to be a drearily monotonous struggle for existence, under conditions which might be supposed to render existence an intolerable burden. But then he can love and suffer as we know civilized men and women love and suffer; and love and suffering will invest the harshest, coarsest life with a certain grace and consecration.

There was once a young Kirghiz, named Polat, who was affianced to Muna Aim, the comeliest maiden in the aul, or community, of Tugluk. Her father, Ish Djan, had received the customary kalym, or wedding present, and the marriage day had been appointed. But before it arrived, "the blind fury with the abhorred shears" had "slit" Polat's "thin-spun life;" and Muna Aim was set free from her promise. Suluk, Polat's brother, came forward, however, and, in his anxiety to recover his brother's property, which she had received as her dower, claimed her as his wife. The claim was supported by her father; but Muna Aim, who had sufficient means to live on, considered herself a widow, and refused to marry. She was driven from her father's kibitka; and taking her camel, with her sheep and goats, her clothes and carpets, she bought a little kibitka for herself, and lived alone, but not unhappy. For her heart was really with Azim, a young Kirghiz belonging to another aul, and she had consented to marry Polat only in obedience to her father. A second sacrifice she was determined not to make. But the old women grew very angry with Muna Aim, as she continued to enjoy her independence. "What is the matter with her?" they cried. "She will not go to her husband, but lives alone like an outlaw." She was an innovator, boldly breaking through a traditional custom, and they resolved to "reason" with her. Their arguments were those which the strong too often employ against the feeble; they hurled at her bad names, and they scratched her face and pulled her hair. Still she would not yield; and in contentment she milked her sheep and goats, drove them to the pasture, and drew water for them from the well, waiting for some happy turn of fortune which might unite her with her Azim.

At last Suluk also resolved to try the effect of "reason." With three or four friends he repaired one night to her kibitka, and broke it open, resolved to carry her off to his tent, and compel her to be his wife. Love and despair, however, lent her so wonderful an energy, that she resisted all their efforts. They dragged her to the door; but she clutched at the door-posts with her hands, and held so firmly, that to make her let go they were forced to draw their knives and slash her fingers. When they succeeded in hauling her into the open air, her clothes were torn from her body, and she was covered with blood from head to foot. She continued her brave struggle; and Suluk, leaping on his horse and catching her by her beautiful long hair, dragged her at his horse's heels, until it came out by the roots, and he was compelled to leave her on the ground, naked, bleeding, half dead.

Information of this outrage, however, reached the Yarim-Padshah (or "half emperor"), as the tribes of Central Asia call the redoubtable General Kauffmann; and he despatched a party of Cossacks to seize its author. Suluk was speedily captured, and sent, a prisoner, to Siberia; while the faithful and courageous Muna Aim recovered her health and her braids of long dark hair, and in the winter met the lover for whom she had endured so much, and was happily married.

Thus the reader will perceive that romance flourishes even in the wildernesses of the Kyzil-Kum; and that a Kirghiz woman can be elevated by a true love like an English maiden.

Continuing his ride after the Russians, Mr. MacGahan, when near Irkibai, came upon the ruins of an ancient city. It had once been about three miles in circumference, walled, and on three sides surrounded by a wide and deep canal, on the fourth by the Yani-Daria. The wall had been strengthened by watch-towers, and on the summit of a hill in the centre stood two towers thirty to forty feet in height. The whole was built of sun-dried brick, and was fast crumbling into shapeless mounds. At Irkibai Mr. MacGahan met with every courtesy from the commandant, but nothing was known of the whereabouts of General Kauffmann. There were but two courses before the traveller—to return, or go forward. Mr. MacGahan was not the man to retrace his steps until his work was done, if it were possible to do it; and he resolved on continuing his progress to the Oxus. On the 7th of May he rode forward. At first he followed the regular caravan route, which, as many traces showed, had also been that of the Russian division, under the Grand-Duke Nicholas. It crosses the thirsty desert—twenty leagues without a well. Fair enough is it to the eye, with its rolling lines of verdant hills; but the hills are only sand, and the verdure consists of a coarse soft weed that, when it flowers, exhales a most offensive odour. Beneath the broad leaves lurk scorpions and tarantulas, great lizards, beetles, and serpents. The traveller, if he lose his way in this deadly waste of delusion, may wander to and fro for days, until he and his horse sink exhausted, to perish of thirst, with no other covering for their bones than the rank and noxious herbage.

Across the gleaming burning sands, while the sun smote them pitilessly with his burning arrows, rode our brave traveller and his companions. Their lips cracked with thirst, and their eyes smarted with the noontide glare, and their weary horses stumbled in the loose shifting soil; but rest they durst not until they reached the well of Kyzil-Kak. How glad they were to throw themselves down beside it, while some kindly Kirghiz, who had already refreshed their camels and horses, drew for them the welcome water! MacGahan made a short halt here, feeding his horses, and sharing with his attendants a light meal of biscuits and fresh milk, supplied by the

Kirghiz, and then—the saddle again! Meeting with a caravan, he learned from its Bashi, or leader, that the Russian army was at Tamdy—that is, instead of being, as he had hoped, within a day's march, it must be upwards of two hundred miles distant; and as it was just on the point of starting for Aristan-Bel-Kudluk, which was still further south, it was impossible to say when he might overtake it. His disappointment was great; but his cry was still "Onwards!" By nine o'clock next morning the indefatigable traveller reached the foot of the grey, bare, treeless heights of the Bukan-Tau. Though but a thousand feet in elevation, they presented, with their glancing peaks, their conical summits, their deep valleys, and awful precipices, all the characteristics of an Alpine range of mountains. Resting there for some hours, he took up, on the morrow, a line of march around their northern slope, and gradually descended into the plain. From some Kirghiz he ascertained that the Grand-Duke Nicholas had joined General Kauffmann two days before, and that the united Russian army had then marched for Karak-Aty. The problem of overtaking it seemed more incapable than ever of a satisfactory solution. But, on studying his map, he found that from the point which he had reached it was no further to Karak-Aty than to Tamdy, and he instantly resolved to follow up a caravan route to the south, which promised to lead to the former.

At noon he rode into the little valley of Yuz-Kudak, or the "Hundred Wells." It was completely bare of vegetation, except a little thin grass, but was brightened by a small, narrow runlet, which led, in less than a quarter of a mile, to the water. There, along the valley, bubbled about twenty-five or thirty wells or springs; in some the water trickling over the surface, in others standing at a depth of from five to ten feet. Thence, to the next well, was a distance of twenty-five miles. The country was sandy, but high and broken up, with a low range of mountains on the left, extending north-east and south-west. Next day Mr. MacGahan fell in with a Kirghiz aul, where he was hospitably entertained by a chief named Bii Tabuk. From him he learned that Kauffmann had left Karak-Aty and arrived at Khala-Ata, one hundred miles further to the south, and that the shortest way to Khala-Ata lay right across the desert in the direction of the Oxus, a little west of south. As there was no road, nor even a sheep path, Mr. MacGahan sought for a guide, and eventually engaged a young Kirghiz at the exorbitant fee of twenty-five roubles. Then, having enjoyed a couple of days' rest, he started before sunrise on that interminable hunt after General Kauffmann, which seemed to promise as romantic a legend as the voyage of Jason in search of the Golden Fleece, or Sir Galahad's famous quest of the Sangreal.

He had not ridden far, when, as the issue of a little intrigue between his Tartar, his old guide, Mushuf, and his new guide, the last named suddenly refused to proceed unless, in addition to the twenty-five roubles, he received a horse or the money to buy one. With prompt decision MacGahan dismissed the guide, and when Ak-Mamatoff showed a disposition to be recalcitrant, threatened him with his revolver. This display of firmness and courage immediately produced a satisfactory effect. Ak-Mamatoff humbled himself, and to prove the sincerity of his penitence, rode to a neighbouring aul, and procured another and more trustworthy guide. Afterwards they all breakfasted, and once more rode across the sandy wastes in the direction of Khala-Ata. Sand, sand, sand, everywhere sand. The horses struggled with difficulty through the huge drifts, and on the second night one of them gave up, and had to be left behind. Sand, sand, sand, everywhere sand; by day as by night, and all so lonely and silent! For fifteen days MacGahan had bravely plodded through the dreary, inhospitable desert—when and how would his journey end? Still he persevered: stumbling through the low coarse brushwood, sliding down into deep sandy hollows; again, clambering painfully up steep ascents, where the horses panted and laboured, and strove with the heavy inexorable sand; over the hard-bound earth, where their hoof's rang as on a stone pavement; late in the night, he was glad to fling himself on the sand to snatch a brief repose.

"We have scarcely shut our eyes," says this intrepid, indefatigable traveller, "when we are called by the guide to renew the march. It is still night, but the desert is visible, dim and ghostly under the cold pale light of the rising moon. Vegetation has entirely disappeared; there is scarcely a twig even of the hardy saxaul. Side by side with us move our own shadows, projected long and black over the moonlit sand, like fearful spectres pursuing us to our doom.

"Thin streaks of light begin to shoot up the eastern sky. The moon grows pale, the shadows fade out, and at last the sun, red and angry, rises above the horizon. After the sharp cold of the night its rays strike us agreeably, suffusing a pleasant sensation of warmth over our benumbed limbs. Then it grows uncomfortably warm, then hot, and soon we are again suffering the pangs of heat and thirst; our eyes are again blinded by the fiery glare, and our lungs scorched by the stifling noonday atmosphere."

Throughout that day the ride was continued, and even far into the night. Early next morning the traveller reached the summit of the mountain range behind which lies Khala-Ata. With feelings of eager expectancy and hope, he spurred forward his horse, and with his field-glass looked down upon the bleak bare plain which stretched far away in the direction of Bokhara; there, at the distance of eight miles, he saw a dome-like mound, encircled by small tents, which shone in the morning sunlight, and at various points were grouped masses of soldiers in white uniform, and the sheen of steel. At last, then, he had overtaken Kauffmann!

Though weary and spent, and covered with the dust of the desert, it was with a cheerful heart that, at about six o'clock on the morning of the 16th of May, he rode into the camp and fortress of Khala-Ata, after a ride of five hundred miles and a chase of seventeen days. All the more bitter was his disappointment when, on asking the young officer on duty to direct him to the quarters of General Kauffmann, he was informed that the general had left Khala-Ata, five days before, and by that time must certainly have reached the Amu-Darya. The chase, then, had been fruitless; the rider, daring and indefatigable as he had showed himself, had missed his mark. The commandant at Khala-Ata proved to be a Colonel Weimam, who received the special correspondent with marked discourtesy, and refused to allow him to continue his search for General Kauffmann, unless he first obtained that general's permission. The sole concession he would make was, that he would send on Mr. MacGahan's letters of introduction, and then, if the Russian commander-in-chief expressed a wish to see him, he would be at liberty to go. This arrangement, however, would evidently involve a delay of ten or twelve days. In the mean time the army would cross the Oxus, would capture Khiva, and the special correspondent's "occupation" would be "gone." Anxiously did Mr. MacGahan meditate on the course it would be best for him to adopt. To break through the Russian lines and effect his escape seemed impracticable. In all probability, the swift-footed and ferocious Turcoman cavalry were hanging in General Kauffmann's rear; and how, without an escort, was he to make his way through their ranks? Yet the more he reflected, the more he became convinced that this was his only chance of reaching the Russian army in time to witness the capture of Khiva. The difficulties in the way, apart from the danger, were enormous. His horses were exhausted; he had neither provisions nor forage, nor any means of procuring them; and he might reckon on Colonel Weimam's despatching a squadron of Cossacks to pursue and arrest him. Ascertaining, however, that the colonel was about to move forward with a couple of companies of infantry, one hundred Cossacks, and two field-pieces, he resolved on the bold plan of quitting the camp with the cavalry, trusting to the darkness to escape detection, and afterwards making a wide circuit to pass the detachment. Several days passed by in wretched inaction. The heat was oppressive; clouds of dust filled the atmosphere, and almost choked the unfortunate victims exposed to its irritating influence; provisions were painfully scarce, and Colonel Weimam absolutely refused to sell or give a grain of barley to the traveller's starving horses. At last, about one a.m. on the 14th of May, the Russian detachment marched out of camp, and struck to the westward, in the direction of Adam-Kurulgan and the Amu-Daria. Mr. MacGahan and his men were on the alert. "I dropped silently," he says, "in the rear of the Cossacks, who led the column, followed by my people, and when we had gained the summit of the low sand-hill, a mile from the camp, over which the road led, I as silently dropped out again, turned my horses' heads to the west, and plunged into the darkness."

Once more he was in the open desert, once more he was free, and he could not repress a feeling of exultation, though he was suffering from hunger, his horses were spent with starvation, and at any moment he might fall into the hands of the murderous Turcomans. A more daring enterprise, or one conceived in a more resolute and intrepid spirit, is hardly recorded, I think, in the annals of adventure. When he supposed himself at a sufficient distance from the Russian column, he turned sharp round to the west, and made as straight as he could for the Amu-Darya, expecting to reach it before Colonel Weimam. But after a hard day's ride, he found, as he approached Adam-Kurulgan, that the Russian soldiers were before him! There seemed no alternative but to return to Khala-ata or surrender himself to the obnoxious and despotic Weimam. Yes; if he could get water for his exhausted beasts he might avoid Adam-Kurulgan altogether, and still pursue his wild ride to the Oxus! Some Kirghiz guides, on their way to Khala-Ata, informed him that twenty miles further on was Alty-Kuduk, or the "Six Wells;" it was not on the road to the Amu, but some four miles to the north, and Kauffmann had left some troops there. This news revived his drooping spirits. "Forward!" he cried, and away through the deep sand-drifts the little company toiled and struggled. He lost another of his horses, and the survivors were almost mad with thirst; but his cry was still "Forward!" He himself longed for water, with a longing unknown to those who have not travelled in the arid desert and under the burning sun, for hours and hours, without moistening the parched lips; but his only thought was "Forward!" On the following day the brave man's persistency was rewarded. He reached the camp of Alty-Kuduk, met with a most friendly reception from all its inmates, and obtained meat and drink for himself and his men, and barley and water for his horses.

A day's rest, and he was again in the saddle (May 27th). It was soon apparent by the dead camels that lined the road that he had got into the trail of the Russian army, and from time to time he could recognize the tracks of cannon. Then he came upon the bodies of Turcoman horses, which, as he afterwards learned, had been slain in a skirmish two days before. Towards sunset the character of the country changed: the rolling sand dunes disappeared, and the traveller entered upon a level plain, which sank away into a lower kind of terrace. The day drew rapidly to a close: lower and lower down the western sky sunk the blood-red sun; at last it dropped below the horizon, and as the sky flashed momently with broad streaks of red and purple and golden light, the shimmer of water became visible in the distance. It was the Oxus!

It was long after dark when MacGahan reached the river. He refreshed his horses with its waters, and then encamped for the night. At daylight he ascended a hill, and looked out upon the scene. The broad, calm river, winding north and south, sparkled before him, like a belt of silver on a golden mantle. But where was the Russian army? Where was General Kauffmann?

Nowhere could he discover a trace of human habitation, of tent or kibitka. Nowhere could he see a single picket, not even a solitary Cossack.

Again was MacGahan disappointed. I have read of an old superstition which represents a cup of gold as the prize of the fortunate mortal who shall find the exact spot where a rainbow touches the earth. And I have read that men, believing it, have pursued the radiant iris with eager footsteps, only to find her eluding them when most they think themselves sure of grasping her. So was it with our special correspondent. He had hoped to overtake the Russians at Myn-Bulak, but they had vanished; at Khala-Ata, but he was too late; and again on the Oxus, but they had disappeared. He was almost tempted to look upon himself as the victim of a portentous delusion. Would there really be a Kauffmann? Was the expedition to Khiva other than a myth?

The tracks of cannon and the ashes of extinct campfires reassured him on these points; and, rallying his energies, he set out once more on his strange quest, following the course of the Oxus. That day he rode five and forty miles. At night he encamped, but as Khivans might be prowling in the vicinity, he resolved to keep watch. For hours he paced up and down in the darkness, a darkness that would have been death stillness but for the murmur of the flowing river; and at length he caught a flash of light. To him, like the light which Columbus saw on the eve of the discovery of the New World, it portended the end of his adventure; for it proceeded, as he knew, from either a Khivan or a Russian bivouac. In the morning he started early, and had ridden but a short distance, when loud upon his ears broke the rolling thunder of artillery! Then he knew that the army was close at hand, and engaged in desperate combat with its Khivan enemies.

A few miles more, and Mr. MacGahan reached a sand-hill which afforded him an extensive view of the valley of the river. The opposite bank was crowded with horsemen, who were galloping to and fro, while a couple of cannon placed in front of a small pit were busily discharging missiles. On his own side the Russians were posted in loose order, and looking quietly on; their artillery replying to the Khivan fire with whizzing shells. "It was a curious scene," says our traveller; "and I suppose the old Oxus, since the time it first broke from the ice-bound springs of Pamir, had never heard such music as this. Five times before had the Russians attempted to reach this very spot, and five times had they failed. Five times had they been driven back, beaten, and demoralized, either by the difficulties of the way, the inclemency of the season, or the treachery of the Khivans. The one detachment which had succeeded in capturing Khiva had afterwards been slaughtered to the last man; and now the Russians stood at last, this bright morning, on the banks of that historic river, with their old enemy once more before them." The Khivans soon retired, leaving the opposite bank entirely free. Mr. MacGahan then started down the river to join the Russian army, and in a short time found himself in their midst, overwhelmed with friendly attentions. News of his gallant ride across the Kyzil-Kum had preceded him, so that he was received as a man who had quietly done a truly heroic thing. His first duty was to pay his respects to the object of his prolonged quest, General Kauffmann. The general, wrapped up in a Bokharan khalat or gown, was seated in an open tent, drinking tea and smoking a cigarette; a man of middle age, bald, rather short of stature, beardless, but wearing a thick moustache, prominent nose, blue eyes, and a pleasant kindly countenance. He shook hands with MacGahan, asked him to sit down, and remarked, with a smile, that he appeared to be something of a "molodyeltz" (a brave fellow). After questioning him respecting his adventures, he briefly told the story of his campaign up to that time, and gave him full and free permission to accompany the army the rest of the way to Khiva. By the Grand-Duke Nicholas Mr. MacGahan was received with equal courtesy.

The traveller now develops into the special correspondent, and his record of travel changes into a chronicle of military events. It would be inconsistent with our purpose to follow minutely his narrative of the Khivan war; but we shall endeavour to select such passages as throw some light on the nature of the country and the character of its inhabitants.

II.

The Khivans, according to Mr. MacGahan, are generally medium-sized, lean, muscular fellows, with long black beards, and no very agreeable physiognomy. They dress in a white cotton shirt, and loose trousers of the same material, over which is worn a khalat, or long tunic, cut straight, and reaching to the heels. The Khivan khalat, with its narrow stripes of dirty brown and yellow, differs very much indeed from the beautiful and brilliant khalat of the Bokhariots. Most of the Khivans go barefoot, and they cover their head with a tall, heavy, black sheepskin cap, which is heavier, uglier, and more inconvenient than even the bearskin of our household troops. In the neighbourhood of Khiva they chiefly cultivate the soil, and their prowess as horticulturists deserves to be renowned. For miles around their capital the country blooms with well-kept gardens, where fruit trees of all kinds flourish, and little fields of waving corn. The houses and farmyards are enclosed by stout walls, from fifteen to twenty feet high, solidly buttressed, and flanked by corner towers. The entrance is through an arched and covered gateway, closing with a massive timber gate. The farmhouse, a rectangular building, from twenty-five to seventy-five yards square, is built of dried mud, worked into large blocks like granite, and measuring three or four feet square and as many thick. There is always a little pond of clear water close at hand, and this is shaded by three or four large elms, while the enclosures are planted with elms and poplars.

Khiva surrendered to the Russians on the 9th. Mr. MacGahan entered it in company with the victorious troops, but confesses to experiencing a feeling of disappointment. The grand or magnificent he had not expected; but his dreams of this Oriental city, secluded far away in the heart of the desert, had pictured it as impressive and picturesque, and they proved entirely false. Through narrow, dirty, and crooked streets, he advanced to the citadel. Entering by a heavy arched brick gateway, he came in sight of a great porcelain tower, shining brilliantly with green, and brown, and blue, and purple. This tower, about one hundred and twenty-five feet high, measured about thirty feet in diameter at the base, and tapered gradually towards the top, where its diameter was about fifteen feet. It was covered all over with burnt tiles, arranged in a variety of broad stripes and figures, as well as with numerous verses of the Koran. With the Khan's palace, it forms one side of a great square, enclosed by the walls of the citadel; the opposite side being occupied by a new médressé, and the other two sides by sheds and private houses.

In the palace nothing is worthy of notice except the Khan's audience chamber, or great hall of state. Of this you can form a good idea if you will tax your imagination to conceive a kind of porch, opening on an inner court, measuring about thirty feet high, twenty feet wide, and ten feet deep, and flanked on either side by towers ornamented with blue and green tiles. The floor was raised six feet, and the roof supported by two curved, slender wooden pillars. The other rooms were mostly dark and ill ventilated. At the back of the hall of state was the Khan's treasury, a low vaulted chamber, the walls and ceilings of which were covered with frescoes of vines and flowers, executed on the most fantastic principles of colouring. The gold, silver, and precious stones had been removed, but not so the weapons, of which there was a most various assortment: swords, guns, daggers, pistols, revolvers, of almost every shape and description. Two or three sabres were of English manufacture. There were also many of the beautiful broad, slightly curved blades of Khorassan, inlaid with gold;

slender Persian scimitars, their scabbards blazing with turquoises and emeralds; and short, thick, curved poniards and knives from Afghanistan, all richly enamelled, and their sheaths set in precious stones. In the hurry of the Khan's departure, beautiful carpets had also been left behind, silk coverlets, cushions, pillows, khalats, and rich and rare Kashmir shawls.

In another apartment were found about three hundred volumes of books, some old telescopes, bows and arrows, and several fine suits of armour, which doubtlessly belonged to the era of the Crusades, when the chivalry of Europe encountered the Saracens on the plains of Syria and Palestine.

In the course of his wanderings Mr. MacGahan lighted upon the Khan's harem, where his favourite Sultana and some other women still remained. As he was an American—or, rather, because they supposed him to be an Englishman—the ladies gave him a cordial reception, and entertained him to tea. They were eight in number: three were old and exceedingly ugly; three middle-aged or young, and moderately good looking; one was decidedly pretty; and the other whom Mr. MacGahan speaks of as the Sultana, was specially distinguished by her superior intelligence, her exquisite grace of movement, and her air of distinction. She wore a short jacket of green silk, embroidered with gold thread; a long chemise of red silk, fastened on the throat with an emerald, slightly open at the bosom, and reaching below the knees; wide trousers, fastened at the ankles; and embroidered boots. She had no turban, and her hair was curled around her well-shaped head in thick and glossy braids. Curious earrings, composed of many little pendants of pearls and turquoises, glanced from her ears, and round her wrists gleamed bracelets of solid silver, traced with gold.

The chamber in which these ladies sat was ten feet wide, twenty long, and twelve high. Parts of the ceiling were embellished with coloured designs, rude in conception and execution. Against one side of the room were placed elegant shelves, supporting a choice assortment of the finest Chinese porcelain. The floor was strewn with carpets, cushions, coverlets, shawls, robes, and khalats, all in admired disorder, together with household utensils, arms, an English double-barrelled hunting rifle, empty cartridges, percussion caps, and—strange contrast!—two or three guitars. It was evident that preparations for flight had been begun, and the principal valuables already removed.

The Khan soon found that nothing was to be gained by flight, and as the Russians were disposed to treat him leniently, he decided on returning to Khiva, and surrendering to the great Yarim-Padshah, the victorious Kauffmann. Mr. MacGahan, who was present at the interview, describes the Asiatic potentate, Muhamed Rahim Bogadur Khan, as at that time a man of about thirty years of age, with a not unpleasing expression of countenance; large fine eyes, slightly oblique, aquiline nose, heavy sensual mouth, and thin black beard and moustache. He was about six feet three inches high, with broad shoulders and a robust figure. "Humbly he sat before Kauffmann, scarcely daring to look him in the face. Finding himself at the feet of the Governor of Turkistan, his feelings must not have been of the most reassuring nature. The two men formed a curious contrast; Kauffmann was not more than half as large as the Khan, and a smile, in which there was apparent a great deal of satisfaction, played on his features, as he beheld Russia's historic enemy at his feet. I thought there never was a more striking example of the superiority of mind over brute force, of modern over ancient modes of warfare, than was presented in the two men. In the days of chivalry, this Khan, with his giant form and stalwart arms, might have been almost a demi-god; he could have put to flight a regiment single-handed, he would probably have been a very Cœur de Lion; and now the meanest soldier in Kauffmann's army was more than a match for him."

The capital of this Asiatic potentate is, as I have hinted, deficient in remarkable characteristics. With three or four exceptions, the buildings are all of clay, and present a miserable appearance. There are two walls—an outer and an inner; the interior enclosing the citadel, which measures a mile in length by a quarter of a mile in breadth, and in its turn encloses the Khan's palace and the great porcelain tower. The outer wall is on an average twenty-five feet high, and it is strengthened by a broad ditch or moat. There are seven gates. The area between the walls is at one point converted into a kind of cemetery; at another it is planted out in gardens, which are shaded by elms and fruit trees, and watered by little canals. Of the houses it is to be said that the interior is far more comfortable than the wretched exterior would lead the traveller to anticipate. Most of them are constructed on the same plan. You pass from the street into a large open court, all around which are arranged the different apartments, each opening into the court, and seldom having any direct communication with each other. Facing the north stands a high porch, with its roof some seven or eight feet above the surrounding walls; this serves to catch the wind, and bring it down into the court below on the principle of a wind-sail aboard ship. The free circulation of air thus maintained is, undoubtedly, very pleasant in the summer heat, but in a Khivan winter it must have its disadvantages.

With twenty-two médressés, or monasteries, and seventeen mosques, is Khiva endowed. Of the latter, the most beautiful and the most highly esteemed is the mosque Palvan-Ata, which raises its tall dome to a height of sixty feet, shining with tiles of glaring green. The interior of the dome is very striking: it is covered, like the exterior, with tiles, but these are adorned with a beautiful blue tracery, interwoven with verses from the Koran. In a niche in the wall, protected by a copper lattice-work, are the tombs of the Khans; and Palvan, the patron-saint of the Khivans, is also buried there.

From the mosques we pass to the bazár, which is simply a street covered in, like the arcades so popular in some English towns. The roof consists of beams laid from wall to wall across the narrow thoroughfare, supporting planks laid close together, and covered with earth. On entering, you are greeted by a pleasant compound scent of spices, by all kinds of agreeable odours, and by the confused sounds of men and animals. As soon as your eyes grow accustomed to the shade, they rest with delight on the rich ripe fruit spread everywhere around you in tempting masses. Khiva would seem to be the paradise of fruit epicures. There are apricots, and grapes, and plums, and peaches, and melons of the finest quality and indescribable lusciousness. But if you want more solid fare, you can enjoy a pilaoff with hot wheaten cakes, and wash down the repast with stimulating green tea. After which, refreshed and thankful, you may sally forth to make your purchases of boots or tobacco or khalats, cotton stuffs or silk stuffs, calico from Manchester, muslin from Glasgow, robes from Bokhara, or Russian sugar. This done, you are at leisure to survey for a while the motley crowd that surges to and fro. The Uzbeg, with his high black sheepskin hat and long khalat, tall, well-formed, swarthy, with straight nose and regular features; the Kirghiz, in coarse dirty-brown khalat, with broad, flat, stolid countenance; the Bokhariot merchant, with turban of white and robe of many colours; the Persian, with quick, ferret-like eyes, and nimble, cat-like motions; and the Yomud Turcoman, with almost black complexion, heavy brows, fierce black eyes, short upturned nose, and thick lips. These pass before you like figures in a phantasmagoria.

Weary with the noise and shifting sights, you gladly accept an invitation to dine with a wealthy Uzbeg, and accompany him to his residence. The day is very warm; in a cloudless sky reigns supreme the sun; and you rejoice when you find that your host has ordered the banquet to be spread in the pleasant garden, amid the shade of green elms and the sparkle of running waters. Your first duty is to remove your heavy riding-boots, and put on the slippers which an attendant hands to you; your second is to make a Russian cigarette, and drink a glass of nalivka, or Russian gooseberry wine, as a preparation for the serious work that awaits you. Then a cloth is spread, and the dinner served. Fruits, of course—apricots, melons, and the most delicious white mulberries; next, three or four kinds of dainty sweetmeats, which seem to consist of the kernels of different nuts embedded in a kind of many-coloured toffee. Into a frothy compound, not unlike ice-cream with the ice left out, you dip your thin wheaten cakes, instead of spoons. Various kinds of nuts, and another glass of nalivka, precede the principal dish, which is an appetizing pilaoff, made of large quantities of rice and succulent pieces of mutton, roasted together.

The dinner at an end, large pipes are brought in. Each consists of a gourd, about a foot high, filled with water; on the top, communicating with the water through a tube, rests a bowl, containing the fire and tobacco. Near the top, on either side, and just above the water, is a hole; but there is no stem. The mode of using it is this: you take up the whole vessel in your hand, and then blow through one of the holes to expel the smoke. Next, stopping up one hole with your finger, you put your mouth to the other, and inhale the smoke into your lungs. You will probably be satisfied with three or four whiffs on this gigantic scale.

Mr. MacGahan had an opportunity of seeing the interior of an Uzbeg house, and he thus describes it:—

"There is little attempt at luxury or taste in the house of even the richest; and in this respect the poorest seems almost on an equality with the most opulent. A few carpets on the floor; a few rugs and cushions round the wall, with shelves for earthenware and China porcelain; three or four heavy, gloomy books, bound in leather or parchment; and some pots of jam and preserved fruit, generally make up the contents of the room. There are usually two or three apartments in the house different from the others, in having arrangements for obtaining plenty of light. In these rooms you find the upper half of one of the walls completely wanting, with the overhanging branches of an elm projecting through the opening. The effect is peculiar and striking, as well as pleasant. From the midst of this room—with mud walls and uneven floor, with the humblest household utensils, and perhaps a smoking fire—you get glimpses of the blue sky through the green leaves of the elm tree. A slightly projecting roof protects the room from rain; in cold weather, of course, it is abandoned. Two or three other rooms are devoted to the silkworms, the feeding and care of which form the special occupation of the women. The worms naturally receive a great deal of attention, for their cocoons pay a great part of the household expenses."

But let us suppose that an Uzbeg host closes up the entertainment he has provided for us with a dance.

The dancers are two young boys—one about eight, the other about ten years of age—with bare feet, a little conical skull-cap on their shaven heads, and a long loose khalat drooping to their ankles. The orchestra is represented by a ragged-looking musician, who sings a monotonous tune to the accompaniment of a three-stringed guitar. The boys begin to dance; at first with slow and leisurely movements, swaying their bodies gracefully, and clapping their hands over their heads to keep time to the music. But as this grows livelier, the boys gradually become more excited; striking their hands wildly, uttering short occasional shouts, turning somersaults, wrestling with each other, and rolling upon the ground.

Towards nightfall, torches will be brought on the scene; some being thrust into the ground, and others fastened to the trunks and branches of trees. The comelier of the juvenile dancers now attired himself as a girl, with tinkling bells to his wrists and feet, and a prettily elaborate cap, also decked with bells, as well as with silver ornaments, and a long pendent veil behind. He proceeds to execute a quiet and restrained dance by himself, lasting, perchance, for about a quarter of an hour; and the other boy coming forward, the two dance together, and enact a love-scene in a really eloquent pantomime. The girl pretends to be angered, turns her back, and makes a pretence of jealousy, while the lover dances lightly around her, and endeavours to restore her to amiability by caresses and all kinds of devices. When all his efforts fail, he sulks in his turn, and shows himself offended. Thereupon the lady begins to relent, and to practise every conciliatory art. After a brief affectation of persistent ill humour, the lover yields, and both accomplish a merry and animated measure with every sign of happiness.

When the Russians left Khiva in the month of August, Mr. MacGahan's mission was ended. He had been present with them at the fall of Khiva, and in the campaign which they afterwards undertook—it would seem, with little or no justification—against the Yomud Turcomans. On the return march he accompanied the detachment in charge of the sick and wounded, descending the Oxus to its mouth, and then proceeding up the Aral Sea to the mouth of the Syr-Daria. The voyage on the Aral occupied two days and a night. Having entered the Syr-Daria, thirty-six hours' sailing brought the flotilla to Kasala—the point from which, as we have seen, Mr. MacGahan had started, some months before, on his daring ride through the desert. After a sojourn of three days, he started in a tarantass for Orenburg.

It will be owned, I think, that Mr. MacGahan's enterprise was boldly conceived and boldly executed; that he displayed, not only a firm and manly courage, but a persistent resolution which may almost be called heroic. He showed himself possessed, however, of even higher qualities; of a keen insight into character, a quick faculty of observation, and a humane and generous spirit.

COLONEL EGERTON WARBURTON,
AND EXPLORATION IN WEST AUSTRALIA.

THE north-west of the "island-continent" of Australia seems to have been discovered almost simultaneously by the Dutch and Spaniards about 1606. Twenty years later, its west coast was sighted; and in 1622 the long line of shore to the south-west. Tasmania, or, as it was first called, Van Diemen's Land, was visited by the Dutch navigator Tasman in 1642. Half a century passed, and Swan River was discovered by Vlaming. The real work of exploration did not begin, however, until 1770, when Captain Cook patiently surveyed the east coast, to which he gave the name of New South Wales. In 1798, in a small boat about eight feet long, Mr. Bass, a surgeon in the navy, discovered the strait that separates Tasmania from Australia, and now perpetuates his memory. He and Lieutenant Flinders afterwards circumnavigated Tasmania; and Flinders, in 1802 and 1803, closely examined the south coast, substituting, as a general designation of this "fifth quarter of the world," Australia for the old boastful Dutch name of New Holland. He also explored the great basin of Port Philip, and discovered the noble inlets of St. Vincent and Spencer Gulfs. In 1788 the British Government selected Botany Bay, on the east coast, as a place of transportation for criminals; and from this inauspicious beginning sprang the great system of colonization, which, developed by large and continual emigration from the mother country, has covered Australia with flourishing States. Tasmania became a separate colony in 1825; West Australia, originally called Swan River, in 1829; South Australia in 1834; Victoria in 1851; Queensland in 1859. Meanwhile, the exploration of the interior was undertaken by a succession of bold and adventurous spirits, starting at first from New South Wales. The barrier of the Blue Mountains was broken through, and rivers Macquarie, Darling, and Lachlan were in time discovered. In 1823 Mr. Oxley surveyed the Moreton Bay district, now Queensland, and traced the course of the Brisbane. In 1830 Captain Sturt explored the Murray, the principal Australian river, to its confluence with Lake Victoria. In 1840 Mr. Eyre, starting from Adelaide, succeeded, after enduring severe privations, in making his way overland to King George's Sound. In the following year he plunged into the interior, which he believed to be occupied by a great central sea; he found only the swamp and saline bays of Lake Torrens. Captain Sturt, in 1845, penetrated almost to the southern tropic in longitude 130° E., traversing a barren region as waterless and as inhospitable as the Sahara. About the same time Dr. Ludwig Leichhardt, with some companions, successfully passed from Moreton Bay to Port Errington; but, in 1848, attempting to cross from east to west, from New South Wales to the Swan River, he and his party perished, either from want of provisions or in a skirmish with the natives. In the same year Mr. Kennedy, who had undertaken to survey the northeast extremity of Australia, was murdered by the natives. Thus Australian exploration has had its martyrs, like African. In 1860 Mr. M'Douall Stuart crossed the continent from ocean to ocean, or, more strictly speaking, from South Australia to a point in lat. 18° 40' S., about two hundred and fifty miles from the coast of the Gulf of Carpentaria. The hostility of the natives prevented him from actually reaching the coast. In August, 1860, a similar expedition was projected by some gentlemen belonging to the colony of Victoria; and, under the command of Robert O'Hara Burke, it started from Melbourne for Cooper's Creek, whence it was to proceed to the northern coast. Some of the members, namely, Burke, Mr. Wills, the scientific assistant, and King and Gray, two subordinates, succeeded in reaching the Gulf of Carpentaria; but on their return route they suffered from want of provisions, and all perished except King. In 1862 Mr. M'Douall Stuart renewed his bold project of crossing the continent, and starting from Adelaide, arrived in Van Diemen's Bay, on the shore of the Indian Ocean, July 25th. Numerous other names might be added to this list; but we shall here concern ourselves only with that of Colonel Egerton Warburton, as one of the most eminent and successful of Australian explorers.

Peter Egerton Warburton was born in August, 1813. After passing through the usual examination in the East India Company's college at Addiscombe, he entered the Bombay army in 1834, and served in India until 1853, passing the greater part of the time in the Adjutant-General's Department, and rising through each grade until he attained his majority, and was appointed Deputy Adjutant-General at head-quarters. But, attracted by the prospects opened up to colonists in New Zealand, he resigned the service, intending to proceed thither with his wife and family. Eventually, circumstances led to his preferring South Australia as a field for his energies; and soon after his arrival at Adelaide he was selected to command the police force of the whole colony—an onerous post, which he held with distinction for thirteen years. He was afterwards made commandant of the volunteer forces of the colony of South Australia. In August, 1872, the South Australian Government resolved on despatching an expedition to explore the interior between Central Mount Stuart and the town of Perth, in West Australia, and chose Colonel Warburton as its leader. Afterwards, the Government drew back, and the cost of the expedition was eventually undertaken by two leading colonists, Messrs. Elder and Hughes, who authorized Colonel Warburton to organize such a party and prepare such an outfit as he considered necessary, and provided him with camels and horses. It was arranged that the party should muster at Beltana Station, the head-quarters of the camels; thence proceed to the Peake, lat. 28° S., one of the head-quarters of the inland telegraph; and, after a détour westward, make for Central Mount Stuart, where they would receive a reinforcement of camels, and, thus strengthened, would be able to cross the country unknown to Perth, the capital of Western Australia.

With his son Richard as second in command, Colonel Warburton left Adelaide on the 21st of September, 1872; reached Beltana Station on the 26th; and on the 21st of December arrived at Alice Springs (1120 miles from Adelaide), the starting-point of his journey westward. The party consisted of himself, his son, T. W. Lewis, two Afghan camel-drivers, Sahleh and Halleem, Denis White (cook and assistant camel-man), and Charley, a native lad. There were four riding and twelve baggage camels, besides one spare camel; the horses being left at Alice Springs. All needful preparations having been completed, the explorers quitted the station on the 15th of April, 1873, and turned their faces westward.

For the first five days not a drop of water was seen, and on the fifth, of the supply carried with them only one quart was left, which it was necessary to reserve for emergencies. When they encamped for the night, no fire was lighted, as without water they could not cook. Next day, the 20th, Lewis and the two Afghans were sent, with four camels, to refill the casks and water-bags at Hamilton Springs, about twenty-five miles distant. Meanwhile, a shower of rain descended; all the tarpaulins were quickly spread, and two or three buckets of water collected. What a change! All was now activity, cheerfulness, heartfelt thanksgiving. A cake and a pot of tea were soon in everybody's hands, and in due time Lewis returned with a full supply of water, to increase and partake in the general satisfaction.

Keeping still in a general westerly direction, they crossed extensive grassy plains, relieved occasionally by "scrub" or bushes, and coming here and there upon a spring or well. "The country to-day," writes Warburton, on one occasion, "has been beautiful, with parklike scenery and splendid grass." In the "creeks," as the water-courses are termed in Australia, they sometimes found a little water; more often, they were quite dry. "This is certainly," he writes, "a beautiful creek to look at. It must at times carry down an immense body of water, but there is none now on its surface, nor did its bed show spots favourable for retaining pools when the floods subsided." On the 9th of January they struck some glens of a picturesque character. At the entrance of the first a huge column of basalt had been hurled from a height of three hundred feet, and having fixed itself perpendicularly in the ground, stood like a sentry, keeping guard over a fair bright pool, which occupied the whole width of the glen's mouth—a pool about fifteen feet wide, fifty feet long, and enclosed by lofty and precipitous basaltic cliffs. At the entrance, the view does not extend beyond thirty yards; but, on accomplishing that distance, you find that the glen strikes off at a right angle, and embosoms another pool of deep clear water, circular in shape, and so roofed over by a single huge slab of basalt that the sun's rays can never reach it. There is a second glen, less grand, less rugged than the former, but more picturesque. At the head of it bubble and sparkle many springs and much running water.

The surrounding country was clothed with porcupine-grass (spinifex)—a sharp thorny kind of herbage, growing in tussocks of from eighteen inches to five feet in diameter. When quite young, its shoots are green; but as they mature they assume a yellow colour, and instead of brightening, deepen the desolate aspect of the wilderness. "It is quite uneatable even for camels, who are compelled to thread their way painfully through its mazes, never planting a foot on the stools, if they can possibly avoid it. To horses on more than one occasion it has proved most destructive, piercing and cutting their legs, which in a very short time become fly-blown, when the animals have either to be destroyed or abandoned. The spiny shoots are of all heights, from the little spike that wounds the fetlock to the longer blade that penetrates the hock. It is one of the most cheerless objects that an explorer can meet, and it is perhaps unnecessary to say that the country it loves to dwell in is utterly useless for pastoral purposes."

Coming to a range of granite, steep, bare, and smooth, Colonel Warburton clambered up its face on hands and knees, to find there a fine hole or basin in the rock, perfectly round and nearly full of water. This hole was, of course, the work of nature, and, strange to say, was on the point of a smooth projecting part of the rock, where it would have seemed impossible that any water could lodge. How it was wrought in such a place one cannot imagine, but the position was so prominent as to be visible from the plain at a considerable distance.

Another day the travellers fell in with a bees' hive;—unfortunately, it was empty. The Australian bee is stingless, and very little larger than our common house-fly, but its honey is remarkably sweet. The nest, or "sugar-bag," as the bushmen call it, is generally made in a hollow tree. They also saw some specimens of the crested dove—one of the loveliest of the Australian pigeons. In truth, it is hardly surpassed anywhere in chasteness of colouring and elegance of form, while its graceful crest greatly enhances the charm of its appearance. It frequently assembles in very large flocks, which, on visiting the lagoons or river banks for water, during the dry seasons, generally congregate on a single tree or even branch, perching side by side, and afterwards descending in a body to drink; so closely are they massed together while thus engaged, that dozens may be killed by a single discharge of a gun. Their flight is singularly swift; with a few quick flaps of the wings they gain the necessary impetus, and then sail forward without any apparent exertion.

The diamond-sparrow, or spotted pardalote, was also seen. This bird inhabits the whole of the southern parts of the Australian continent, from the western to the eastern border, and is very common in Tasmania. It is nearly always engaged in searching for insects among the foliage both of the tallest trees and the lowest shrubs, in the garden and orchard as in the open forest; and it displays in all its movements a remarkable activity, clinging about in every variety of position, both above and beneath the leaves, with equal facility. Its mode of nest-building differs from that of every other member of the genus to which it belongs. It first excavates, in some neighbouring bank, a hole just large enough to admit of the passage of its body, in a nearly horizontal direction, to the depth of two or three feet; at the end of this burrow or gallery, it forms a chamber; and in this chamber it deposits its nest, which is beautifully woven of strips of the inner bark of the Eucalypti, and lined with finer strips of the same or similar materials. In shape it is spherical, about four inches in diameter, with a lateral hole for an entrance. To prevent the ingress of rain the chamber is raised somewhat higher than the mouth of the hole. Mr. Gould, the Australian naturalist, speaks of these nests as very difficult to detect; they can be found, he says, only by watching for the ingress or egress of the parent birds, as the entrance is generally concealed by herbage or the overhanging roots of a tree. Why so neat a structure as the diamond-sparrow's nest should be constructed at the end of a gallery or tunnel, into which no light can possibly enter, is beyond comprehension; it is one of those wonderful results of instinct so often brought before us in the economy of the animal kingdom, without our being able to explain them. The diamond-sparrow rears two broods, of four or five each, in the course of the year. Its song or call is a rather harsh, piping note of two syllables, frequently repeated.

The great difficulty which besets the Australian explorer is the want of water. He travels day after day across open grassy plains, relieved by few variations of surface, except the sand ridges, to meet with neither spring nor watercourse. Sometimes he comes upon the native wells, but these, very frequently, are dry or almost dry; he digs well after well himself, but no water rises. Colonel Warburton's party suffered severely from this deficiency. They met with much trouble, moreover, through the straying of their camels. Thus, one evening, "Charley," who acted as camel-herd, reported that they had run away southward. He traced their tracks for several miles, and observed that one camel had broken its hobbles. [302] Halleem, the Afghan camel-driver, then mounted the Colonel's riding camel, "Hosee," and started in search of them at five o'clock on a Sunday evening. He was to push on for five or six miles, then camp for the night, and at dawn follow up the tracks vigorously, so as to overtake the truants, and return by mid-day.

Monday came, but Halleem and the camels came not with it. Sahleh, who had been exploring in the vicinity of the camp with a gun, returned in the evening with the startling information that he had seen Hosee's *return* track, coming near the camp, and then striking off in a north-easterly direction. Colonel Warburton now also learned for the first time that Halleem was occasionally subject to fits, and that while they lasted he knew not what he was doing or where he was going. It was evident that such a man ought not to have been trusted alone, and it became a question whether Halleem had lost his camel or his wits; the latter seemed more probable, as Hosee, if he had come near the other camels, would certainly have joined them.

Next day, Monday, July 22nd, the Colonel writes:—"I sent my son and Charley with a week's provisions on our back tracks, to try for Halleem first; but, in the event of not finding his *foot* tracks, to continue on, and endeavour to recover the camels. Lewis also went in the other direction, to run up Hosee's tracks; so that I hoped that by one or other of these means I should learn what had become of Halleem. Unfortunately, Lewis, supposing he had only a few hours' work, took neither food nor water. Now, 6 p.m., it is beginning to rain, and Lewis has not returned. I know he will stick to the tracks as long as he can, but I wish he were back; if Halleem be demented, he may urge the camel on sixty or seventy miles without stopping, and thus get a start in his mad career that will make it impossible for Lewis to help him.

"23rd. It has rained lightly all night. Lewis is still absent; I am greatly grieved at his having nothing to eat.

"1 p.m. Lewis returned; he had camped with Richard, and so was all right.

"It appears from his report that Sahleh, whilst out 'birding,' must have stumbled upon a mare's nest, for Lewis soon abandoned the track he started on, and turned after Richard to find Halleem's first camp. They did not find this, but they fell on his tracks of next day, steadily following the runaway camels; it is clear, therefore, that Sahleh has done his countryman some injustice, and caused much unnecessary alarm. . . . Richard returned, having seen Halleem, and promised to take out provisions to meet him on his return.

"26th. Sahleh shot an emu (*Dromaius Novoe Hollandicæ*), a welcome addition to our larder. Every scrap of this bird was eaten up, except the feathers. The liver is a great delicacy, and the flesh by no means unpalatable.

"27th and 28th. Sent provisions to Ethel Creek for Halleem.

"29th. The camel-hunters returned in the evening, but without the camels. This is a double loss; the camels are gone, and so is our time; our means of locomotion are much reduced, whilst the necessity of getting on is greatly increased. Halleem has, however, done all he could do; he followed the camels nearly one hundred miles, but as they travelled night and day, whilst he could only track them by day, he never could have overtaken them. No doubt these animals will go back to Beltana, where alarm will be created as soon as they are recognized as belonging to our party."

Such is the Colonel's simple, unaffected account of what was really an annoying and perplexing incident.

At this date (July 29th) the explorers had accomplished seventeen hundred miles. The country continued to present the same general features—plains yellow with porcupine-grass, alternating with low hills of sand; but as they advanced, the sand-hills became more numerous, and among them lay numerous half-dry salt lagoons of a particularly cheerless aspect. Dense spinifex—high, steep sand-ridges, with timber in the flats, and nothing for the camels to eat but low scrubby bushes;—that horses should cross such a region is obviously impossible. The want of water again became urgent. From the burnt ground clouds of dust and sand were thrown up by the wind, almost choking the travellers, and intensifying their thirst. They were temporarily relieved by coming upon a native well. But the country still wore the same cheerless aspect of inhospitality; the desolate arid plain extended in every region—a desert of sand, which wearied the travellers by its monotony. Even when they arrived at the so-called basaltic hills, there was no water, no sign of green and pleasant vegetation. It was quite an excitement when, for the first time, they descried some flock-pigeons. The birds were very wild, and they could kill only three or four, but they were excellent eating, and made quite a dainty dish. Soon after this cheerful episode, Lewis, who had been sent on a short excursion south in quest of water, returned with intelligence of an Eden oasis which he had discovered in the wilderness. A beautiful clump of large gum trees flourished at the bottom of a small creek, which was hemmed in by a high sand-hill, and afterwards broke through a rocky ridge sprinkled with fine, clear, deep water-holes, one hundred feet in circumference. The rich green foliage of the gum trees contrasted vividly with the red sand-hills on either side, and the bare rocky barrier in front. To this delightful spot of greenery, bustard, bronze-wing pigeons, owls, and other birds resorted.

Colonel Warburton, however, was averse to retrace his steps, even to enjoy a halt in such an "earthly paradise;" and, pushing forward, was rewarded for his persistency by discovering a fine large lake of fresh water, haunted by ducks, flock-pigeons, and parrots. He halted on its borders for a couple of days.

Of the bronze-wing pigeon, to which allusion has just been made, it may be affirmed that it prevails in every part of Australia. In some individuals the forehead is brown, in others buff white; the crown of the head and occiput, dark brown, shading into plum colour; sides of the neck, grey; upper surface of the body, brown, each feather edged with tawny brown; wings, brown, with an oblong spot of lustrous bronze on the coverts; the tail feathers, deep grey, with a black band near the tip, except the two central, which are brown; under surface of the wing, ferruginous; breast, deep wine-colour, passing into grey on the under parts; bill, blackish grey; legs and feet, carmine red. It is a plump, heavy bird, and, when in good condition, weighs nearly a pound. Its favourite haunts are the dry hot plains, among the bushes or "scrub." Its speed is very surprising; in an incredibly short time it traverses a great expanse of country. Before sunrise it may be seen in full flight across the plain, directing its course towards the creeks, where it quenches its thirst. The traveller who knows its habits can, by observing it, determine, even in the most arid places, whether water is near at hand; if he descry it wending its way from all quarters towards a given point, he may rest assured that there he will obtain the welcome draught he seeks. Mr. Gould says that it feeds entirely upon the ground, where it finds the varieties of leguminous seeds that constitute its food. It breeds during August and the four following months, that is, in the Australian spring and summer, and often rears two or more broods. Its nest is a frail structure of small twigs, rather hollow in form; and is generally placed on the horizontal branch of an apple or gum tree, near the ground. On one occasion, Mr. Gould, during a long drought, was encamped at the northern extremity of the Brezi range, where he had daily opportunities of observing the arrival of the bronze-wing to drink. The only water for miles around lay in the vicinity of his tent, though that was merely the scanty supply left in a few small rocky basins by the rains of many months before. Hence, he enjoyed an excellent opportunity for observing not only the bronze-wing, but all the other birds of the neighbourhood. Few, if any, of the true insectivorous or fissirostral birds came to the water-holes; but, on the other hand, the species that live upon grain and seeds, particularly the parrots and honey-eaters (*Trichoglossi* and *Meliphagi*), rushed down incessantly to the margins of the pools, heedless of the naturalist's presence, their sense of peril vanquished temporarily by their sense of thirst. The bronze-wing, however, seldom appeared during the heat of the day; it was at sunset that, with the swiftness of an arrow, it rushed towards the watering-place. It did not descend at once, says Mr. Gould, to the brink of the pool, but dashed down upon the ground at about ten yards' distance, remained quiet for a while until satisfied of its safety, and then leisurely walked to the water. After deep and frequent draughts, it retired, winging its way towards its secluded nest.

Just before reaching the lake, the Colonel's party made a capture, a young native woman; and they detained her in order that she might guide them to the native wells. On the 1st of September, however, she effected her escape by gnawing through a thick hair-rope, with which she had been fastened to a tree.

Spinifex and sand resumed their predominance as the travellers left the lake behind them. The heat was very great, and crossing the hot sand and the steep hills was trying work. On the 12th, they rejoiced in the discovery of some excellent wells. Then again came spinifex and sand-hills. These troublesome ridges varied considerably in height and in distance from one another; but their elevation seldom exceeded eighty feet, and the space between them was not often more than three hundred yards. They lay parallel to one another, running from east to west; so that while going either eastward or westward the travellers could keep in the intervening hollows, and travel with comparative facility, but when compelled to cross them at a great angle, the feet of the camels ploughed deep in the sand, and the strain upon the poor animals was terrible. Yet the Australian waste is, after all, less wearisome than the sandy deserts of Nubia or the great Sahara; it is sadly deficient in water, but the sand-hills disguise their inhospitality with many varieties of shrubs and flowers, as well as with acacias and gum trees. The shrubs are not edible, and the trees are of no value as timber, but they serve to hide the nakedness of the land.

A grave danger beset them on the 15th. Their master bull (or male) camel had eaten poison, and fell ill; he was of immense value to the travellers, not only on account of his great strength, but because without his help it would be almost impossible to keep the young bulls in order, and they might elope with all the ewe (or female) camels. They administered to him a bottle of mustard in a quart of water—the only available medicine—but without any beneficial effect. In every herd of camels, it is necessary to explain, is found a master bull, who, by his strength, preserves order among his young brethren. These gay cavaliers are always desirous of a harem to themselves; and, if allowed an opportunity, would cut off three or four cows from the herd, and at full speed drive them for hundreds of miles. They are quiet only while under subjection to the master bull, and become intractable if, through illness or accident, his supremacy should be relaxed. Colonel Warburton was surprised at the marvellous instinct of the young bulls in his little camel harem; they knew that their master was ailing almost before the camel-men did, and at once showed signs of insubordination, so that it was necessary to watch them by night and to knee-halter them.

The old camel did not improve, and on the 16th the Colonel was compelled to abandon him. Three misfortunes followed: on the 17th two riding camels were taken ill, having been struck in the loins by the night wind; and on the 18th the same fate befell Richard Warburton's riding camel. Thus, in three days the travellers lost four camels. They endeavoured to make some profit out of the misadventure by "curing" a quantity of camel-meat. The inner portions of the animal were first eaten—not the liver and other dainty parts only, but the whole; every single scrap was carefully consumed, not a shred was wasted. Then, head, feet, hide, tail, all went into the boiling pot. Even the very bones were stewed down, for soup first, and afterwards for the sake of the marrow they contained. The flesh was cut into thin flat strips, and hung upon the bushes for three days to be dried by the sun. The tough thick hide was cut up and parboiled, the coarse hair scraped off with a knife, and the leathery substance replaced in the pot and stewed until, both as to flavour and savour, it bore a disagreeable resemblance to the inside of a carpenter's glue-pot. As may be supposed, such a dish as this was not so nutritious as the roast beef (or mutton) of Old England; but it stifled for a while the cry of an empty stomach. The attack next fell upon the head, which was speedily reduced to a polished skull. As for the foot, like cow-heel or sheep's trotters, it was looked upon as a delicacy, and its preparation was a marvel of culinary skill. First, a good fire was lighted, and allowed to burn down to bright red embers, while the foot, severed at the hock, was scraped and singed as thoroughly as time permitted. The foot was thrust into the glowing coals, burnt for some considerable time, removed, placed on its side on the ground, and deprived of its tough horny sole. After this elaborate series of operations, the reader will doubtless suppose that the delicacy is fit for the table. Not a bit of it! It must be placed in a bucket of water, and kept steadily boiling for six and thirty hours; then, and then only, may it be served up. On the whole, we should not consider it a dish for a hungry man.

The 21st of September was the anniversary of their departure from Adelaide. Two of the party went out on camels to search for water, and two, in a different direction, on foot. As they had only two riding camels left, and these in a weak condition, they threw away their tents, and most of their private property, retaining only their guns and ammunition, and clothing enough for decency. Happily, one of the reconnoitring parties found a well, to which the travellers at once proceeded, and watered the thirsty, weary camels.

After a three days' halt they resumed their advance, but moved very slowly. They were sick and feeble, and the country was difficult to traverse. Another camel had to be abandoned; so that out of seventeen animals, only eight remained. A plague of insects was added to their troubles. Not only did clouds of common flies buzz and worry around them, and legions of ants assail them, but the Australian bee, or honey-fly, tormented them by its pertinacious adhesion to their persons—an unwelcome adhesion, as it is famed for its intolerable smell. To get water they were again compelled to wander from the direct route, and at one time they descended as far south as lat. 20° 2'. Hence they began to suffer from want of provisions, and a grim alternative faced them: if they pressed forward, they ran the chance of losing their camels and dying of thirst; if they halted, they could hope only to prolong their lives on sun-dried camel flesh.

On the 3rd of October their condition was critical. The improvident Afghans, having consumed all their flour and meat, had to be supplied from the scanty rations of the white men, and Colonel Warburton resolved that if water were but once more found, so that he might not be compelled to retrace his steps, he would at all risks push forward to the river Oakover. Another riding camel broke down, and was killed for meat. A well was discovered, but the supply of water was so small that only one bucketful could be obtained in three hours, and on the second day it ran dry. On the 8th, having slightly recruited their animals, the undaunted travellers again moved forward; but one of the camels was still so feeble that Colonel Warburton and his son took it in turns to walk. The Colonel had the first stage, and, owing to stoppages from loads slipping off at the sand-hills, he soon struck ahead of the camels. Suddenly, hearing a noise behind him, he turned;—nine armed blacks were rushing full upon him! He halted to confront them, and they too stopped, at fifteen yards apart; two of them, in bravado, poised their spears, but, on his advancing pistol in hand, immediately lowered them, and a parley followed, in which, however, as neither understood the other's language, there was very little edification.

The blacks were all chattering round him, when he heard a shot, as he supposed, on his "right front." In reality it was fired from quite an opposite direction; but he was unwilling to answer the signal, because he did not wish to lose one of the three charges of his pistol. Moreover, the natives might have supposed that the single discharge had exhausted his resources, and have made an attack upon him. He accompanied them to their camp, and got a little water. The women and children would not approach him, but, thanks to his grey beard, the men similarly equipped welcomed him readily. There was a general passing of hands over each other's beards—a sign of friendship, it is to be presumed; for, after this little ceremony, the intercourse was conducted on the most amicable terms. Eventually the Colonel resumed his walk across the hot glaring sand-hills, until he thought he had covered the required distance, and that the camels would soon overtake him; then he stopped, lighted a fire, smoked a pipe, and would have indulged in a short nap, had the ants been agreeable. Finding that sleep was impossible, he resolved on returning to the camp of the blacks for some more water; but, at that moment, his son and Lewis arrived with Charley, who had followed up his tracks, and he found that he must retrace his steps, having gone astray. Exhausted by heat, hunger, and fatigue, he could scarcely stagger along; but his companions supported his tottering feet, and in the evening he reached their encampment.

A good supply of water had been discovered, and, notwithstanding the alarming scarcity of provisions, it was indispensable that they should halt by it for some days, in order to give the camels an opportunity of partially recovering their strength. Without them the explorers could hardly hope to cross the wide and weary wilderness in which they were involved. Their rapidly diminishing store of food they endeavoured to eke out by killing such feathered spoil as came within their range—Gular parrots, and bronze-wing and top-knot pigeons—and by a mess of boiled salt-plant (*Salicornia*). On the 14th they resumed their weary march.

An entry or two from Colonel Warburton's journal will afford a vivid idea of his distressed condition at this period:—

"19th. This is Sunday. How unlike one at home! Half a quart of flour and water at four a.m.; a hard, sinewy bit of raw, that is, sun-dried, but uncooked, camel-meat for dinner at two p.m.; supper uncertain, perhaps some roasted acacia seeds: this is our bill of fare. These seeds are not bad, but very small and very hard; they are on bushes, not trees, and the natives use them roasted and pounded.

"20th. Got a pigeon; and some flour and water for breakfast. We can only allow ourselves a spoonful of flour each at a time, and it won't last many days even at this rate.

"Killed a large camel for food at sunset. We would rather have killed a worse one, but this bull had, in the early part of our journey, got a very bad back, and was unable to work for a long time. . . .

"21st. Cutting up and jerking camel-meat. The inside has given us a good supper and breakfast. This is a much better beast than the old, worn-out cow we killed before, and we have utilized every scrap, having had a sharp lesson as to the value of anything we can masticate. . . .

"25th. All the camel-meat has been successfully jerked, and we have lived since the 20th on bone-broth and gristle. The birds were getting shy, so when we killed the camel we gave them a rest; to-day we go at them again. I hope the water-searchers will return this evening; our prospects are not very bright under any circumstances, but if we get water anywhere between south and west we shall have a prospect of overcoming the difficulties and dangers that threaten us. . . .

"29th. A short rain squall passed over us last evening; it has cooled the ground a little. Economy is, of course, the order of the day in provisions. My son and I have managed to hoard up about one pound of flour and a pinch of tea; all our sugar is gone. Now and then we afford ourselves a couple of spoonfuls of flour, made into paste. When we indulge in tea the leaves are boiled twice over. I eat my sun-dried camel-meat uncooked, as far as I can bite it; what I cannot bite goes into the quart pot, and is boiled down to a sort of poor-house broth. When we get a bird we dare not clean it, lest we should lose anything.

"More disasters this morning. One of our largest camels very ill; the only thing we could do for it was to pound four boxes of Holloway's pills, and drench the animal. . . . One of the Afghans apparently wrong in his head. . . . In the evening the camel was still very sick."

The animal, however, was better on the following day, and the expedition again toiled onward across the sands. Very troublesome were the ants, which seemed to have undertaken a deliberate campaign against the much-suffering travellers. They were small black ants, and in such numbers that a stamp of the foot on the ground started them in thousands. When the wearied men flung themselves down in the shade of a bush to obtain the solace of half an hour's sleep, these pestilent persecutors attacked them, making their way through their scanty clothing, and dealing sharp painful nips with their strong mandibles.

On the evening of the 1st of November, they began their "rush" or forced march for the Oakover river, and across the wearisome sand-hills actually accomplished five and twenty miles. Colonel Warburton then felt unable to continue the journey, thirst, famine, and fatigue having reduced him to a skeleton, while such was his weakness that he could scarcely rise from the ground, or when up, stagger half a dozen steps forward. "Charley" had been absent all day, and when he did not return at sunset, much alarm was felt about him. The Colonel knew not what to do. Delay meant ruin to them all, considering their want of food and water; yet to leave the camp without the Colonel seemed inhuman, as it was dooming him to certain death. Until nine o'clock in the evening they waited. Then a start was made, but before they had gone eight miles, the poor lad joined them. Notwithstanding the fatigue of the previous night's travelling, the lad had actually walked about twenty miles; he had fallen in with a large party of natives, and accompanied them to their water. "It may, I think, be admitted," says Colonel Warburton, "that the hand of Providence was distinctly visible in this instance."—Is it not in *every* instance?—"I had deferred starting until nine p.m., to give the absent boy the chance of regaining the camp. It turned out afterwards that if we had expedited our departure by ten minutes, or postponed it for the same length of time,

Charley would have crossed us; and had this happened, there is little doubt that not only myself, but probably other members of the expedition, would have perished from thirst. The route pursued by us was at right angles with the course pursued by the boy, and the chances of our stumbling up against each other in the dark were infinitesimally small. Providence mercifully ordered it otherwise, and our departure was so timed that, after travelling from two to two hours and a half, when all hope of the recovery of the wanderer was almost abandoned, I was gladdened by the 'cooee' of the brave lad, whose keen ears had caught the sound of the bells attached to the camels' necks. To the energy and courage of this untutored native may, under the guidance of the Almighty, be attributed the salvation of the party. It was by no accident that he encountered the friendly well. For fourteen miles he followed up the tracks of some blacks, though fatigued by a day of severe work, and, receiving a kindly welcome from the natives, he had hurried back, unmindful of his own exhausted condition, to apprise his companions of the important discovery he had made."

At the native camp, Colonel Warburton's party obtained some kangaroo meat, and a good supply of fresh water. They rested for twenty-four hours, and the repose and the food together temporarily reinvigorated them. At this time their position was lat. 20° 41', and long. 122° 30'; so that they were only three days' journey from the Oakover. Forward they went, the country still presenting the two main features of sand and spinifex; forward they went, over the cheerless, monotonous plains, broken by sand ridges; growing weaker every day, but losing not one jot of hope or resolution. The annals of travel present few examples of more heroic tenacity and persistent purpose; few records of suffering more patiently borne, or of obstacles more steadfastly overcome. The highest energy, perseverance, and fortitude were necessary to the leader of an exploring expedition through so forlorn a wilderness, and these were never wanting on the part of Colonel Warburton, whose name, amongst the pioneers of civilization in Australia, must always be held in honour.

On the 11th of November, the seven members of the expedition were living wholly on sun-dried strips of meat, as devoid of nutriment as they were of taste; and as these were almost exhausted, they had to consider the probability of having to sacrifice another camel. They had no salt—a terrible deprivation; no flour, tea, or sugar. Next day, they were surrounded by sand-hills, and no water was visible anywhere. It was certain that, unless some providentially opportune help arrived, they could not live more than twenty-four hours; for the burning heat and the terrible country could not be endured without water. Not a snake, kite, or crow could they discover; one little bird, the size of a sparrow, was all that their guns could procure. Writing in his journal, the Colonel calmly says:—"We have tried to do our duty, and have been disappointed in all our expectations. I have been in excellent health during the whole journey, and am so still, being merely worn out from want of food and water. Let no self-reproaches afflict any one respecting me. I undertook the journey for the benefit of my family, and was quite equal to it under all the circumstances that could reasonably be anticipated, but difficulties and losses have come upon us so thickly for the last few months that we have not been able to move; thus our provisions are gone, but this would not have stopped us could we have found water without such laborious search. The country is terrible. I do not believe men ever traversed so vast an extent of continuous desert."

Early on the 14th Charley sighted in the distance a native camp, and while the remainder of the party, with the camels, kept out of sight, he advanced alone towards it. The blacks received him kindly and gave him water, but when he "cooed" for the party to come up, they seem to have thought he had entrapped them, and instantly speared him in the back and arm, cut his skull with a tomahawk, and nearly broke his jaw. After perpetrating this cruelty, they fled ignominiously. Colonel Warburton took possession of the fire they had kindled, and rejoiced at obtaining water. Charley's wounds were serious, but they were bound up as carefully as circumstances permitted, and it is satisfactory to state that he recovered from them. Another camel was killed, and Charley was nursed upon soup. This supply of meat enabled the expedition to continue its march towards the Oakover, which receded apparently as they advanced; and they toiled onward painfully, with the hot sun and hot wind exhausting their small resource of energy, the ants tormenting them at night, the sand and spinifex oppressing them by their monotony. On the 25th, to save themselves from starvation, they killed another camel, and all hands were employed in cutting up and jerking the meat. At last, on the 4th of December, they camped on a rocky creek, tributary to the Oakover, and were able to take leave of the dreadful desert which had so long hemmed them in on every side. Their spirits revived, for there was no longer a scarcity of water and they hoped that the river would supply them with the means of subsistence.

But they had soon reason to feel that their difficulties were not all at an end. It was pleasant to look on the beautiful trees and profuse vegetation of the creek, but the charms of nature will not satisfy stomachs that have had no food for two days. So, on the evening of the 6th, a third camel was killed. Next day a few small fish were caught; they were greatly relished, and proved of real benefit. The 8th was happily marked by another banquet of fish; but as they had no net or fishing apparatus, it was by no means easy work to catch them. Still, the travellers did not grow stronger; want of rest and of wholesome food, and the strain of continuous exertion and anxiety for so long a period, had undermined the whole system, and they could not rally.

On the 11th they struck the Oakover in lat. 21° 11' 23". This must be a noble river, writes the Colonel, when the floods come down. The bed is wide and gravelly, fringed with magnificent cajeput or paper-bark trees. How grateful was its lovely and shady refuge from the hot fierce sun after the terrible sand-hills among which the travellers had wandered so long!

On the 13th Lewis and an Afghan driver, on the only two camels that could travel, were sent forward to search for the station of Messrs. Harper and Co., and procure some help both in food and carriage. During his absence the Colonel and his companions lived, to use an expressive phrase, from hand to mouth. They could not get the fish to bite; but one day Richard Warburton shot a teal, and they rescued from the talons of a hawk a fine black duck, which supplied them with a splendid dinner. They were compelled, however, to fall back upon their last camel, though he was so lean and worn-out that he did not cut up well. On the 23rd they rejoiced in the capture of a couple of wood-ducks, and they also secured a little honey—a delightful novelty for persons who for many weeks had been deprived of the strengthening and useful properties of sugar. Still, these occasional "tidbits" could not supply the want of regular and nutritious food; and all the travellers could hope for was to stave off actual famine. Day after day passed by, and Lewis did not return. Colonel Warburton had calculated that he would be absent about fourteen days; but the seventeenth came, and yet there was no sign of Lewis. Writing in his journal, Colonel Warburton, on December 20th, sums up his position in a few pithy and pregnant sentences:—"We have abundance of water, a little tobacco, and a few bits of dried camel. Occasionally an iguana or a cockatoo enlivens our fare; and, lastly, I hope the late rain will bring up some thistles or some pig-weed that we can eat. Our difficulties are, to make our meat last, though, so far from doing us good, we are all afflicted with scurvy, diarrhoea, and affection of the kidneys from the use of it. We cannot catch the fish; we cannot find opossums or snakes; the birds won't sit down by us, and we can't get up to go to them. We thought we should have no difficulty in feeding ourselves on the river, but it turns out that, from one cause or another, we can get very little, and we are daily dropping down a peg or two lower." But a few hours after making this entry, the Colonel's long period of suffering and anxiety was at an end. He and his son were lying down near the little hut of boughs which they had constructed as a shelter, and listlessly eyeing the boy Charley, who had climbed a tree to look for honey, when they were startled by his cry—whether a yell of pain or shout of joy, it was impossible to determine. But in a moment the cause of his emotion was satisfactorily explained; out from the thick brushwood trotted a string of six horses, driven by the gallant Mr. Lewis, accompanied by another white man from a station on the De Grey river. They brought an ample supply of nutritious food, and on the following day some additional stores came up on camels. Mr. Lewis's apparent delay was soon explained; the station, which belonged to Messrs. Grant, Harper, and Anderson, was one hundred and seventy miles distant.

On the 3rd of January Colonel Warburton started down the river. For the first few days he had to be lifted on his horse's back, but with good food and moderate exercise he regained something of his old strength, and the journey to the station was accomplished in a week and a day. Ten days were then given to rest under the hospitable roof of Messrs. Grant, and on the 21st he started for Roebourne, one hundred and seventy miles further, arriving there on the 26th. His after stages were Lepack, Fremantle, Perth, Albany. At Glenelg, in South Australia, the Colonel and his companions arrived on Easter Sunday, having travelled by land four thousand miles, and by sea two thousand miles.

The casualties are quickly recorded: the Colonel lost the sight of one eye, and his son's health was seriously shaken. Out of seventeen camels, only two arrived safely at the station on the De Grey river.

It is almost needless to say that everywhere in West Australia Colonel Warburton was received with the public honours due to a man who has courageously and successfully accomplished a work of equal difficulty and danger. He was entertained in the most generous and cordial manner, and the high utility of his labours was liberally acknowledged. On his return to South Australia he met, of course, with an enthusiastic welcome. A great banquet was given to the explorers, and the Legislative Assembly voted the sum of £1000 to the leader, and £500 to be divided among the subordinates. In 1874 the Royal Geographical Society of London conferred upon him its gold medal, and a few months later the Queen appointed him a Companion of the Order of St. Michael and St. George.

Here closes a simple but stirring narrative, of which it is not, perhaps, too much to say, as has been said, that scarcely has a record of terrible suffering more nobly borne been given to the world. Hunger and thirst, intense physical exhaustion, the burning heat of a tropic sun, the glowing sands of an arid desert—not a single circumstance was wanting that could test the heroic endurance and patient heroism of the explorers. The country through which they toiled day after day was barren, inhospitable, desolate; a wilderness of coarse yellow herbage, a sombre waste of sand-hills. Their hearts were never cheered by bright glimpses of gorgeous scenery, of forests clothed with magnificent vegetation, of rivers pouring their ample waters through sylvan valleys; everywhere the landscape was melancholy and unprofitable. He who, with his life in his hand, penetrates the frozen recesses of the Polar World, and dares its storms of snow and its icy winds, has at least the inspiration to support him that springs from the grandeur of huge cliffs of ice and vast glaciers and white-gleaming peaks outlined against a deep blue sky. But in the wide Australian interior the landscape is always marked by the same monotony of dreariness, the same uniformity of gloom; and it tests and taxes the traveller's energies to rise superior to its depressing influences.

The reader, therefore, will feel that "the Municipal Council and inhabitants of Fremantle" used no language of undeserved eulogy when, in their address of welcome to Colonel Egerton Warburton, they said—

"The difficulties to be overcome in the work of Australian exploration are acknowledged to be as formidable as are to be found in any part of our globe, and to meet these difficulties requires a combination of intelligence, energy, perseverance, and fortitude that few men possess; and the fact that you have surmounted all obstacles, and borne up under so many privations, has awakened in all our minds the deepest feelings of gratitude and admiration." [324]

MAJOR BURNABY,
AND A RIDE TO KHIVA.

I.

THAT vast and various region of sandy deserts and fertile valleys, of broad open plains and lofty highlands, which extends eastward from the Caspian Sea to the borders of Afghanistan, and from Persia northward to the confines of Siberia, is known to geographers by the name of Turkistan, or "the country of the Turks." Across it, from north to south, strikes the massive chain of the Bolor-tagh, dividing it into two unequal portions. The western division is popularly known as Independent Tartary, or Great Bokhara; it covers an area of nearly 900,000 square miles—that is, it is ten times as large as Great Britain—and it consists of the arid sandy plain of the Caspian and Aral Seas, and of the hilly districts which skirt the ranges of the Bolor-Tagh, the Thian-Shan, and the Hindu Kush. The eastern division, or Upper Tartary, probably contains 700,000 square miles, and extends from Asiatic Russia on the north to Thibet and Kashmir on the south, from Mongolia on the east to the Bolor-Tagh on the west. The Thian-Shan separates its two provinces, which the Chinese call Thian-Shan-Pe-lû and Thian-Shan-Nan-lû. The reader's attention, however, will be here directed only to Western Turkistan, which is divided into the Khanates of Khokan (north-east), Badakshan (south-east), Bokhara (east), and Khiva (west). To the north stretch the steppes of the nomadic Kirghiz; to the south the hills and dales are occupied by the hordes of the Turkomans. Its two great rivers are the Amu-Daria and the Syr-Daria, the ancient *Oxus* and *Jaxartes*,—the former traversing the centre, and the latter the south of the district, on their way to the great Arabian Sea; and the valleys through which they flow, as well as those of their tributary streams, are mostly fertile and pleasant. As might be inferred from the character of the country, the chief resources of the population are the breeding of domestic animals, and the cultivation of the soil; but in the towns of Khokand, Bokhara, Urgondji, and Karshi, a brisk manufacturing industry flourishes, which disposes of its surplus produce, after the local demand is satisfied, to the merchants of Russia, Persia, India, and China.

Since 1864, the supremacy of Russia has been steadily advancing in Western Turkistan. In ordinary circumstances, the extension of the power of a civilized nation over a number of semi-barbarous states, constantly engaged in internecine warfare, is regarded as a just and legitimate movement, or, at all events, as one that is inevitable and calls for no expression of regret; but the eastward progress of Russia has long been considered, by a large party in England, as a menace to the safety of our Indian empire. Every fresh step of the Russian armies has therefore excited alarm or created suspicion among those who are known as Russophobists. How far their fear or their mistrust is justifiable or dignified it is not our business in these pages to inquire; but it has been necessary to allude to it because it was this Russophobism which impelled Major (then Captain) Burnaby to undertake the difficult, if not dangerous, task of visiting Western Turkistan, that he might see with his own eyes what the Russians were doing there. The Russians had recently conquered Khokand and Khiva; it was thought they were preparing for further annexations; and Major Burnaby determined on an effort to reach Khiva, which during the Russian campaign had been visited, as we have seen, by Mr. MacGahan, the war correspondent of the *New York Herald*. Having obtained leave of absence from his regiment, the Royal Horse Guards, Major Burnaby rapidly equipped himself for his adventurous journey. He was well aware that the Russian authorities did not welcome the inquisitive eyes of English travellers, and that from them he could expect no assistance. His confidence in his resources, however, was great; he felt *totus in se ipso*; and he did not intend to be baffled in his object by anything but sheer force. The climate was another difficulty. The cold of the Kirghiz desert is a thing unknown in any other part of the world, even in the Arctic wastes and wildernesses; and he would have to traverse on horseback an enormous expanse of flat country, extending for hundreds of miles, and devoid of everything save snow and salt-lakes, and here and there the species of bramble-tree called saxaul. The inhabitants of Western Europe can form no conception of the force of the winds in Turkistan. They grumble at the pungent, irritating east; but they little imagine what it is like in countries exposed to the awful vehemence of its first onset, before its rigour has been mitigated by the kindly ocean, and where its wild career is unimpeded by trees or rising land, by hills or mountains. Uninterruptedly it blows over dreary leagues of snow and salt, absorbing the saline matter, and blighting or almost gashing the faces of those unfortunates who are exposed to its fury. But no fear of the east wind prevailed over Major Burnaby's patriotic curiosity. He provided against it as best he could: warm were the garments specially made for him; his boots were lined with fur; his hose were the thickest Scottish fishing stockings; his jerseys and flannel shirts of the thickest possible texture; and he ordered for himself a waterproof and airproof sleeping-bag, seven feet and a half long, and two feet round. A large aperture was left on one side, so that the traveller might take up his quarters in the interior, and sleep well protected from the wintry blasts. For defensive purposes he took with him his rifle, a revolver, cartridges, and ball. His cooking apparatus consisted of a couple of soldier's messtins. A trooper's hold-all, with its accompanying knife, fork, and spoon, completed his kit; and, by way of instruments, he carried a thermometer, a barometer, and a pocket sextant.

On the 30th of November, 1875, Major Burnaby left London. He arrived at St. Petersburg on the 3rd of December, and immediately set to work to obtain the necessary authorization for his proposed journey, which he defined as a tour to India *viâ* Khiva, Merv, and Kabul; in other words, across Central Asia and Afghanistan. All that he *did* obtain was a communication to the effect that the commandants in Russian Asia had received orders to assist him in travelling through the territory under their command, but that the Imperial Government could not acquiesce in his extending his journey beyond its boundaries, as it could not answer for the security or the lives of travellers except within the Emperor's dominions— a self-evident fact. The reply was evidently intended to discourage Major Burnaby; but Major Burnaby was not to be discouraged. It is not in the English character to be daunted by a consideration of prospective or possible dangers; certainly, it is not in the character of English officers. So the adventurous guardsman started by railway for Orenburg, the great centre and depôt of Central Asiatic traffic. At Riajsk he obtained a vivid illustration of the heterogeneous character of the Russian empire, the waiting-room being crowded with representatives of different nationalities. Here stalked a Tartar merchant in a long parti-coloured gown, a pair of high boots, and a small yellow fez. There a fur trader, in a greasy-looking black coat, clutched his small leather bag of coin. Here an old Bokharan, in flowing robes, was lulled by opium into a temporary forgetfulness of his troubles. There Russian peasants moved to and fro, with well-knit frames, clad in untanned leather, which was bound about their loins by narrow leather belts, studded with buttons of brass and silver. Europe and Asia met together in the waiting-room at Riajsk station.

The railway went no further than Sizeran, where Major Burnaby and a Russian gentleman hired a troika, or three-horse sleigh, to take them to Samara. The distance was about eighty-five miles; but as the thermometer marked 20° below zero (R.), the travellers found it necessary to make formidable preparations. First they donned three pairs of the thickest stockings, drawn up high above the knee; next, over these, a pair of fur-lined low shoes, which in their turn were inserted into leather goloshes; and, finally, over all, a pair of enormously thick boots. Allow for extra thick drawers and a pair of massive trousers; and add a heavy flannel under-shirt, a shirt covered by a thick wadded waistcoat and coat, and an external wrap in the form of a large shuba, or fur pelisse, reaching to the heels; and you may suppose that the protection against the cold was tolerably complete. The head was guarded with a fur cap and vashlik, *i.e.* a kind of conical cloth headpiece made to cover the cap, and having two long ends tied round the throat. Thus accoutred, the travellers took their places in the troika, which, drawn by three horses harnessed abreast, and with jingling bell, rapidly descended the hill, and dashed on to the frozen surface of the river Volga. Along the solid highway furnished by the ice-bound stream, past frozen-in shipping and sledges loaded with various kinds of wares, sped the troika; sometimes, in its turn, outstripped by other troikas,— drivers and passengers all alike white with glittering hoar-frost, until they seemed a company of grey-beards. The solid river flashed like a burnished cuirass in the rays of the morning. Here the scene was varied by a group of strangely patterned blocks and pillars; there a fountain gracefully shooting upwards with shapely Ionic and Doric columns, reflected a myriad prismatic hues from its diamond-like stalactites. Here a broken Gothic arch overhung the shining highway; there an Egyptian obelisk lay half buried beneath the snow. Such were the fantastic shapes into which the strong wind had moulded the ice as it was rapidly formed.

Regaining the main road, Major Burnaby and his companion sped on towards Samara. Their first halting-place was a farmhouse, called Nijny Pegersky Hootor, twenty-five versts from Sizeran, where some men were winnowing corn after a fashion of antediluvian simplicity. Throwing the corn high up into the air with a shovel, they allowed the wind to blow away the husks, and the grain fell upon a carpet laid out to catch it. As for the farmhouse, it was a square wooden building, containing two low but spacious rooms. A large stove of dried clay was so placed as to warm both apartments; and above it, a platform of boards, not more than three feet from the ceiling, supplied the family with sleeping accommodation. On the outside of the building a heavy wooden door opened into a small portico, at one end of which stood the obraz, or image—as usual an appendage to a Russian house, as were the Lares and Penates, or household gods, to a Roman house. The obrazye are made of different patterns, but usually represent a saint or the Trinity; they are executed in silver-gilt on brass relief, and adorned with all kinds of gewgaws.

A fresh team having been obtained, the travellers resumed their journey; but the cold had increased, the wind blew more furiously, and their suffering was severe. In thick flakes fell the constant snow, and the driver had much ado to keep the track, while the half-fed horses floundered along heavily, and frequently sank up to the traces in the gathering drift. The cracks of the whip resounded from their jaded flanks like pistol-shots. With sarcastic apostrophes the driver endeavoured to stimulate their progress:—

"Oh, sons of animals!" (whack!)

"Oh, spoiled one!" (whack!) This to a poor, attenuated brute.

"Oh, woolly ones!" (whack, whack, whack!) Here all were upset into a snow-drift, the sleigh being three-parts overturned, and the driver flung in an opposite direction.

The sleigh was righted; the travellers once more took their seats; and on through the darkening day they drove, until they came to a long straggling village, where the horses stopped before a detached cottage. Benumbed with the bitter cold, Major Burnaby and his companion dashed inside, and made haste, in front of a blazing stove, to restore the suspended circulation. Then, while the women of the house made tea in a samovar, or urn, they unfroze in the stove some cutlets and bread which they had carried with them, and proceeded to enjoy a hearty repast. In one hour's time they were ready to start; but their driver demurred. The snowstorm was heavy; wolves prowled along the track; the river ice might give way. It was better to wait until the morning, when, with beautiful horses, they might go like birds to the next station. The two travellers could do nothing with him, and were compelled to resign themselves to pass the night on the hard boards, in an atmosphere infested by many unpleasant smells. A good hour before sunrise all were again in motion. The Major and his companion abandoned their heavy troika, and engaged two small sleighs with a pair of horses to each, one for themselves and one to carry their luggage.

It was a glorious winter morning, and the sun came forth like a bridegroom to run his course, invested with indescribable pomp of colour. First, over the whole of the eastern horizon extended a pale blue streak, which seemed, like a wall, to shut off the vast Beyond. Suddenly its summit changed into rare lapis-lazuli, while its base became a sheet of purple. From the darker lines shot wondrous waves of grey and crystal; and in time the purple foundations upheaved into glowing seas of fire. The wall broke up into castles, battlements, and towers—all with magical gleams, which gradually floated far away, while the seas of flame, lighting up the whole horizon, burst through their borders and swelled into a mighty ocean. The sight was one on which the eye of man could scarcely gaze. The sunny expanse of the winter-bound earth reflected as in a mirror the celestial panorama. Shafts of light seemed to dart in rapid succession from earth to sky, until at last the vast luminous orb of day rose from the depth of the many-coloured radiance, and with its surpassing glory put everything else to shame.

The travellers reached Samara—a well-built prosperous town, situated on a tributary of the Volga. There Major Burnaby parted from his companion, whose road thenceforward lay in a different direction, and proceeded to make his preparations for a drive across the steppes to Orenburg.

He started next morning, in a sleigh which he had purchased, and had caused to be well repaired, and took the road towards Orenburg. The country was flat and uninteresting; buried beneath a white shroud of sand, with a few trees scattered here and there, and at intervals a dreary-looking hut or two. The first post-station, for changing horses, was Smeveshlaevskaya, twenty versts (a verst is two-thirds of an English mile); the next, Bodrovsky, where Burnaby arrived a little after sunset. After drinking a few glasses of tea to fortify himself against the increasing cold (25° below zero, R.), he pushed forward in the hope of reaching Malomalisky, about twenty-six and a half versts, about nine p.m. But plunging into the heart of a terrible snowstorm, he and his driver were so blinded and beaten, and the horses so jaded by the swiftly forming snow-drifts, that he was compelled to give the order to return, and to pass the night at Bodrovsky.

At daybreak the resolute guardsman was on his way. In the course of the day he fell in with General Kryjonovsky, the governor of the Orenburg district, who was bound for St. Petersburg; and a brief conversation with him showed that the authorities, as he had suspected, by no means approved of his expedition to Khiva. At one of the stations, the man assigned to him as driver had been married only the day before, and undertook his duties with obvious reluctance. His sole desire was to return as quickly as possible to his bride, and with this intent he lashed his horses until they kicked and jumped in the most furious contortions. The Major was thrown in the air, and caught again by the rebound; upset, righted, and upset again; gun, saddle-bags, cartridge-cases, and traveller, all simultaneously flying in the air. After a third of these rough experiences, the Major resolved to try the effect of a sharp application of his boot.

"Why do you do that?" said the driver, pulling up his horse. "You hurt, you break my ribs."

"I only do to you what you do to me," replied the Major. "You hurt, you break my ribs, and injure my property besides."

"Oh, sir of noble birth," ejaculated the fellow, "it is not my fault. It is thine, oh moody one!" to his offside horse, accompanied by a crack from his whip. "It is thine, oh spoilt and cherished one!" to his other meagre and half starved quadruped (whack!) "Oh, petted and caressed sons of animals" (whack, whack, whack!), "I will teach you to upset the gentleman."

At length, after a journey of four hundred versts, Orenburg was reached. At this frontier town, situated almost on the verge of civilization, our traveller was compelled to make a short sojourn. He had letters of introduction to present, which procured him some useful friends; a servant to engage, provisions to purchase, information to collect about the route to Khiva, and his English gold and notes to convert into Russian coin. Through the good offices of a Moslem gentleman, he was able to engage a Tartar, named Nazar—not five feet high—as a servant; and after some delay he obtained from the military chief a podorojoraya, or passport, as far as Kasala, or Fort No. 1. This pass ran as follows: "By the order of His Majesty the Emperor Alexander, the son of Nicolas, Autocrat of the whole of Russia, etc., etc. From the town of Orsk to the town of Kasala, to the Captain of the English service, Frederick, the son of Gustavus Burnaby, to give three horses, with a driver, for the legal fare, without delay. Given in the town of Orenburg, 15th December, 1875."

The next day, Frederick, "the son of Gustavus Burnaby," with his Tartar servant, took their departure from Orenburg, and in a few minutes were trotting along the frozen surface of the river Ural. Every now and then they fell in with a caravan of rough, shaggy, undersized camels, drawing sleighs laden with cotton from Tashkent; or a Cossack galloped by, brandishing his long spear; or a ruddy-faced Kirghiz slowly caracolled over the shining snow. Three stations were passed in safety, and Burnaby resolved on halting at the fourth, Krasnojorsk, for refreshment. But as the afternoon closed in, the Tartar driver began to lash his weary jades impatiently; as an excuse for his vehemence, pointing to the clouds that were rising before them, and the signs of a gathering snowstorm. Soon the air was filled with flakes; the darkness rapidly increased; the driver lost his way, and, at length, the team came to a standstill, breast deep in a snow-drift. What was to be done? It was equally impossible to go forward or to return; there was no wood in the neighbourhood with which to kindle a fire, no shovel with which to make a snow house; nothing could the belated wayfarer do but endure the bitter cold and the silent darkness, and wait for morning. Burnaby suffered much from the exposure, but the great difficulty was to prevent himself from yielding to the fatal lethargy which extreme cold induces—from falling into that sleep which turns inevitably into death. How he rejoiced when the day broke, and he was able to despatch the driver on one of the horses for assistance; and how he rejoiced when the man returned with three post horses and some peasants, and the road was regained, and the journey resumed, and the station reached at last! There they rested and refreshed themselves, before, with invigorated spirits, they dashed once again into the snow-bound depths of the steppes.

After a while the aspect of the country grew more cheery. The low chain of mountains to the north-east was sometimes abruptly broken, and a prominent peak thrust its summit into the interval. Through the fleecy snow various coloured grasses were visible. Olive-tinted branches, and dark forests of fir and pine, contrasted strongly with the whitely shining expanse that spread as far as the eye could see. Spider-like webs of frozen dew hung from the branches. The thin icicles glistened like prisms with all the colours of the rainbow. Thus, through a succession of fairy landscapes, such as the dwellers in Western lands can form but a faint idea of, the travellers dashed onward to Orsk.

Then the face of the country underwent another change. They were fairly in the region of the steppes—those wide and level plains which, during the brief summer, bloom with luxuriant vegetation, and are alive with the flocks and herds of the nomads, but in the long drear winter, from north to south and east to west, are buried deep beneath frozen snow. Wherever you direct your gaze it rests upon snow, snow, still snow; shining with a painful glare in the mid-day sun; fading into a dull, grey, melancholy ocean as noon lapses into twilight. "A picture of desolation which wearies by its utter loneliness, and at the same time appals by its immensity; a circle of which the centre is everywhere, and the circumference nowhere." Travel, in this world-beyond-the-world, in this solitude which Frost and Winter make all their own, tests the courage and endurance of a man, for it makes no appeal to the imagination or the fancy, it charms the eye with no pleasant pictures, suggests no associations to the mind. But it has its dangers, as Major Burnaby experienced. He had left the station of Karabootak (three hundred and seventeen miles from Orsk), and as the road was comparatively smooth, and the wind had subsided, he leaned back in his sleigh and fell asleep. Unluckily he had forgotten to put on his thick gloves, and his hands, slipping from the fur-lined sleeves of his pelisse, lay exposed to the full potency of the cold air. In a few minutes he awoke with a feeling of intense pain; and looking at his hands, he saw that the finger-nails were blue, blue too the fingers and back of the hands, while the wrists and lower part of the arms had assumed the hue of wax. They were frost-bitten! He called his servant, and made him rub the skin with some snow in the hope of restoring the vitality. This he did for some minutes; but, meanwhile, the pain gradually ascended up the arms, while the lower portion of the arms was dead to all feeling, all sensation. "It is no good," said Nazar, looking sorrowfully at his master; "we must drive on as fast as possible to the station."

The station was some miles off. Miles? Each mile seemed to the tortured traveller a league; each league a day's journey; the physical pain consumed him, wore him down as mental anguish might have done. But at last the station was reached; Burnaby sprang from the sleigh, rushed into the waiting-room, and to three Cossacks whom he met there showed his hands. Straightway they conducted him into an outer apartment, took off his coat, bared his arms, and plunged him into a tub of ice and water up to the shoulders. He felt nothing.

"Brother," said the eldest of the soldiers, shaking his head, "it is a bad job; you will lose your hands."

"They will drop off," remarked another, "if we cannot get back the circulation."

"Have you any spirit with you?" asked a third.

Nazar, on hearing this inquiry, immediately ran out, and returned with a tin bottle containing naphtha for cooking purposes; upon which the Cossacks, taking the Major's arms out of the icy water, proceeded to rub them with the strong spirit.

Rub, rub, rub; the skin peeled under their horny hands, and the spirit irritated the membrane below. At last a faint sensation like tickling—we are using the Major's own words—pervaded the elbow-joints, and he slightly flinched.

"Does it hurt?" asked the eldest Cossack.

"A little."

"Capital, brothers," he continued; "rub as hard as you can;" and after continuing the friction until the flesh was almost flayed, they suddenly plunged his arms again into the ice and water. This time, the pain was sharp.

"Good," exclaimed the Cossacks. "The more it hurts, the better chance you have of saving your hands." And after a short time they let him remove his arms from the tub.

"You are fortunate, little father," said the eldest Cossack. "If it had not been for the spirit your hands would have dropped off, even if you had not lost your arms."

"Rough, kind-hearted fellows were these poor soldiers," adds Major Burnaby; "and when I forced on the oldest of them a present for himself and comrades, the old soldier simply said, 'Are we not all brothers when in misfortune? Would you not have helped me if I had been in the same predicament?'"

The Major shook his hand heartily, and retired to the waiting-room to rest upon the sofa, as the physical shock he had undergone had for the moment thoroughly prostrated him. Moreover, his arms were sore and inflamed, the spirit having in some places penetrated the raw flesh; and several weeks elapsed before he thoroughly recovered from the effects of his carelessness.

At Terekli, about five hundred miles from Orenburg, our traveller entered the province of Turkistan, and found himself in the region which acknowledges the authority of General Kauffmann—a restless and ambitious soldier, to whose energy much of Russia's recent advance eastward would seem to be due. He still pushed forward with characteristic resolution, braving the terrors of the climate and the dangers of the road in his determined purpose to reach Khiva. At one station no horses were to be obtained, and, instead, three gigantic camels were harnessed to the tiny sleigh. A strange spectacle! "I have tried many ways of locomotion in my life, from fire-balloons to bicycles, from canoes and bullocks to cows, camels, and donkeys; whilst in the East the time-honoured sedan of our grandfathers has occasionally borne me and my fortunes; but never had I travelled in so comical a fashion. A Tartar rode the centre camel. His head-gear would have called attention, if nothing else had, for he wore a large black hat, which reminded me of an inverted coal-scuttle, whilst a horn-like protuberance sticking out from its summit gave a diabolical appearance to his lobster-coloured visage. The hat, which was made of sheepskin, had the white wool inside, which formed a striking contrast to the flaming countenance of the excited Tartar. He had replaced the usual knout used for driving, by a whip armed with a thin cord lash, and he urged on his ungainly team more by the shrill sounds of his voice than by any attempt at flagellation, the Tartar seldom being able to get more than four miles an hour from the lazy brutes.

"All of a sudden the camel in the centre quickly stopped, and the rider was precipitated head-over-heels in the snow. Luckily, it was soft falling; there were no bones broken, and in a minute or two he was again in the saddle, having changed the system of harnessing, and placed one of the camels as leader, whilst the other two were driven as wheelers. We got on very fairly for a little while, when the foremost of our train having received a rather sharper application of the lash than he deemed expedient remonstrated with his rider by lying down. Coaxing and persuasion were now used; he was promised the warmest of stalls, the most delicious of water, if he would only get up. But this the beast absolutely declined to do, until the cold from the snow striking against his body induced him to rise from the ground.

"We now went even slower than before. Our driver was afraid to use his whip for fear of another ebullition of temper on the part of the delinquent, and confined himself to cracking his whip in the air. The sounds of this proceeding presently reaching the ears of the leader, perhaps made him think that his companions were undergoing chastisement. Anyhow, it appeared to afford him some satisfaction, for, quickening his stride, he compelled his brethren behind to accelerate their pace; and after a long, wearisome drive we arrived at our destination."

Under the influence of milder weather the aspect of the country rapidly modified and brightened, and instead of a uniform sheet of frozen snow, broad patches of vegetation met the eye. On these the Kirghiz horses were browsing with evident delight. How they live through the winter is a mystery, as their owners seldom feed them with corn, and they are compelled to trust to the scanty grasses which may still be partially alive underneath the snow. Nor are they in any way protected from the cold. As a necessary consequence, the spring finds them reduced to mere skeletons, whose ribs are barely covered by their parchment-like skin; but they soon gain in flesh and strength when once the rich pasturage of the steppes is at their disposal. Their powers of endurance are wonderful; and without rest, or water, or food, they will accomplish surprising distances, maintaining a first-rate speed. An instance is on record of a Kirghiz chief having galloped two hundred miles, over a rocky and mountainous ground, in twenty-four hours. A Russian detachment of cavalry, mounted on Kirghiz horses, marched 333 miles in six days.

Major Burnaby was soon apprised that he was nearing the Sea (or Lake) of Aral by the salt breeze which blew persistently in his face. The whole district for miles around was impregnated with salt, and the springs and streams had all a brackish taste and strong saline flavour. At Nicolaivskaya his road touched close upon the north-eastern extremity of the sea. This great inland basin of brackish water is separated from the Caspian by the dense plateau of Ust-Urt. It measures about 260 miles from north to south, and 125 from east to west. On the north-east it receives the waters of the Syr-Daria, or Jaxartes; on the south-east those of the Amu-Daria, or Oxus. As it is on the same level with the Caspian, we may reasonably suppose that both seas were at one time connected. Owing to the excessive evaporation which takes place, it is understood to be decreasing in size.

At Kasala, or Fort No. 1, our traveller struck the Syr-Daria, some forty or fifty miles above its outlet in the Aral. Kasala is inhabited by nomad Kirghiz, who pitch their kibitkas in its outskirts in the winter, to resume their migratory life with the first breath of spring; by Russian and Tartar merchants, who dwell in one-storied houses, built of brick or cement; and by a motley population of Greeks, Khivans, Bokharans, Tashkentians, and Turcomans generally, attracted thither by the hope of gain. Owing to its geographical position, it is the centre of a considerable trade; for all goods to Orenburg from Western Turkistan must pass through it. Its civil population numbers about 5000 souls; its garrison consists of about 350 infantry and 400 cavalry, and it is also the head-quarters in winter of the sailors of the Aral fleet, which is made up of four small steamers of light draught. As for the fort, it is simply an earthwork, constructed in the shape of a half-star, with a bastion on the south extending to the bank of the Syr-Daria. A dry ditch, thirty feet broad by twelve feet deep, and a parapet, eight feet high and twelve feet thick, surround it. Sufficiently strong to overawe the Kirghiz, it could offer no effective resistance to an European force.

Major Burnaby paid a visit to a Kirghiz kibitka, or tent, and his description of it may be compared with Mr. Atkinson's. Inside it was adorned with thick carpets of various hues, and bright-coloured cushions, for the accommodation of the inmates. In the centre a small fire gave out a cloud of white smoke, which rose in coils and wreaths to the roof, and there escaped through an aperture left for the purpose. The fuel used is saxaul, the wood of the bramble tree, and it emits an acrid, pungent odour. The women in the tent had their faces uncovered; they received their visitor with a warm welcome, and spread some rugs for him to sit down by their side. They were all of them moon-faced, with large mouths, but good eyes and teeth.

The master of the kibitka, who was clad in a long brown robe, thickly wadded to keep out the cold, poured some water into a large caldron, and proceeded to make tea, while a young girl handed round raisins and dried currants. A brief conversation then arose. The Kirghiz were much surprised to learn that their visitor was not a Russian, but had come from a far Western land, and were even more surprised to find that he had brought no wife with him—a wife, in the opinion of the Kirghiz, being as indispensable to a man's happiness as a horse or camel. In entering into matrimony, the Kirghiz have one great advantage over the other Moslem races; they see the girls whom they wish to marry, and are allowed to converse with them before the bargain is concluded between the parents, one hundred sheep being the average price given for a young woman.

On the 12th of January Major Burnaby left Kasala for Khiva. His retinue consisted of three camels, loaded with a tent, forage, and provisions, his Tartar servant, who bestrode the largest camel, and a Kirghiz guide, who, like himself, was mounted on horseback. His provisions included stchi, or cabbage soup, with large pieces of meat cut up in it, which, having been poured into two large iron stable buckets, had become hard frozen, so that it could be easily carried slung on a camel's back. He also took with him twenty pounds of cooked meat. A hatchet, to chop up the meat or cut down brushwood for a fire, and a cooking lamp, with a supply of spirit, formed part of his equipment.

Crossing the icy surface of the Syr-Daria, our traveller once more plunged into the solitude of the steppes, bravely facing the storm-wind and the ridges of snow which rolled before it, like the wave-crests of a frozen sea. After a five hours' march, he called a halt, that the camels might rest and be fed—for they will feed only in the daytime; wherefore it is wise to march them as much as possible during the night. Their ordinary pace is about two miles and a third in an hour; and the best plan is to start at midnight, unload them for about two hours in the day to feed, and halt at sunset: thus securing sixteen hours' work per day, and accomplishing a daily journey of at least thirty-seven miles.

The kibitka was soon raised. "Imagine," says our traveller, "a bundle of sticks, each five feet three inches in length, and an inch in diameter; these are connected with each other by means of cross sticks, through the ends of which holes are bored, and leather thongs passed. This allows plenty of room for all the sticks to open out freely; they then form a complete circle, about twelve feet in diameter, and five feet three in height. They do not require any pressing into the ground, for the circular shape keeps them steady. When this is done, a thick piece of cashmar, or cloth made of sheep's wool, is suspended from their tops, and reaches to the ground. This forms a shield through which the wind cannot pass. Another bundle of sticks is then produced. They are all fastened at one end to a small wooden cross, about six inches long by four broad; a man standing in the centre of the circle raises up this bundle in the air, the cross upwards, and hitches their other ends by means of little leather loops one by one on the different upright sticks which form the circular walls. The result is, they all pull against each other, and are consequently self-supporting; another piece of cloth is passed round the outside of this scaffolding, leaving a piece uncovered at the top to allow the smoke to escape. One stick is removed from the uprights which form the walls. This constitutes a door, and the kibitka is complete."

While the Major and his followers were enjoying a meal of rice and mutton, and a glass of hot tea, three Khivans rode up to them—a merchant and his two servants. The Khivan merchant was strongly built, and about five feet ten inches in height. He wore a tall, conical black Astrakhan hat; an orange-coloured dressing-gown, thickly quilted, and girt about the loins with a long, red sash; and over all, enveloping him from hand to foot, a heavy sheepskin mantle. His weapons consisted of a long, single-barrelled gun, and a short, richly mounted sabre. An exchange of civilities followed, and then both parties retired to rest. At about three o'clock in the morning, after some difficulty with his guide and camel-driver, the Major resumed his march, and for six hours the weary tramp and toil over the frost-bound plain continued. At nine a halt was called, soup was made, and the party breakfasted. By the time they were ready to set out again, the Khivan merchant's caravan had come up, and all went on together.

In advance rode the guide, singing a song in praise of mutton, and descriptive of his partiality for that succulent meat. The Kirghiz poets make the sheep the special subject of their metrical eulogium; in truth, it fills in their poetry as conspicuous a place as the dove in the love-songs of the Latin bards. Nor is to be wondered at. The sheep represents the wealth, the property of the nomads. During the summer and autumn they live upon their milk, and never think of killing them except to do honour to a guest by serving up before him a leg of mutton. In the winter they are, of course, obliged very frequently to sacrifice the highly esteemed animal, but they live upon horseflesh and camel's flesh as much as they can. Their clothing is furnished by the sheep, being made entirely of sheep's wool wrought into a coarse homespun. Finally, if they want to buy a horse, a camel, or a wife, they pay in sheep; and a man's worth in the world is reckoned by the numbers of his flock.

On the following day, in the course of their march, the travellers came upon a Kirghiz encampment, the members of which were considerably excited by Major Burnaby's announcement of his desire to purchase a whole sheep. The head of the principal kibitka, accompanied by a pretty Kirghiz girl, hastened to conduct him to the sheepfold, that he might select an animal, and the fattest of the flock became his for the small sum of four roubles. The pretty young girl acted as butcher, receiving the skin and head in acknowledgment of her trouble, and the carcase was conveyed to the Major's tent, where it was duly cooked, and devoured by his followers, who showed the most intense appreciation of his liberality.

The march being resumed, Major Burnaby made for a place called Kalenderhana, instead of the Russian settlement of Petro-Alexandrovsky, having a shrewd suspicion that if he went thither, as the governor of Kasala had desired, he would, in some way or other, be prevented from reaching Khiva. Pushing forward steadily, he left his Khivan merchant far behind, and strode across an undulating country in the direction of south-south-west. Next he came into a salt district, barren and dreary; and afterwards reached the desert of Jana-Daria, the dried-up bed of a river, which is lost in the sand. Still continuing his march, he came upon an unbounded ocean of sand, which, in the glaring sunshine, glittered like a sea of molten gold. When this was traversed, the country grew pleasanter and more fertile. Traces of game appeared. Sometimes a brown hare darted through the herbage; while in the distance herds of saigak, or antelopes, bounded with elastic tread across the sward. A chain of mountains running east and west rose up before the wanderer's path, and presented a picturesque spectacle, with their broken crests, sharp pinnacles, and masses of shining quartz.

Upon their rugged sides could be traced the furrows ploughed by the torrents which the spring lets loose and feeds with its abundant rains. Through a dark and deep defile, about seven miles long, the little company penetrated the mountain barrier of the Kazan-Tor, and descended into a broad plain, overspread by a network of canals for irrigation, where a striking indication of the desultory but ceaseless hostilities waged between the Kirghiz and the Turcomans was presented in the rude fortifications, a high ditch and a wattled palisade, that encircled every little village. Kalenderhana was fortified in this manner. Here Major Burnaby was warmly welcomed, and in great state escorted to his Kirghiz guide's house, or kibitka, where a curious throng quickly surrounded him, and proceeded to examine, and comment unreservedly upon, every part of his attire. Major Burnaby, if less outspoken, was not less curious, and carefully noted that the hostess was a good-looking woman, clad in a flowing white dressing-gown, with a whiter turban, folded many times around her small head. The brother-in-law, a short hump-backed fellow, had a horse to sell, which Major Burnaby expressed his willingness to purchase, if he went to Khiva. The guide had been ordered by the Russian governor of Kasala to conduct the Englishman to Petro-Alexandrovsky, and at first he was reluctant to run the risk of punishment; but the domestic pressure put upon him could not be resisted, and he agreed to go to Khiva, on condition that the Major completed his bargain with the horse-dealer. This was at last arranged, and a Tartar being sent forward with a letter to the Khan, requesting permission to visit his capital, the traveller resumed his journey, with Nazar proudly seated astride the new purchase.

A brief ride carried them to the bank of the great Amu-Daria, the Oxus of Alexander the Great, which at this time was frozen over, presenting a solid highway of ice, half a mile in breadth. There they met with some Khivan merchants—stalwart men, with dark complexions and large eyes, dressed in long red thickly wadded dressing-gowns and cone-shaped black lambskin hats. A caravan of camels was crossing the river, and numerous arbas, or two-wheeled carts, each drawn by one horse, passed to and fro. Every man whom they encountered saluted them with the customary Arab greeting, "*Salam aaleikom!*" to which the response was always given, "*Aaleikom salam!*" Soon after crossing the frozen river, Major Burnaby determined to halt for the night; and the guide began to look about for suitable quarters. He pulled up at last by the side of a large, substantial-looking square building, built of clay. A rap at the high wooden gates brought out an old man bent nearly double with age, who, on hearing that the travellers wanted a night's hospitality, immediately called to his servants to take charge of the horses and camels, and across the square-walled courtyard ushered Major Burnaby into his house. The guest-room was spacious and lofty. One end of it was covered with thick carpets; this was the place of honour for visitors. In the centre a small square hearth was filled with charcoal embers, confined within a coping about three inches high. On the coping stood a richly chased copper ewer—which might have been dug out of the ruins of the buried Pompeii, so classic was it in shape and appearance—with a long swan-like neck, constructed so as to assist the attendant in pouring water over the hands of his master's guests before they began their repast. On one side of the hearth was a square hole about three feet deep, filled with water, and reached by a couple of steps. It was the place of ablution—something like the *impluvium* in a Roman villa—and its sides were lined with ornamental tiles. The windows were represented by two narrow slits, each about two feet long by six inches wide, while some open wooden trellis-work supplied the place of glass.

After a brief absence the host reappeared, carrying in his hand a large earthenware dish full of rice and mutton, while his servants followed, with baskets of bread and hard-boiled eggs. A pitcher of milk was also produced, and an enormous melon, weighing quite twenty-five pounds. When the host and his visitor had completed their repast, they began to converse, the Khivan asking many questions about the countries which the Englishman had travelled. To his inquiry whether there were camels in England, Major Burnaby replied with an amusing description of our railways and locomotives.

"We have trains," he said, "composed of arbas with iron wheels; they run upon long strips of iron, which are laid upon the ground for the wheels to roll over."

"Do the horses drag them very fast?" asked the Khivan.

"We do not use live horses, but we make a horse of iron and fill him with water, and put fire under the water. The water boils and turns into steam. The steam is very powerful; it rushes out of the horse's stomach, and turns large wheels which we give him instead of legs. The wheels revolve over the iron lines which we have previously laid down, and the horse, which we call an engine, moves very quickly, dragging the arbas behind him; they are made of wood and iron, and have four wheels, not two, like your arbas in Khiva. The pace is so great that if your Khan had an iron horse and a railway, he could go to Kasala in one day."

Next morning, after remunerating his host for his hospitality, Major Burnaby proceeded towards the goal of his daring enterprise. He passed through the busy trading town of Oogentel, the first in Khivan territory on the road from Kalenderhana, and, as an Englishman, attracted the attention of the population. This attention grew into wild excitement, when he found his way to a barber, intent upon getting rid of a beard of thirteen weeks' growth. In Oogentel the people shave their heads and not their chins; so that the traveller's desire to have his chin shaved, instead of his head, begat an extraordinary sensation. An increasing crowd gathered round the barber's shop; moullahs (or priests), camel-drivers, and merchants jostling one another in their anxiety to obtain good points of view, like the London populace on the Lord Mayor's Show day. The thought occurred to Major Burnaby that this fanatical Moslem multitude might not be displeased if the barber cut an unbeliever's throat, and it was not without a qualm he resigned himself to his hands. No such catastrophe happened, however; but the barber, rendered nervous by the accumulated gaze of hundreds of eyes, let slip the thin strip of steel which did duty for a razor, and inflicted a slight wound on his customer's cheek. As no soap was used, and the substitute for a razor was innocent of "edge," the operation was sufficiently disagreeable; and if the crowd were sorry, Major Burnaby was heartily rejoiced when it came to an end and he was free to continue his journey.

At nine versts from Oogentel he and his party crossed the canal of the Shabbalat, and rode through a barren tract of sand until they arrived at a cemetery. The tombs were made of dried clay, and fashioned into the strangest shapes; while over several of the larger floated banners or white flags, from poles ten or twelve feet high, indicating the last resting-place of some unknown and unchronicled hero. *Multi fortes vixerunt ante Agamemnona*; but they have found no bard to record their deeds of prowess in immortal verse. The Khivan warriors who fell in defence of their wild father-land must sleep for ever in nameless graves.

At a village called Shamahoolhur, the traveller was received with true Khivan hospitality. His entertainer was a fair-looking man, with a genial address and a hearty glance in his dark eyes, and appeared, from his surroundings, to be possessed of considerable wealth. He was a sportsman, and kept several hawks; these birds being used in Khiva to fly at the saigahs and hares. The bird strikes his victim between its eyes with a force which stuns or confuses it, so that it can make no resistance or attempt at escape when the hounds seize it.

"Do you not hunt in this way in your country?" said the Khivan.

"No; we hunt foxes, but only with hounds, and we ourselves follow on horseback."

"Are your horses like our own?" he asked.

"No; they are most of them stouter built, have stronger shoulders, and are better animals; but though they can gallop faster than your horses for a short distance, I do not think they can last so long."

"Which do you like best, your horse or your wife?" inquired the man.

"That depends upon the woman," I replied; and the guide, here joining in the conversation, said that in England they did not buy or sell their wives, and that I was not a married man.

"What! you have not got a wife?"

"No; how could I travel if I had one?"

"Why, you might leave her behind, and lock her up, as our merchants do with their wives when they go on a journey!"

The next morning Major Burnaby encountered on the road the messenger he had despatched to Khiva. He was accompanied by two Khivan noblemen, one of whom courteously saluted the English traveller, and explained that the Khan had sent him to escort him into the city, and bid him welcome.

They rapidly approached the capital, and above its belt of trees could see its glittering crown of minarets and domes. The landscape round about it was very pleasant to see, with its leafy groves, its walled orchards, and its avenues of mulberry trees; and recalled to the traveller's mind the descriptions which figure in the pages of Oriental story-tellers. A swift ride brought the party to the gates of Khiva. The city is built in an oblong form, and surrounded by two walls; of which the outer is not less than fifty feet in height, and constructed of baked bricks, with the upper part of dried clay. This forms the first line of defence. At a quarter of a mile within it rises the second wall, somewhat lower than the first, and protected by a dry ditch. It immediately surrounds the tower. The space between the two walls is used as a market, and high above the throng of vendors and buyers, and the press of cattle, horses, sheep, and camels, rises the cross-beam of the ghastly gallows, on which all people convicted of theft are executed.

But as we have already spoken of this now famous city, we must confine ourselves in these pages to Major Burnaby's individual adventures. Lodging was provided for him in the house of his escort, and directly on his entry he was served with refreshments. Afterwards he was conducted to the bath. In the evening a succession of visitors arrived; and it was late when the Major was at liberty to seek repose.

II.

In the afternoon of the following day two officials arrived from the Khan, with an escort of six men on horseback and four on foot, to conduct the English officer to the palace. Mounting his horse, he rode forth, preceded by the six horsemen, and with an official on either side; the rear being brought up by Nazar, with some attendants on foot, who lashed out freely with their long whips when the staring crowd drew inconveniently near the *cortége*. Fresh sightseers arrived every moment, for the name of England exercises a charm and a power in Khiva, where people are never weary of talking of the nation which holds in fee the gorgeous Indian empire, and is regarded as the rival and inevitable foe of the White Czar. The very housetops were lined with curious eyes. Through the hum and din of voices the Englishman proceeded to the Khan's residence; a large building, with pillars and domes reflecting the sun's rays from their bright glazed tiles. At the gates stood a guard of thirty or forty men with flashing scimitars. The company passed into a small courtyard, from which a door opened into a low passage, and this led to some squalid corridors, terminating in a large square room, where was seated the treasurer, with three moullahs, busily engaged in counting up his money. He made a sign to the attendants, and a large wooden box was at once pushed forward, and offered to Major Burnaby as a seat. An interval of fifteen minutes, as the playwrights say, followed. Then a messenger entered the room, and announced that the Khan was at liberty to receive the stranger. Away through a long corridor, and across an inner courtyard, to the reception-hall—a large dome-shaped tent or kibitka. A curtain was drawn aside, and the Englishman found himself face to face with the celebrated Khan.

The portrait he draws of the Khivan potentate differs in some particulars from that drawn by Mr. MacGahan (see p. 283):—"He is taller than the average of his subjects, being quite five feet ten in height, and is strongly built. His face is of a broad massive type; he has a low square forehead, large dark eyes, a short straight nose, with dilated nostrils, and a coal-black beard and moustache. An enormous mouth, with irregular but white teeth, and a chin somewhat concealed by his beard, and not at all in character with the otherwise determined appearance of his face, must complete the picture. He did not look more than eight and twenty, and had a pleasant genial smile, and a merry twinkle in his eye, very unusual amongst Orientals; in fact, a Spanish expression would describe him better than any English one I can think of. He is *muy simpatico*. . . . The Khan was dressed in a similar sort of costume to that generally worn by his subjects, but it was made of much richer materials, and a jewelled sword was lying by his feet. His head was covered by a tall black Astrakhan hat, of a sugar-loaf shape."

Tea having been served in a small porcelain cup, the Khan entered into conversation with his visitor, through the medium of Nazar, a Kirghiz interpreter, and a moullah. At first it turned upon the relations existing between England and Russia, the Crimean War, the Indian Government, and other branches of *la haute politique*; the Khan displaying a quick and clear intelligence. At last he said—

"You do not have a Khan at the head of affairs?"

"No," replied Burnaby, "a Queen; and her Majesty is advised as to her policy by her ministers, who for the time being are supposed to represent the opinion of the country."

"And does that opinion change?"

"Very frequently; and since your country was conquered we have had a fresh Government, whose policy is diametrically opposite to that held by the previous one; and in a few years' time we shall have another change, for in our country, as the people advance in knowledge and wealth, they require fresh laws and privileges. The result of this is, they choose a different set of people to represent them;" and the Major entered on a brief exposition of constitutional principles, which to the Khan must surely have been unintelligible.

"Can your Queen have a subject's head cut off?"

"No, not without a trial before our judges."

"Then she never has their throats cut?" [the Khivan punishment for murder].

"No."

"Hindostan is a very wonderful country," continued the Khan; "the envoy I sent there a few years ago [359] has told me of your railroads and telegraphs; but the Russians have railroads, too."

"Yes," replied Burnaby; "we lent them money, and our engineers have helped to make them."

"Do the Russians pay you for this?" he inquired.

"Yes; so far they have behaved very honourably."

"Are there not Jews in your country like some of the Jews at Bokhara?"

"One of the richest men in England is a Jew."

"The Russians do not take away the money from the Jews?"

"No."

Here the Khan said a few words to his treasurer, and then remarked, in allusion to the tribute he pays to Russia annually:—"Why do they take money from me, then? The Russians love money very much." As he said this, he shook his head sorrowfully at the treasurer; and the latter, assuming a dolorous expression, poured out with a pitiful accent the monosyllable "Hum!" which, in Khivan language, seems to convey as pregnant a meaning as Lord Burleigh's shake of the head in "The Critic."

With a low bow from the Khan, the interview terminated.

On the following day Major Burnaby visited the Khan's gardens, which lie about three-quarters of a mile from the town. They are five in number, surrounded by high walls of sun-dried clay, and each from four to five acres in extent. Entering one of them, our traveller discovered that it was neatly laid out and trimly kept. The fruit trees, arranged in long avenues, were carefully cut and pruned; apple, pear, and cherry trees abounded. In the spring melons are grown on a large scale; and in the summer trellis-work arbours of vines, loaded with grapes, afford a delightful shelter from the sun's fierce glare. In a small summer-palace here, the Khan holds his court in June and July, and on a raised stone daïs outside sits to administer justice.

Returning to Khiva, Burnaby visited the prison and the principal school—the invariable accompaniments of civilization, however imperfect. But may we not hope that, some day, the school will destroy the gaol, and relieve civilization from the reproach of barbarism that still attaches to it? Meanwhile, Nazar was preparing for the Major's contemplated expedition to Bokhara, his tour to Merv and Meshed, and his journey from Persia into India, and so back to England. It was the 27th of January, and he had determined to spend only one more day in Khiva. But his plans were upset by an unexpected incident. On the morning of the 28th, just after his return from a ride through the market, he was "interviewed" by two strangers, who presented him with a letter from the commandant of Petro-Alexandrovsky, the Russian fort he had so determinedly avoided. It was to the effect that a telegram, which had been forwarded *viâ* Tashkent, awaited him at the fort, whither he must be pleased to repair to receive it. How or why any person should consider him of importance enough to despatch a telegram so many thousands of miles, and should go to the expense a sending it from Tashkent where the telegraph ends, to Khiva, a distance of nine hundred miles, by couriers with relays of horses, Burnaby could not understand. But there was no help for it. He must hasten to Petro-Alexandrovsky, where he did not want to go, and abandon his trip to Bokhara and Merv, where he very much wished to go. So he paid a visit to the bazar, and afterwards took leave of the Khan, who bestowed upon him the honourable gift of a khalat, or dressing-gown, and on the 29th bade adieu to Khiva.

He reached Petro-Alexandrovsky on the second day, and found that the important telegram which had travelled so far was one from the Duke of Cambridge, Field-Marshal Commanding-in-Chief, requiring his immediate return to European Russia. He found also that the Russian Government had given orders for his return by the shortest route to Kasala. All hope of further exploration and adventure in Central Asia had to be abandoned. Before leaving Petro-Alexandrovsky, the disappointed traveller had an opportunity of accompanying a coursing party, and sharing in a day's novel sport. There were horses and men of all kinds and shapes, Russians, Bokharans, Kirghiz, short-legged men on giant steeds, and long-legged men on short-legged horses. A short colonel, said to be well versed in the pastime, acted as master of the hunt. Behind him were led seven or eight greyhounds in couples; while a stalwart Khivan bore on his elbow a hooded falcon, graceful enough to have figured in Mr. Tennyson's poetical little drama. Amid a storm of cries and shouts and yells, the hunters rode forward at a rattling pace, crossing a flat open country, intersected by a ditch or two; until, after an eight miles' run, they arrived at the cover, a narrow tract of bush and bramble-covered ground stretching down to the bank of the frozen Oxus. Forming in a line, at a distance of twenty yards from one another, the horsemen rode through bush and bramble. A sharp yell from a Kirghiz, and after a startled hare, which had left its covert, dashed Russians, Bokharans, Englishman, and hounds. On they went, down the slippery river bank, across the shining ice, towards a dense bit of copse, where it looked as if poor puss might find an asylum from her pursuers. But at this moment the falcon was launched into the air. A swift swooping flight, and whir of wings, and in a second it was perched on its victim's back, while around it gathered the well-trained dogs, with open mouths and lolling tongues, not daring to approach the quarry. The master galloped up, seized the prize, and in a few minutes more the hunt was resumed; nor did the horsemen turn their faces homeward until five hares had rewarded their chivalrous efforts.

In company with two Russian officers, and an escort of ten Cossacks, Major Burnaby, after a pleasant sojourn at Petro-Alexandrovsky, set out on his return to Kasala. As the weather was warmer, and the snow had begun to melt, the three officers travelled in a tarantass, drawn by six Kirghiz horses; the said tarantass closely resembling a hansom cab which, after its wheels have been removed, has been fastened in a brewer's dray. It has no springs, and it runs upon small but solid wooden wheels. They had gone but a few miles before they came again into a land of snow; the horses had to be taken out, and a couple of camels substituted. At night they bivouacked, resuming their journey before daybreak. It was a picturesque sight:—"First, the Cossacks, the barrels of their carbines gleaming in the moonlight, the vashlik of a conical shape surmounting each man's low cap, and giving a ghastly appearance to the riders. Their distorted shadows were reflected on the snow beneath, and appeared like a detachment of gigantic phantoms pursuing our little force. Then the tarantass, drawn by two large camels, which slowly ploughed their way through the heavy track, the driver nodding on his box but half awake, the two officers in the arms of Morpheus inside, and the heavy woodwork creaking at each stride of the enormous quadrupeds. In the wake of this vehicle strode the baggage camels. The officers' servants were fast asleep on the backs of their animals, one man lying with his face to the tail, and snoring hard in spite of the continued movement; another fellow lay stretched across his saddle, apparently a good deal the worse for drink. He shouted out at intervals the strains of a Bacchanalian ditty. Nazar, who was always hungry, could be seen walking in the rear. He had kept back a bone from the evening meal, and was gnawing it like a dog, his strong jaws snapping as they closed on the fibrous mutton. I generally remained by our bivouac fire an hour or so after the rest of the party had marched, and seated by the side of the glowing embers, watched the caravan as it vanished slowly in the distance."

At mid-day, on the 12th of February, Burnaby and his companions galloped across the frozen highway of the Syr-Daria, and into the streets of Kasala, having ridden three hundred and seventy one miles in exactly nine days and two hours. He remained at Kasala for a few days, endeavouring to obtain permission to return to European Russia *viâ* Western Siberia; but his application failed, and he was informed that the authorization he had received to travel in Russian Asia had been cancelled. There was nothing to be done, therefore, but to complete the necessary preparations for his journey to Orenburg. A sleigh was hired, and amid a chorus of farewells from his Russian acquaintances, who showed themselves more friendly than their Government, he started on his homeward route, having undergone some novel experiences, and seen Khiva, but gathered no information of any value to geographers or men of science. In fact, the chief interest attaching to Major Burnaby's expedition is personal: it shows that he was a man of much energy, resolution, and perseverance, and he may fairly be complimented on the good use he made of these qualities in his bold but unsuccessful Ride to Khiva. [364]

SIR SAMUEL BAKER,

AND THE SOURCES OF THE NILE.

I.

OF late years the Lake Regions of Central Africa have offered a fertile and attractive field to the explorer. The interest of the public in African discovery, which had for some time been dormant, was revived in 1849, by the achievements of Dr. Livingstone, who, starting from the south, crossed the tropic of Capricorn, and penetrated to the shores of Lake Ngami. In 1853 to 1856 the same great traveller traced the course of the river Leeambye or Zambési, and traversed the entire breadth of the "black continent" from Angola on the west coast to Zanzibar on the east. In 1865 he resumed his labours, striking into the very heart of Africa, with the view of tracing out the Sources of the Nile, and entering into a fertile country, the resources of which he found to be capable of immense development. For the first two or three years of his absence his letters and despatches reached England with some degree of regularity, but at length a veil of silence fell across his path, and it began to be feared that he, like other explorers, had fallen a victim to his enthusiasm. An expedition in search of the missing traveller was equipped by Mr. Gordon Bennett, proprietor of the *New York Herald*, in 1871, and placed in charge of Mr. Henry M. Stanley, who had the good fortune to find Livingstone at Ujiji, near Unyanyembé, on the 10th of November. He remained with him until the 14th of March, 1872, when he returned to England with his diary and other documents. Dr. Livingstone at this time reported that, in his belief, the Nile springs up about six hundred miles to the south of the southernmost point of Lake Victoria Nyanza. In November, 1872, a relief or auxiliary expedition, under Lieutenant V. Lovett Cameron, started from Zanzibar; but in October, 1873, while at Unyanyembé, its leader received the intelligence of Livingstone's death, which had taken place at Ujiji, and soon afterwards the corpse arrived in charge of his faithful followers. Cameron then took up the work of exploration, and in spite of immense difficulties, great mental and physical suffering, and obstacles of every kind, he made his way to Lake Tanganyika, thence to Nyangwé, and after identifying the Lualaba with the Kongo, struck to the southward, and passing through regions hitherto unexplored, struck the west coast at Benguela. As a result of his observations, Lieutenant Cameron thus sketches the river system of Africa:—

"The basin of the Nile is probably bounded on the south-west by the watershed reached by Dr. Schweinfurth; on the south of the Albert Nyanza, by the high lands between that lake and the Tanganyika, whence the watershed pursues a tortuous course to Unyanyembé (where, I believe, the basins of the Nile, Kongo, and Lufiji approach each other), and then follows a wave of high land running east till it turns up northwards along the landward slopes of the mountains dividing the littoral from the interior. Passing by Mounts Kilima Njaro and Kenia, it extends to the mountains of Abyssinia, where the sources of the Blue Nile were discovered by Bruce [1770], and so on to the parched plains bordering the Red Sea, where no rains ever fall. The western boundary of the Nile basin is, of course, the eastern portion of the desert.

"The basins of the Niger and the Ogowai cannot yet be defined with any degree of exactitude, and the northern boundary of the basin of the Kongo has still to be traced.

"The Zambési drains that portion of the continent south of the Kongo system, and north of the Kalahari desert and the Limpopo, the northern boundary of the Transvaal Republic; some of its affluents reaching to within two hundred and fifty miles of the west coast.

"The mighty Kongo, king of all the African rivers, and second only to the Amazon (and perhaps to the Yang-tse-Kiang) in the volume of its waters, occupies a belt of the continent lying on both sides of the equator, but most probably the larger area belongs to the southern hemisphere. Many of its affluents fork into those of the Zambési on a level tableland, where the watershed is so tortuous that it is hard to trace it, and where, during the rainy season, floods extend right across between the head-waters of the two streams.

"The Kelli, discovered by Dr. Schweinfurth, may possibly prove to be the Lowa, reported to me as a large affluent of the Lualaba [or Kongo] to the west of Nyangwé; or, if not an affluent of the Lualaba, it most probably flows either to the Ogowai or the Tchadda, an affluent of the Niger."

In 1874 another expedition of discovery was fitted out, at the joint expense of the proprietors of the London *Daily Telegraph* and the *New York Herald*, and Mr. H. M. Stanley was appointed to the command. In 1875 he reached Lake Victoria Nyanza, and through the good offices of Mtesa, King of Uganda, obtained a flotilla of canoes, with which he circumnavigated the lake. It proved to be the largest basin of fresh water in the world, occupying the immense area of sixty thousand square miles. Mr. Stanley next pushed on to Lake Albert Nyanza; afterwards circumnavigated the northern half of Lake Tanganyika; struck westward to the Lualaba at Nyangwé (1876), and thence descended the Lualaba as far as the Isangila

Falls (June, 1877), whence he crossed the country to Kalinda, on the west coast.

But we must now return to 1857, when Captains Burton and Speke, under the auspices of the Royal Geographical Society of London, started from Zanzibar to explore the inland lacustrine region; and discovered, to the south of the equator, Lake Tanganyika, which they partially explored in a couple of canoes. Captain Burton being taken ill, Speke pushed on to the north alone, and discovered the immense basin now known as the Victoria Nyanza, which he immediately conceived to be the great reservoir and head-waters of the Nile. To ascertain the truth of this supposition, he started again from the east coast in October, 1860, accompanied by Captain Grant; crossed the great equatorial table-land of the interior; reached the Victoria Nyanza; skirted its shores until they discovered its main outlet, which proved to be the Nile, and then traced the course of the famous river to Gondokoro, whence, by way of Assouan, Thebes, and Cairo, they proceeded to Alexandria. Their well-directed energy had to a great extent solved the geographical problem of ages, and dispelled the cloud-land in which the Nile springs had so long been hidden:—

> "The mystery of old Nile was solved; brave men
> Had through the lion-haunted inland past,
> Dared all the perils of desert, gorge, and glen,
> Found the far Source at last."

With heroic patience they had accomplished on foot their journey of thirteen hundred miles, and shown that the parent stream of the Nile, even in its earliest course a considerable river, was fed by the vast reservoir of the "Victorian Sea." What remained to be discovered was the feeders of this vast basin, and which among them was indeed the primary source of the Nile. Some fresher light was thrown on the subject by Sir Samuel Baker, [369] who, with his wife, underwent some remarkable experiences in Central Africa, and earned a right to be included among our Heroes of Travel. Let us now follow him "through scorching deserts and thirsty sands; through swamp and jungle and interminable morass; through difficulties, fatigues, and sickness," until we stand with him on that high cliff where the great prize burst upon his view, and he saw before him one of the chief sources of the Nile in the Luta N'zige, or Albert Lake.

Accompanied by his courageous and devoted wife, who insisted upon sharing his labours and his perils, he sailed up the Nile from Cairo on the 15th of April, 1861. In twenty-six days they arrived at Kousko, whence they crossed the Nubian desert, so as to cut off the western bend of the river, touching it again at Abou Hamed. Eight days more and they reached Berber, where they remained until the 11th of June. A year was spent in exploring the Abyssinian frontier and the Abyssinian tributaries of the Nile; and the travellers made their appearance at Khartûm on the 11th of June, 1862. Khartûm is a densely populated, unclean, and pestiferous town, in lat. 15° 29', at the junction point of the White and Blue Nile; it is the capital of the Soudan, and the seat of a governor-general. Twenty years ago it was also the centre of a cruel and desolating slave-trade, but the exertions of Sir Samuel Baker and Colonel Gordon have done much to lessen its proportions.

Having engaged a Nile boat, or dahabeeyah, and two larger noggens or sailing barges, with an escort of forty armed men, and forty sailors, and accumulated four months' supplies of provisions, Sir Samuel set sail from Khartûm on the 18th of December, 1862. On Christmas Day he was slowly ascending the river, the banks of which were fringed with immense forests. These trees are the soont (*Acacia Arabica*), which produce an excellent tannin; the fruit is used for that purpose, and yields a rich brown dye. The straight smooth trunks are thirty-five feet high, and about eighteen inches in diameter. When in full foliage they look well from a distance, but on a closer approach the forest is seen to be a desolate swamp, completely overflowed; "a mass of fallen dead trees protruding from the stagnant waters, a solitary crane perched here and there upon the rotten boughs; floating water-plants massed together, and forming green swimming islands, hitched generally among the sunken trunks and branches; sometimes slowly descending with the sluggish stream, bearing, spectre-like, storks thus voyaging on nature's rafts to freer lands unknown." This kind of scenery—depressing enough, no doubt—continues for a considerable distance, and so long as it lasts deprives the Nile of that romance with which it has been invested by the imagination of poets. There is neither beauty nor interest in it; and one is surprised to see the low flat banks studded with populous villages. The flooded plains, however, afford abundant pasture for the herds of the Shillooks, who in their choice of a locality are governed by considerations of utility, and not by the principles of æstheticism.

The junction of the Sobat takes place in lat. 9° 21'. This tributary, at the point of confluence, is a hundred and twenty yards broad, and flows at the rate of two miles and a half per hour. Still the Nile valley presents the same characteristics—broad tracts of marsh and grasses; dull, monotonous levels, unrelieved by any vividness of colour. After receiving the Bahr-el-Ghazal, the White Nile turns abruptly to the south-east, and winds upward through a flat country, which, in the rainy season, is resolved into a system of extensive lakes. Its highway is half choked with floating vegetation, which nurtures innumerable clouds of mosquitoes. The people on its banks belong to the Nuehr tribe; the women pierce the upper lip, and wear an ornament about four inches long, of beads upon a iron wire, which projects like the horn of a rhinoceros. The men are both tall and robust, and armed with lances. They carry pipes that will hold nearly a quarter of a pound of tobacco; when the supply of "the weed" fails, they substitute charcoal.

The monotony of the voyage was broken one day by the appearance of a hippopotamus close to Sir Samuel's boat. He was about half grown, and in an instant a score of men jumped into the water to seize him. The captain caught him by the hind-leg; and then the crowd rushed in, and, with ropes thrown from the vessel, slipped nooses over his head. A grand struggle ensued, but as it seemed likely to result in a victory for the hippopotamus, Sir Samuel slew him with a rifle ball. The Arab seamen, who have an extraordinary appetite, like the old school-men, for the most trivial arguments, observing that the animal had been "bullied" and scarred by some other and stronger hippopotamus, plunged into a fierce contention on the point whether he had been misused by his father or his mother. As they could not agree, they referred the question to the arbitration of Sir Samuel, who pacified both parties by the felicitous suggestion that perhaps it was his uncle! They set to work at once with willing vigour to cut up the ill-treated hippopotamus, which proved to be as fat as butter, and made most excellent soup.

Continuing their "up-river" course, the voyagers came to the country of the Kegtah tribe. Such savages as they saw were equally uncivilized and emaciated. The young women wore no clothing, except a small piece of dressed hide across the shoulders; the men, instead of the hide, assumed a leopard-skin. There was greater appearance of intelligence in the termites, or white ant, than in these poor half-starved wretches. The white-ant hills here rise like castle-towers above the water of the marshes. Their inmates build them ten feet high in the dry season, and when the rains come, live high and dry in the upper stories. Humanity, meanwhile, sickens in the stagnant swamp, and lingers out a miserable existence. The Bohr and Aliab tribes are a degree higher in the scale of civilization, but the Shir go beyond them. They are armed with well-made ebony clubs, two lances, a bow and arrows; they carry upon their backs a neatly made miniature stool, along with an immense pipe. The females are not absolutely naked; they wear small lappets of tanned leather as broad as the hand; at the back of the belt which supports this apron is a tail, depending to the lower portions of the thighs—a tail of finely cut strips of leather, which has probably given rise to the Arab report that a tribe in Central Africa had tails like horses. The huts here, and all along the Nile, are circular, with entrances so low that the inmates creep in and out on hands and knees. The men decorate their heads with tufts of cock's feathers; their favourite attitude, when standing, is on one leg, while leaning on a spear, the uplifted leg reposing on the inside of the other knee.

All the White Nile tribes are quick to collect their harvest of the lotus, or water-lily, seed, which they grind into flour, and make into a kind of porridge. The seed-pod of the white lotus resembles an unblown artichoke, and contains a number of light red grains about the size of the mustard-seed, but in shape like those of the poppy, and like them in flavour. The ripe pods are strung upon reeds about four feet long, formed into large bundles, and carried from the river to the villages, to be dried in the sun, and stored away until wanted.

The 1st of February was a "white day" in the voyagers' calendar, for on that day the scenery of the river underwent a welcome improvement. The marshes gave place to dry ground; the well-wooded banks rose four feet above the water level; the thickly populated country bloomed like an orchard. At Gondokoro the picture was fresh and pleasant, with a distant view of high mountains, and neat villages nestling under the shade of evergreen trees. Gondokoro is not a town, but merely a station of the ivory traders, and for ten months of the year is almost a solitude. Its climate is hot and unhealthy. Sir Samuel Baker did not meet with a friendly reception. The men who profited by the slave-trade regarded him with suspicion; they believed he had come to watch their doings, and report them to the world. Their hostility, however, did not disturb his composure, and he amused himself in riding about the neighbourhood, and studying the place and its inhabitants. He admired the exquisite cleanliness of the native dwellings, which almost rose to the standard of the famous village of Brock. Each house was enclosed by a hedge of the impenetrable euphorbia, and the area within was neatly plastered with a cement of ashes, cow-dung, and sand. Upon this well-kept surface stood one or more huts, surrounded by granaries of neat wicker-work, thatched, resting upon raised platforms. The huts are built with projecting roofs for the sake of shade, and the entrance is not more than two feet high. On the death of a member of the family, he is buried in the yard, his resting-place being indicated by a pole crowned by a bunch of cock's feathers, and ornamented with a few ox-horns and skulls. Each man carries with him, wherever he goes, his weapons, pipe, and stool, the whole (except the stool) being held between his legs when he is standing. The Gondokoro natives belong to the Bari tribe: the men are well grown; the women are not prepossessing, with good features, and no sign of negro blood, except the woolly hair. They tattoo themselves on stomach, sides, and back, and anoint their persons with a peculiar red clay, abounding in oxide of iron. Their principal weapon is the bow and arrow; the arrow they steep in the juice of euphorbia and other poisonous plants.

At the secret instigation of the slave-traders, Sir Samuel Baker's escort broke out into open mutiny, declaring that they had not meat enough, and demanding leave to carry off the oxen of the natives. The ringleader, an Arab, was so violent that Sir Samuel ordered him to receive twenty-five lashes. The vakeel, Saati, advanced to seize him, when many of the men rushed to his rescue; and Sir Samuel was compelled to interfere. The Arab then rushed at his employer; but Sir Samuel knocked him back into the middle of the crowd, caught him by the throat, and called to the vakeel for a rope to bind him; but in an instant all the mutineers sprang forward to his assistance. How the affair would have ended seems doubtful; but as the fray took place within ten yards of the boat, Lady Baker, who was ill with fever in the cabin, witnessed the whole of it, and seeing her husband surrounded, rushed out, forced her way into the middle of the crowd, and called on some of the least mutinous to assist. For a moment the crowd wavered, and Sir Samuel seized the opportunity to shout to the drummer-boy to beat the drum. Immediately, the drum beat, and in his loudest tones Sir Samuel ordered the men to "fall in." The instinct of discipline prevailed: two-thirds of the men fell in, and formed in line, while the others retreated with the ringleader, declaring he was badly hurt. Then Sir Samuel insisted upon their all forming in line, and upon the ringleader being brought forward. At this critical moment, Lady Baker, with true feminine tact, implored her husband to forgive the man if he kissed his hand and begged for pardon. The men were completely conquered by this generosity, and called on their ringleader to apologize, and that all would be right. Thus the affair ended; but Sir Samuel rightly foresaw in it the promise of future troubles. According to the custom of the White Nile, the men had five months' wages in advance; he had therefore no control over them; yet he and his wife were about to penetrate into the midst of a probably hostile native population, with an escort on whose faithfulness no reliance could be placed.

On the 15th of February, Captains Speke and Grant arrived at Gondokoro, from the Victoria Nyanza, and the meeting between them and Sir Samuel was necessarily very cordial. The information they communicated had a material effect upon his plans. He found that they had been unable to complete the actual exploration of the Nile—that a most important portion remained to be determined. It appears that in lat. 2° 17' N. they had crossed the Nile, after tracking it from the Victoria Lake; that the river then turned suddenly to the west, and that they did not touch it again until they arrived in lat. 3° 32' N., when it was then flowing from the west-south-west. The natives, and Kamrasi, King of Unyoro, had assured them that the Nile from the Victoria Nyanza, which they had crossed in lat. 2° 17' N., flowed westward for several days' journey, and at length fell into a large lake called the Luta N'zige ("Dead Locust"); that this lake came from the south, and that the Nile, on entering its northern extremity, almost immediately made its exit, and as a navigable river continued its course to the north through the Koshi and Madi countries. Circumstances prevented Speke and Grant from pushing their explorations as far as the Luta N'zige; and the question that remained to be answered was, What was the exact position of this lake in the basin of the Nile? what was its relation to the great river?

This question Sir Samuel Baker resolved upon settling. Speke and Grant sailed from Gondokoro, homeward bound, on the 26th, and he immediately began to prepare for his journey to the Luta N'zige. His preparations were delayed, however, by the mutinous conduct of his escort, and the obstacles thrown in his path by the nefarious ivory-traders and slave-hunters; and it was the 26th of March before he was able to effect a start. Then, with his escort reduced in number to fifteen men, with two faithful servants, Richard and the boy Saat, and a heavily loaded caravan of camels and donkeys, with Lady Baker mounted on a good strong Abyssinian hunter, Tétel ("Hartebeest"), and Sir Samuel himself on his horse Filfil ("Pepper"), and the British flag waving proudly above the *cortége*, they left Gondokoro, and began their march into Central Africa.

The country was park-like, but dried up by the hot weather. The soil was sandy, but firm, and numerous evergreen trees enlivened the landscape, which was further animated by clusters of villages, each surrounded by a fence of euphorbia. It varied greatly in character as the travellers advanced; sometimes presenting a magnificent forest, sometimes a dense jungle, sometimes a labyrinth of ravines, through which the caravan made its way with difficulty. The view of the valley of Tollogo was exceedingly picturesque. An abrupt granite wall rose on the east side to a height of about a thousand feet; from this perpendicular cliff huge blocks had fallen, strewing the bottom with a confused mass of fragments, among which the natives had built their village. A slow stream wound its way in the hollow, which was nowhere more than half a mile wide, in the shade of numerous fig trees. At Ellyria Sir Samuel narrowly escaped a hostile encounter with an ivory-trader's party, but through the firmness and skilfulness of himself and his wife, not only was it avoided, but friendly relations were established with its leader. No supplies, however, could be procured from the natives, whose character Sir Samuel paints in the darkest colours. Of the village of Wakkala he gives a pleasant description. The soil was very rich, and the ground being protected from the burning sun by the large trees, there was a wealth of luscious grass; while the good pasturage, the extensive forest, and a plentiful supply of water insured a not less plentiful supply of wild animals—antelopes in numerous varieties, rhinoceros, buffaloes, elephants, and giraffes. The next town was Latomé, where the traveller's presence of mind and courage were tested by another mutiny; but again he succeeded in defeating the intentions of the insurgents, and reducing them to obedience.

Along the foot of the Lafut mountains, which attain a general elevation of six to seven thousand feet, the travellers pursued their way. Desertions reduced their escort by five men, but they abated not their high hopes or spirit of daring enterprise. They duly arrived at Tarangdlé, famous for its fine trees—the chief settlement of the Latookas, a fine, frank, and warlike race, who resemble the Irish in their readiness to join either in a feast or a fray. The town contains three thousand houses, each of which, as well as the town itself, is protected by an iron-wood palisade. The cattle are kept in large kraals, and at various points high platforms are erected, where sentinels keep watch and ward both day and night. The cattle are the wealth of the country, and so rich are the Latookas in them, that ten or twelve thousand head are housed in every large town. The natives are constantly on guard to prevent the depredations of neighbouring tribes.

"The houses of the Latookas," says Sir Samuel, "are generally bell-shaped, while others are precisely like huge candle-extinguishers, about twenty-five feet high. The roofs are neatly thatched, at an angle of about 75°, resting upon a circular wall about four feet high; thus the roof forms a cap descending to within two feet and a half of the ground. The doorway is only two feet and two inches high, thus an entrance must be effected upon all-fours. The interior is remarkably clean, but dark, as the architects have no idea of windows. It is a curious fact that the circular form of hut is the only style of architecture adopted among all the tribes of Central Africa, and also among the Arabs of Upper Egypt; and that, although these differ more or less in the form of the roof, no tribe has ever yet sufficiently advanced to construct a window. The town of Tarangdlé is arranged with several entrances, in the shape of low archways through the palisades; these are closed at night by large branches of the hooked thorn of the kittur bush (a species of mimosa). The main street is broad, but all others are studiously arranged to admit of only one cow, in single file, between high stockades; thus, in the event of an attack, these narrow passages could be easily defended, and it would be impossible to drive off their vast herds of cattle unless by the main street. The large cattle kraals are accordingly arranged in various quarters in connection with the great road, and the entrance of each kraal is a small archway in the strong iron-wood fence, sufficiently wide to admit one ox at a time. Suspended from the arch is a bell, formed of the shell of the Oolape palm-nut, against which every animal must strike either its horns or back, on entrance. Every tinkle of the bell announces the passage of an ox into the kraal, and they are thus counted every evening when brought home from pasture."

While at Latooka Sir Samuel was enabled to gratify his passion for the chase, and his skill and prowess were rewarded by the capture of an elephant. There is a great difference, or rather, there are three great differences between the African and the Asiatic elephant: the back of the former is concave, that of the latter convex; the former has an enormous ear, the latter a comparatively small one; the head of the former has a convex front, while that of the latter exposes a flat surface a little above the trunk. The African animal is much larger than the Asiatic; and while the latter seeks the forest depths during the day, and does not wander forth upon the plains till towards evening, the former remains all day in the vast open prairies, where the thick grass springs to a height of twelve feet. The African elephant feeds chiefly on the foliage of trees; the Asiatic is an extensive grass feeder.

The natives hunt the elephant for the sake of the flesh and the tusks. Sometimes he is caught in pitfalls; at other times, the grass of the prairies is fired, and the elephants gradually driven back into a confined area, where they are surrounded and speared to death. Or, should a number of elephants be in the neighbourhood of a village, about a hundred men, armed with heavy-bladed lances, post themselves in as many trees, while a multitude of natives gradually drive the animals towards this ambush, when such as pass near enough are speared between the shoulders. The Bagara Arabs are famous elephant hunters. Armed with bamboo lances, tipped with a sharp iron head, two of them, mounted on good horses, sally forth to secure a prize. On coming in sight of a herd, they single out the finest tusker and separate him from the others. One man then leads the charge, and the animal, hotly pursued, turns against the horse, which the rider so manages as to draw the elephant further and further after him, while carefully keeping a safe distance ahead. The other man, meanwhile, is at the elephant's heels, and suddenly dismounting, while at full gallop, plunges his spear into its body about two feet below the junction of the tail, driving it with all his strength into the abdomen, and then withdrawing it. If successful in his thrust, he remounts his horse and escapes, or takes to flight on foot, pursued by the elephant, until the attention of the latter is drawn to his first assailant, who in his turn rides up, and inflicts a wound. Sometimes the first wound proves fatal; sometimes the process is repeated twice or thrice before the animal succumbs; and sometimes the elephant overtakes his enemy, in which case the latter must expect no mercy.

On the 2nd of May, 1863, leaving five men in charge of his camp and baggage, Sir Samuel started for Obbo, crossing the Kanisti river, and travelling through a bold and romantic highland country. He found the vegetation of Obbo rich and various; the soil produced nine kinds of yams, and many capital kinds of fruit. Tobacco flourishes, and ground nuts are plentiful. As for the people, they attire themselves in the skin of an antelope or goat, wearing it mantle-wise across their shoulders; but when on the warpath, they paint their body with red and yellow stripes. Sir Samuel was received with all the honours by Katchiba, the chief of Obbo, and entertained with a grand dance, in which more vigour was displayed than elegance. About a hundred men formed a ring; each holding in his hand a small cup-shaped drum, formed of hollowed wood, over the perforated end of which was lightly stretched the skin of an elephant's ear. In the centre was placed the chief dancer, wearing, suspended from his shoulders, an immense drum, also covered with elephant's ear. The dance commenced with a wild but agreeable chorus, the time being kept by the big drum, and the small *tympana* striking in at certain periods, with so much precision as to give the effect of a single instrument. The figures varied continually, and the whole terminated with a "grand galop" in double circles, at a tremendous pace, the inner ring revolving in a contrary direction to the outer.

Sir Samuel returned to Latooka, and collecting his baggage and escort, started again for Obbo on the 13th of June. Here he and his wife remained for several months, waiting for a favourable opportunity to resume their southward march. Their quinine was exhausted, and consequently they suffered much from fever. Sir Samuel, in lieu of horses, purchased and trained for their contemplated journey three robust oxen, named respectively, "Beef," "Steaks," and "Suet." He also obtained a supply of porters to carry his luggage, and arranged with Ibrahim, the friendly trader, that he should accompany him to Unyoro with a guard of one hundred men. It was the 5th of January, 1864, before the expedition started. On the very first day, however, one of the oxen bolted; and Sir Samuel was compelled to purchase another of one of the Turks at the price of a double-barrelled gun. Three days' march through a beautiful country brought them to the Asua river, in lat. 3° 12' N. Its bed was almost dry. On the 13th they arrived at Shooa. This is characterized as a lovely place. A noble mountain of granite ascended in a sheer precipice for about eight hundred feet from its base; perfectly abrupt on the eastern side, the other parts were of gradual inclination, covered with fine forest trees, and picturesquely studded with villages. The surrounding country, with its trees and rivulets and greensward, might have been taken for an English park, but for the granite rocks that rose at intervals like the gray ruins of ancient castles.

Shooa is a land of milk and honey. The travellers found fowls, butter, and goats abundant and ridiculously cheap; and as beads were highly valued, they effected some good bargains. The women flocked to see the white lady, bringing her gifts of milk and flowers, and receiving beads and bracelets in return. They were gentle in manner, and evidently anxious to establish friendly relations. Sir Samuel was struck by the superior cultivation of the country. Large quantities of sesamum were grown and carefully harvested, the crop being collected in oblong frames about twenty feet long and twelve feet high. These were inclined at an angle of about 60°; the pods of the sesamum plants hanging on one facet, so that the frames resembled enormous brushes. When fully dried, the crop was removed to the granaries, of which there were two kinds: the wicker-work plastered over with cow-dung, supported on four posts, with a thatched roof; and a simpler contrivance, which may be thus described:—A stout pole, twenty feet long, was fixed upright in the earth, and, at about four foot from the ground, a bundle of strong and long reeds was tied tightly round it. Round these reeds, at intervals, were fastened hoop of wicker-work, until the structure assumed the shape of an inverted umbrella half expanded. When this is filled with grain, fresh reeds are added, until the work has extended to within a few feet of the top of the pole. The whole is then crowned with a covering of reeds, securely strapped, and resembles nothing in the world so much as one of those cigars which slightly bulge in the middle.

At Shooa all Sir Samuel's Obbo porters absconded, being afraid to enter Kamrasi's country, and he found so much difficulty in supplying their places, that he resolved on leaving behind him every article that was not absolutely indispensable. How different an appearance his expedition presented to that which it had worn on leaving Khartûm! It was shorn of all its "pride and circumstance;" but its leader remained as resolute and as hopeful as ever, and started from Shooa on the 18th of January, determined to press forward to the Luta N'zige. After passing Fatiko, a village perched like an eagle's eyrie on a rocky table-land, he entered upon a sea of prairies, an immense undulating expanse of verdure, dotted with a few palms. As his guide lost the road, Sir Samuel proposed to clear the country to the south by firing the prairies, and a strangely picturesque spectacle was the result. In a few minutes the flames roared before them, and waves upon waves of fire, and clouds upon clouds of smoke, rolled away to the far horizon. Flocks of buzzards and swarms of beautiful fly-catchers thronged to the spot, to prey upon the innumerable insects that endeavoured to escape from the approaching conflagration, which continued to extend until arrested by a reedy swamp.

On the 22nd, the expedition reached the Victoria White Nile, or, as it is sometimes called, the Somerset river, and proceeded through the magnificent forest that crowned its bank to the Karuma Falls. The river here was about a hundred and fifty yards wide, and flowed between lofty cliffs, which were green with vines, bananas, and palms. The falls, however, are very insignificant, not exceeding five feet in height. Just above them is a ferry, and Sir Samuel and Lady Baker crossing by it, found themselves in Unyoro, King Kamrasi's country, and in his town or village of Atado. Speke and Grant had left behind them pleasant memories, so that Baker, as their friend and countryman, received a hearty welcome. A large hut was placed at the disposal of his wife and himself, and in exchange for fresh beef—Sir Samuel ordering an ox to be killed for the purpose—the natives furnished liberal quantities of flour, beans, and sweet potatoes. A brisk market was quickly set going, and whole rows of girls and women arrived, bringing baskets filled with the desired provisions. The women, we are told, were neatly dressed in short double-skirted petticoats: many had the bosom bare: others wore a piece of bark-cloth, plaid-wise, across chest and shoulders. Bark-cloth, which is exclusively used throughout Equatorial Africa, is the produce of a kind of fig tree. The bark is stripped off in large pieces, soaked in water, and beaten with a mallet. In appearance it much resembles corduroy, in colour tanned leather; the finer qualities are peculiarly soft to the touch, like woven cotton.

The travellers were struck by the difference between the Unyoro people and the tribes they had previously seen. On the north side of the Nile the natives were either wholly naked, or wore only a piece of skin across their shoulders. The river seemed to mark the limit or *ne plus ultra* of savagedom, for the inhabitants of Unyoro shrank like Europeans from the indecency and shame of nakedness. Their higher civilization was shown also by their manufactures: their smiths were very skilful, and used iron hammers instead of stone; they converted into fine wire the thick brass and copper wire which they received from Zanzibar; and their pottery showed a certain degree of taste in conception.

"The natives," writes Sir Samuel, "are particularly neat in all they do; they never bring anything to sell unless carefully packed in the neatest parcels, generally formed of the bark of the plantain, and sometimes of the inner portions of reeds stripped into snow-white stalks, which are bound round the parcels with the utmost care. Should the plantain cider, 'marossa,' be brought in a jar, the mouth is neatly covered with a finger-like mat of these clean white rushes split into shreds. Not even tobacco is brought for sale unless most carefully packed. During a journey, a pretty, bottle-shaped, long-necked gourd is carried, with a store of plantain cider; the mouth of the bottle is stopped with a bundle of the white rush shreds, through which a reed is inserted that reaches to the bottom; thus the drink can be sucked up during the march without the necessity of halting; nor is it possible to spill it by the movement of walking.

"The natives," he adds, "prepare the skins of goats very beautifully, making them as soft as chamois leather; these they cut into squares, and sew them together as neatly as would be effected by a European tailor, converting them into mantles, which are prized far more highly than bark-cloth, on account of their durability. They manufacture their own needles, not by boring the eye, but by sharpening the end into a fine point, and turning it over, the extremity being hammered into a small cut in the body of the needle to prevent it from catching."

The arrival of Sir Samuel Baker being made known to Kamrasi, he requested him to pay a visit to his capital, and sent a legion of porters to carry his baggage. Lady Baker suffered much from illness on the journey, which she performed in a litter; and Sir Samuel was also attacked by a debilitating fever. His first interview with "the king" took place on the 10th of February. He describes him as a fine-looking man, whose extremely prominent eyes gave a peculiar expression to his countenance; about six feet high; and dressed in a long robe of bark-cloth, draped in graceful folds. The nails of his hands and feet were carefully tended, and his complexion was about as dark a brown as that of an Abyssinian. He sat upon a copper stool, with a leopard-skin carpet spread around him, and was attended by about ten of his principal chiefs. Of his character as a man Sir Samuel Baker speaks in the most unflattering terms; he was grasping, mean, mendacious, and a coward. After some delay, and by dint of repeated bribes, Sir Samuel obtained from him a supply of natives to carry the baggage to the lake, where canoes were to be provided for the voyage to Magango, a village situated at the junction of the Somerset river. He went to take leave of the royal savage, and was astonished by the insolent demand that Lady Baker should be left with him! Sir Samuel drew his revolver; Lady Baker broke out into invectives in Arabic, which the woman, Bachuta, translated as nearly as she could, and with indignant emphasis, into the language of Unyoro; in short, "a scene" ensued! Kamrasi was completely cowed, and faltered out, "Don't be angry! I had no intention of offending you by asking for your wife; I will give you a wife, if you want one, and I thought you might have no objection to give me yours; it is my custom to give my visitors pretty wives, and I thought you might exchange. Don't make it fuss about it: if you don't like it, there's an end of it; I will never mention it again." Sir Samuel received the apology very sternly, and insisted upon starting. Kamrasi did not feel in a position to interpose any further delay, and the march to the lake began.

On the road a very painful incident occurred. The expedition had reached Uafour river, which ran through the centre of a marsh, and, although deep, was so thickly covered with matted and tangled water grass and other aquatic plants, that a natural floating bridge, some two feet in thickness, was available for crossing. The men passed it quickly, sinking merely to the ankles, though beneath the tough vegetation was deep water. It was equally impossible to ride or be carried over this fickle surface; Sir Samuel therefore led the way, and begged his wife to follow on foot as quickly as possible, keeping exactly in his track. The river was about eighty yards wide, and Sir Samuel had scarcely accomplished a fourth of the distance, when, looking back, he was horrified to see her standing in one spot, and sinking gradually through the weeds, while her face was distorted and perfectly purple. She fell, as if stricken dead. Her husband was immediately by her side, and, with the help of some of his men, dragged her through the yielding vegetation, across to the other side. There she was tenderly laid beneath a tree, and her husband bathed her head and face with water, thinking she had fainted. But he soon perceived that she was suffering from a sunstroke; and, removing her to a miserable hut close at hand, he watched anxiously for some sign of returning consciousness. We shall quote his own words in all their pathetic simplicity:

"There was nothing to eat in this spot. My wife had never stirred since she fell by the *coup de soleil*, and merely respired about five times a minute. It was impossible to remain; the people would have starved. She was laid gently upon her litter, and we started forward on our funeral course. I was ill and broken-hearted, and I followed by her side through the long day's march over wild park lands and streams, with thick forest and deep marshy bottoms; over undulating hills, and through valleys of tall papyrus rushes, which, as we brushed through them on our melancholy way, waved over the litter like the black plumes of a hearse. We halted at a village, and again the night was passed in watching. I was wet, and coated with mud from the swampy marsh, and shivered with ague; but the cold within was greater than all. No change had taken place; she had never moved. I had plenty of fat, and I made four balls of about half a pound, each of which would burn for three hours. A piece of a broken water-jar formed a lamp, several pieces of rag serving for wicks. So in solitude the still calm night passed away as I sat by her side and watched. In the drawn and distorted features that lay before me I could hardly trace the same form that for years had been my comfort through all the difficulties and dangers of my path. Was she to die? Was so terrible a sacrifice to be the result of my selfish exile?

"Again the night passed away. Once more the march. Though weak and ill, and for two nights without a moment's sleep, I felt no fatigue, but mechanically followed by the side of the litter as though in a dream. The same wild country diversified with marsh and forest. Again we halted. The night came, and I sat by her side in a miserable hut, with the feeble lamp flickering while she lay, as in death. She had never moved a muscle since she fell. My people slept. I was alone, and no sound broke the stillness of the night. The ears ached at the utter silence, till the sudden wild cry of a hyæna made me shudder as the horrible thought rushed through my brain, that, should she be buried in this lonely spot, the hyæna would . . . disturb her rest.

"The morning was not far distant; it was past four o'clock. I had passed the night in replacing wet cloths upon her head, and moistening her lips, as she lay apparently lifeless on her litter. I could do nothing more; in solitude and abject misery in that dark hour, in a country of savage heathens, thousands of miles away from a Christian land, I beseeched an aid above all human, trusting alone to Him.

"The morning broke; my lamp had just burnt out, and, cramped with the night's watching, I rose from my seat, and seeing that she lay in the same unaltered state, I went to the door of the hut to breathe one gasp of the fresh morning air. I was watching the first red streak that heralded the rising sun, when I was startled by the words, 'Thank God,' faintly uttered behind me. Suddenly she had awoke from her torpor, and with a heart overflowing I went to her bedside. Her eyes were full of madness! She spoke, but the brain was gone!"

II.

Happily, after suffering for some days from brain fever, Lady Baker recovered consciousness, and thenceforward her progress, though slow, was sure. After a brief rest, the march to the lake was resumed by the undaunted travellers; for the devoted wife would not allow any consideration of her comfort or safety to come between her husband and the accomplishment of the work he had undertaken. At a village called Parkani, the guides informed them that they were only a day's journey from the lake. In the west rose a lofty range of mountains, and Sir Samuel Baker had conjectured that the N'zige lay on the other side of it, but he was told that it actually formed its western or further boundary. Only a day's journey! That night Sir Samuel could hardly sleep; his brain was fired with the thought that he was within so short a distance of the Source of the Nile—that in a few hours he might drink of the waters of its mysterious fountain. He was up before sunrise on the 14th of March, and crossing a deep cool valley between the hills, ascended the slope, gained the summit, and there, before him, flashing in the light of morning like a sea of quicksilver or a huge mirror of polished steel, lay the long-sought lake! The height on which he stood was about fifteen hundred feet above its level, so that he could survey the entire expanse of those welcome waters which had created fertility in the heart of the desert, and made the fame and wealth and glory of Egypt. He resolved that thenceforth they should bear a great name, and as the eastern reservoir of the Nile had been named after the Queen of England, he determined that the western should commemorate her lost and lamented consort, Prince Albert. It is therefore now known as the Albert Lake.

With some difficulty, but with a grateful heart, he and his wife descended the steep to the shore of the silent, shining lake, and took up their quarters in a fishing village called Vacovia. It was a wretched place, and the soil was strongly impregnated with salt; but discomforts were forgotten in the joy of a great discovery. Sir Samuel proceeded to collect all the information he could relative to its position. The chief of the village told him that its breadth was immense, but that large canoes had been known to cross from the other side after four days and nights of hard rowing. That other side, the west, was included in the great kingdom of Malegga, governed by King Kajoro, who traded with Kamrasi from a point opposite to Magango, where the lake contracted to the width of one day's voyage. South of Malegga was a country named Tori, and the lake extended into the kingdom of Karagwé, with whose sovereign, Rumanika, Speke and Grant had maintained a friendly intercourse. Karagwé partly bounded the lake on the eastern side, and next to it, towards the north, came Utumbi; then, in succession, came Uganda, Unyoro, Chopé.

The Albert Nyanza formed a vast basin of water, lying far below the general level of the country, and receiving all its drainage. It was surrounded by precipitous cliffs, which left but a narrow strip of sand between them and the swelling waves, and bounded on the west and south-west by huge mountain-ranges, from five to seven thousand feet in altitude. Sir Samuel Baker, after a careful survey, concluded that it was the one great reservoir which received everything, from the passing shower to the roaring mountain torrent that drained from Central Africa towards the north. Speke's Victoria Nyanza was a reservoir situated at a considerable elevation, receiving the waters from the west of the Kitangulé river, its principal feeder; but as the Albert Lake extended much farther north than the Victoria, it took up the river from the latter, and monopolized the entire head-waters of the Nile. In Sir Samuel's opinion the Albert was the great reservoir, while the Nile was the eastern source; the parent streams that created these lakes were from the same origin, and the Kitangulé poured its waters into the Victoria, to be eventually received by the Albert. The discoveries of Mr. Stanley, however, impose on geographers the necessity of considerably modifying Sir Samuel Baker's hypothesis, without detracting from the importance of his discovery. The Albert Lake really holds an inferior position to the Victoria, which unquestionably receives the parent waters of the Nile; but it is not the less one of its great reservoirs.

Having obtained a canoe at Vacovia, Sir Samuel explored the north-eastern coast of the Albert, and after a voyage of thirteen days arrived at Magango, where the Nile, or Somerset river, after a winding course from the Victoria Nyanza, flows calmly into its basin, to quit it again a few miles further north, and make its way towards Egypt and the Mediterranean. At Magango the lake is about seventeen miles wide, but to the north it ends in a long strip or neck which a growth of tall green rushes almost conceals. After leaving the lake, the Nile smoothly descends its green valley, and is navigable for boats until it reaches Agunddo, where it dashes headlong over a precipice of thirty or forty feet.

Having completed his survey of the Albert, as far as his means admitted, Sir Samuel determined, instead of retracing his steps to Kamrasi's residence at 'Mroolli, to trace the course of the Somerset or Nile river up to Karuma Falls, to which point Speke and Grant had followed it downwards. The canoes having been got ready, Baker and his wife began their river voyage. About two miles from Magango the width contracted from 500 to 250 yards. As they proceeded, the river gradually narrowed to about 180 yards, and when the men ceased paddling, they could distinctly hear the roar of water. Arriving at a point where the river made a slight turn, they saw the sandbanks covered with crocodiles; like logs of timber, they lay together. The cliffs on either side were steep and rugged, and the whole picture was rich in various colouring. Foliage of the intensest green clothed each rocky projection, and through a narrow cleft or gap in the precipices the river plunged down before them in one vast leap of about 120 feet. The fall of waters was white as snow, and contrasted magnificently with the dark walls that held it in, while the graceful palms of the tropics and wild plantains increased the beauty of the view. This noble cataract, the grandest on the Nile, Sir Samuel named the Murchison Falls, in honour of the famous geologist and geographer.

It was impossible, of course, to pass the cataract, and the voyagers made haste to land and collect their oxen and attendants in order to resume their journey. The route they took was parallel to the river, which continued to flow in a deep and picturesque ravine. From an island called Palooan, a succession of islets broke its course until near the Karuma Falls. These islets belonged to two chiefs, Rionza and Fowooka, who were bitter enemies of the King of Unyoro, Kamrasi. On arriving at this point, Sir Samuel found that they were at that very time engaged in hostilities, and that it would be impossible for him to continue along the bank of the river. Obstacles of every kind were thrown by the natives in the onward path of the travellers, but in spite of ill health, weakness, and weariness, they slowly pushed forward. Not the least of their troubles was the scarcity of suitable provisions, and they grew so feeble that at last even their brave hearts gave way, and they began to despair of reaching Gondokoro—to resign themselves to the thought of being buried in that inhospitable land. "I wrote instructions in my journal," says Sir Samuel, "in case of death, and told my headman to be sure to deliver my maps, observations, and papers to the English consul at Khartûm; this was my only care, as I feared that all my labour might be lost should I die. I had no fear for my wife, as she was quite as bad as I, and if one should die, the other would certainly follow;— in fact, this had been agreed upon lest she should fall into the hands of Kamrasi at my death. We had struggled to win, and I thanked God that we had won; if death were to be the price, at all events we were at the goal, and we both looked upon death rather as a pleasure, as affording rest; there would be no more suffering; no fever, no long journey before us, that in our weak state was an infliction; the only wish was to lay down the burthen."

From this wretched position Sir Samuel delivered himself, by undertaking to assist Kamrasi in his war against Fowooka. Whether this was a legitimate proceeding on the part of a scientific explorer, who had no interest in the quarrel of either party, may well be doubted, but the alliance led to his obtaining an immediate supply of provisions. Natives were sent to assist him and his wife in their journey to Kamrasi's camp at Kisoona. But what was their surprise to find that the Kamrasi whom they had interviewed at 'Mrooli was not, after all, the real Kamrasi, the King of Unyoro, but his brother, M'Gami, whom Kamrasi had ordered to personate him, in an access of alarm as to the traveller's possible designs. Sir Samuel was indignant at the deception, and it was with some difficulty that M'Gami could prevail upon him to forgive it. At last he consented to visit the king, and something like an amicable understanding was established between them. He was well supplied with provisions of all kinds, and both his wife and himself slowly recovered their health and spirits. By a dexterous use of the British flag he repelled an attempted invasion of Fowooka's warriors; and he rendered various services to Kamrasi, which met, we need hardly say, with no adequate reward. It was the middle of November before, in company with a caravan of ivory-traders under his old friend Ibrahim, Sir Samuel was able to resume his return journey to Gondokoro. The caravan consisted of about seven hundred porters and eighty armed men, with women and children; in all, about one thousand people. To provision such a body was necessarily difficult, and there was no meat, although flour was abundant. Sir Samuel's skill as a hunter was put into requisition to supply a little variety to the bill of fare; and his bringing down a fine hartebeest was an event which gave very general satisfaction.

Five days after leaving the Victoria Nile, the caravan arrived at Shooa, where Sir Samuel and his wife received a hearty welcome. Some months were spent in this pleasant locality, the Turks profiting by the opportunity to make razzias upon the neighbouring tribes, so that, for many miles around, the blackened ruins of villages and the desolated fields bore witness to their reckless cruelty; cattle were carried off in thousands, and a fair and fertile region was converted into a dreary wilderness. The captives made were detained to be sold as slaves. On one occasion, among the victims brought in to the Turkish camp was a pretty young girl of about fifteen. She had been sold by auction, as usual, the day after the return from the razzia, and had fallen to the lot of one of the men. A few days later, there appeared in the camp a native from the plundered village, intent upon ransoming the girl with a quantity of ivory. He had scarcely entered the gateway, when the girl, who was sitting at the door of her owner's hut, descried him, and springing to her feet, ran with all the speed her chained ankles permitted, and flung herself into his arms, with the cry of "My father!" Yes; it was her father who, to rescue his child from degradation, had nobly risked his life in his brutal enemy's camp.

The Turks who witnessed this particular incident, far from being touched by any emotion of pity, rushed on to the unfortunate native, tore him from his daughter, and bound him tightly with cords. At this time Sir Samuel was in his tent, assisting some of his men to clean his rifles. Suddenly, at a distance of less than a hundred paces, he heard three shots fired. The men exclaimed, "They have shot the abid (native)!" "What native?" inquired Sir Samuel; and his men replied by narrating the story we have just recorded. Sir Samuel at first refused to believe it, but it proved to be true in every detail, even in the last; for, bound to a tree, lay the wretched father, shot dead with three balls.

In the month of February the caravan started for Gondokoro. The route lay at first through a fertile and pleasant country, crossing twice the Un-y-Ami river, and touching at its point of junction with the Nile, in lat. 3° 32' N. On the north bank of the Un-y-Ami, about three miles from its mouth, Sir Samuel saw the tamarind tree—the "Shadder-el-Sowar" (or "Traveller's Tree"), as the trading parties called it—which indicated the limit of Signor Miani's explorations from Gondokoro, and the furthest point reached by any traveller from the north prior to Sir Samuel Baker's enterprise. The journey was continued through a fine park-like extent of verdant grass, covered with stately tamarind trees, which sheltered among their branches great numbers of the brilliant yellow-breasted pigeon. Ascending a rocky eminence by a laborious pass, Sir Samuel, from the summit, which was eight hundred feet high, saw before him the old historic river. "Hurrah for the old Nile!" he said, and contemplated with eager gaze the noble scene before him. Flowing from the westward, with many a curve and bend, was the broad sheet of unbroken water, four hundred yards wide, exclusive of the thick belt of reeds on either margin. Its source could be clearly traced for some scores of miles, and the range of mountains on the west bank was distantly visible that the travellers had previously sighted, when on the route from Karuma to Shooa, at a distance of sixty miles. This chain begins at Magango, and forms the Koshi frontier of the Nile. The country opposite to Sir Samuel's position was Koshi, which extends along the *west* bank of the river to the Albert Lake. The country which he was traversing extends, under the name of Madi, along the *east* bank to the confluence of the Somerset Nile, opposite Magango.

The Nile here enters a rocky valley between Gebel Kookoo and the western mountains, and foams and frets around and against rock and island, until, suddenly contracting, it breaks into a roaring torrent, and dashes furiously onward in the shadow of perpendicular cliffs. Waterfall succeeds to waterfall, and it is difficult to identify the swollen, thunderous, angry river with the calm clear stream that brightens the fertile pastures of Shooa. In this part of its course it receives the Asua. Through dense thickets of bamboos, and deep ravines which, in the season of rains, pour their turbid tribute into the great river, the caravan made its way; but in passing through a gorge between two rocky hills it was attacked by a body of the Bari natives, who were lying in ambush. Their bows and arrows, however, proved ineffectual against the musketry of the Turks, and they retired discomfited. This was the last important incident of the journey to Gondokoro, where, after an absence of upwards of two years, Sir Samuel and Lady Baker arrived in safety.

But what was their disappointment to find there neither letters nor supplies! Their friends and agents had long since given them up as dead; never believing that travellers could penetrate into that far and savage south, and return alive. There was no news from home; no money; no conveyance provided to take them back to Khartûm. With characteristic energy Sir Samuel confronted his disappointment, and instead of wringing his hands and waiting for the help that would not come, he set actively to work, engaged a dahabeeyah for the sum of four thousand piastres (£40), removed his baggage on board, collected provisions, took friendly leave of Ibrahim and the traders, and, with the flag of Old England flying at his masthead, set sail from Gondokoro. There is very little to be said about the voyage to Khartûm. Sir Samuel shot some antelopes, and the progress of the dahabeeyah beyond the junction of the Bahr-el-Ghazal was considerably impeded by that natural dam of floating vegetation, intermingled with reeds, sunburnt wood, and mud that here forms so signal an obstruction to the navigation of the Upper Nile. To allow of the passage of boats a canal has been cut, about ten feet wide, but it requires constant clearance, and its transit is not accomplished without considerable difficulty. Two days' hard work from morning till night carried the voyagers through it, and with feelings of relief and exultation they found themselves once more on the open Nile and beyond the dam. But as they floated past the Sobat junction, the terrible plague broke out on board their vessel, carrying off two of the crew, and the boy Saat, who had served them so long and so faithfully. It was a sad conclusion to an expedition which, though fraught with sufferings, trials, and dangers, had, on the whole, been crowned with complete success.

It was the evening of the 5th of May, 1865, when Sir Samuel and Lady Baker entered Khartûm, to be welcomed by the whole European population as if they had risen from the dead. On the 1st of July they left it for Berber. In making the passage of the Cataracts they narrowly escaped shipwreck; their boat, as it sped along under full sail before a high gale of wind, struck broadside upon a sandbank. About sixty yards below rose a ridge of rocks on which it seemed certain that the vessel would be driven, if it cleared the bank; so that to avoid Scylla was to rush into Charybdis. Sir Samuel, however, proved equal to the occasion. An anchor was laid up stream; the crew hauled on the cable, and the great force of the current pressing against the vessels' broadside, she wore gradually round. All hands then laboured to clear away the sand, which, when loosened by their hands and feet, the swift full current rapidly carried away. For five hours they remained in this position, with the boat cracking, and half filled with water; however, a channel was opened at last, and slipping the cable, Sir Samuel hoisted sail, and with the velocity of an arrow, the head of the vessel swung round, and away she went, plunging through the swirling, boiling water, and clearing the rocks by a few inches.

They arrived at Berber, and procuring camels, started east for Souakim on the Red Sea, a distance of two hundred and seventy-five miles. There they obtained passage on board an Egyptian Government steamer, and in five days landed at Suez. Here ends the record of their heroic enterprise. [404]

NOTES

[3] The roc, a gigantic bird, which figures in the Eastern fable of Sinbad the Sailor.

[12] A rich, quaint, walled-up doorway, in semi-Monastic, semi-Byzantine style, still extant in the Corte del Sabbrin, or Corta Sabbonicia, is nearly all that remains of the house of Messer Marco Palo.

[17] A summary of the Russian explorations of the Pamir, by Sievertzof, has been published in Kettler's "Zeitschrift für wissenschaftliche Geographie."

[22] *Cuir-bouilli*, leather softened by boiling, during which process it took any form or impression required, and afterwards hardened.

[35] Probably *malachite*, or carbonate of copper.

[41] The Hon. Robert Lindsay writes:—"At night each man lights a fire at his post, and furnishes himself with a dozen joints of the large bamboo, one of which he occasionally throws into the fire, and the air it contains being rarefied by the heat, it explodes with a report as loud as a musket."—"Lives of the Lindsays," iii. 191.

[89] G. F. Ruxton, "Adventures in Mexico and the Rocky Mountains." London, 1861.

[156] Heinrich Barth, "Travels and Discoveries in North and Central Africa." Second edition. London, 1857.

[159] The scenery of the Tchossowaia valley is warmly praised by Sir Roderick Murchison. "A more picturesque river-gorge," he says, "was certainly never examined by geologists. Between the hamlet of Kinist and Ust-Koiva we passed through scenes even surpassing in beauty those higher up the stream, and to which it would require the pencil of a professed artist to do justice. The river runs in a limestone gorge, in which are cliffs of every variety of form, occasionally exposing large caverns along their vertical faces, with trees and flowers grouped about in the clefts—rocks varying in colour from black to white."—"Geology of the Oural," p. 188.

[166] A four-wheeled waggon, made without either nail, bolt, or springs.

[211] Mrs. Somerville, "Physical Geography," i. 105.

[212] Humboldt, "Ansichten der Natur," i. 8.

[228] T. W. Atkinson, "Oriental and Western Siberia." London, 1858.

[249] It is, in reality, nothing more than a curve of the river, which forms an island of about half a mile in length, called Meschra-el-Reg.

[259] Augustus Petermann, *Mittheilungen*; Dr. Heughlin, "Reise in das Gobiet, des Weissen Nil, etc."

[302] These consist of a few links of chain, with a swivel in the middle, and a steel strap with a buckle at either end. They are fastened round the animal's fore-legs just above the hoof, so as to confine the feet together, and render straying difficult.

[324] Colonel Egerton Warburton, C.M.G., "Journey across the Western Interior of Australia," with Introduction, etc., by C. H. Eden. Edited by H. W. Bates. London, 1875.

[359] During the viceroyalty of Lord Northbrook.

[364] "A Ride to Khiva: Travels and Adventures in Central Asia." By Fred Burnaby, Captain, Royal Horse Guards. Second edition. London, 1876.

[369] Our gallant explorer was not knighted until 1866, but throughout this chapter we shall use the title by which he is so well and so honourably known.

[404] Sir Samuel White Baker, "The Albert Nyanza, Great Basin of the Nile, and Explorations of the Nile Sources." London, 1866.